THE CHRISTIAN SOCIETY

THE
CHRISTIAN SOCIETY

BY

STEPHEN NEILL

FELLOW OF TRINITY COLLEGE,
CAMBRIDGE

GREENWOOD PRESS, PUBLISHERS
WESTPORT, CONNECTICUT

The Library of Congress has catalogued this publication as follows:

Library of Congress Cataloging in Publication Data

Neill, Stephen Charles, Bp.
  The Christian society.

  Reprint of the 1952 ed., issued in series: The
Library of constructive theology.
  1. Church history. I. Title. II. Series.
[BR148.N4 1972]   270   76-141280
ISBN 0-8371-5877-X

Originally published in 1952
by Nisbet & Co. Ltd. London

Reprinted with the permission
of James Nisbet and Company, Ltd.

First Greenwood Reprinting 1972

Library of Congress Catalogue Card Number 76-141280

ISBN 0-8371-5877-X

Printed in the United States of America

GENERAL INTRODUCTION

THE Editors of this series are convinced that the Christian Church as a whole is confronted with a great though largely silent crisis, and also with an unparalleled opportunity. They have a common mind concerning the way in which this crisis and opportunity should be met. The time has gone by when " apologetics " could be of any great value. Something more is needed than a defence of propositions already accepted on authority, for the present spiritual crisis is essentially a questioning of authority if not a revolt against it. It may be predicted that the number of people who are content simply to rest their religion on the authority of the Bible or the Church is steadily diminishing, and with the growing effectiveness of popular education will continue to diminish. We shall not therefore meet the need, if we have rightly diagnosed it, by dissertations, however learned, on the interpretation of the Bible or the history of Christian doctrine. Nothing less is required than a candid, courageous and well-informed effort to think out anew, in the light of modern knowledge, the foundation affirmations of our common Christianity. This is the aim of every writer in this series.

A further agreement is, we hope, characteristic of the books which will be published in the series. The authors have a common mind not only with regard to the problem but also with regard to the starting-point of reconstruc-

tion. They desire to lay stress upon the value and validity
of religious experience and to develop their theology on
the basis of the religious consciousness. In so doing they
claim to be in harmony with modern thought. The
massive achievements of the nineteenth and twentieth
centuries have been built up on the method of observation
and experiment, on experience, not on abstract *a priori*
reasoning. Our contention is that the moral and spiritual
experience of mankind has the right to be considered, and
demands to be understood.

Many distinguished thinkers might be quoted in
support of the assertion that philosophers are now prepared in a greater measure than formerly to consider
religious experience as among the most significant of their
data. One of the greatest has said, " There is nothing
more real than what comes in religion. To compare facts
such as these with what is given to us in outward existence
would be to trifle with the subject. The man who demands
a reality more solid than that of the religious consciousness, seeks he does not know what."[1] Nor does this
estimate of religious experience come only from idealist
thinkers. A philosopher who writes from the standpoint
of mathematics and natural science has expressed the
same thought in even more forcible language. " The fact
of religious vision, and its history of persistent expansion,
is our one ground for optimism. Apart from it, human
life is a flash of occasional enjoyments lighting up a
mass of pain and misery, a bagatelle of transient experience."[2]

[1] F. H. Bradley, *Appearance and Reality*, p. 449.
[2] A. N. Whitehead, *Science and the Modern World*, p. 275.

The conviction that religious experience is to be taken
as the starting-point of theological reconstruction does
not, of course, imply that we are absolved from the labour
of thought. On the contrary, it should serve as the
stimulus to thought. No experience can be taken at its
face value ; it must be criticised and interpreted. Just
as natural science could not exist without experience and
the thought concerning experience, so theology cannot
exist without the religious consciousness and reflection
upon it. Nor do we mean by " experience " anything
less than the whole experience of the human race, so far
as it has shared in the Christian consciousness. As
Mazzini finely said, " Tradition and conscience are the
two wings given to the human soul to reach the truth."

It has been the aim of the writers and the Editors of
the series to produce studies of the main aspects of
Christianity which will be intelligible and interesting to
the general reader and at the same time may be worthy
of the attention of the specialist. After all, in religion we
are dealing with a subject-matter which is open to all and
the plan of the works does not require that they shall
delve very deeply into questions of minute scholarship.
We have had the ambition to produce volumes which
might find a useful place on the shelves of the clergyman
and minister, and no less on those of the intelligent layman. Perhaps we may have done something to bridge
the gulf which too often separates the pulpit from the pew.

Naturally, the plan of our series has led us to give the
utmost freedom to the authors of the books to work out
their own lines of thought, and our part has been strictly
confined to the invitation to contribute, and to suggestions

concerning the mode of presentation. We hope that the series will contribute something useful to the great debate on religion which is proceeding in secret in the mind of our age, and we humbly pray that their endeavours and ours may be blessed by the Spirit of Truth for the building up of Christ's Universal Church.

PREFACE

THE scope of this book is clearly set forth in its title : it is a study of the Christian people as a society of men and women, existing in time and space, acting and reacting continually with its environment.

I have a friend who was for some years a professor of the phenomenology of religion. I was never sure what it was that he was supposed to profess, but I now believe that I have written a book on the phenomenology of the Christian religion. The word *Church* necessarily carries with it theological presuppositions. In this book, I have tried throughout to approach the subject empirically. It is a fact that, since the middle of the First Century A.D., there have been in the world persons who have called themselves and have been called by others Christians. The reason for their taking and being given this title is a real or imaginary relation to one Jesus of Nazareth called Christ, who lived and died in Palestine at the beginning of that century. These persons have lived together in communities, which have continued to exist because of the continued allegiance of their members to this Jesus Christ.

Whether all who have claimed the name Christian have had a right to the name or not is a subject for discussion. Just where the boundaries of the Church are to be drawn is a matter on which Christians are not agreed among themselves. Some would deny to certain others all right to be considered as members of the Church, or would at best admit that they were in some sense members of the soul of the Church, though not of the body. Some groups have been condemned by the general consensus of Christians throughout the centuries as heretical. This book concerns itself with all who have claimed the Christian name, without making preliminary judgments as to their orthodoxy or their standing within the general body of Christian people.

It may be questioned whether it is either possible or useful to make such a study, without first determining the dogmatic bases from which the investigation is to proceed. This is a matter on which opinion may differ. *The Christian Society* was the subject on which I was asked to write, and I have done my best faithfully to fulfil the commission entrusted to me. At the same time, I have been for some years engaged in the study of the doctrine of the Church, and I hope that some day the results of this study may be incorporated in another book. If in this book dogmatic and theological considerations have been left to a very large extent on one side, that has been deliberately done, in accordance with the plan of the work, and not through ignorance of these factors or an underestimate of their importance. It would be possible to treat both aspects in a single book ; it has seemed to me that some things may stand out more clearly if they are treated in separation.

When people speak of the Church, they often do so, as though the Church was a self-existent entity, remaining unchanged through all the vicissitudes of time and its changing situations. In one sense this is true ; I shall have failed in my purpose, if the reader who pursues the theme to the end has not received an impression of the element of continuity in the life of the Christian society in all the forms which it has assumed, and of its essential oneness beneath its tragic history of division and conflict. But in reality the Christian society is an organism acting and reacting with its environment. It is the nature of living organisms that they draw their nourishment from their surroundings, and modify their surroundings in the process. When an organism loses the capacity for adaptation to its environment, it dies. In every age, the Christian society has had to live in relation to its environment. It has undergone many modifications in its organisation and even in its structure. Without this power of adaptation perhaps it too would have died.

Every Christian believes that the Church is a divine society, and that for its inner life it depends wholly on the grace of God revealed in Jesus Christ and perpetually made available through the Holy Spirit. But for those who believe in the Incarnate Son of Man, in whom the divine and the human were for ever made one, it is not difficult to recognise that this divine society lives also a very human life. The difference is that the Son of Man was sinless, whereas the Christian society is marred and weakened by the sin which persists even in those who have been redeemed. It might even be maintained that, had the Christian society been sinless, it would have had no history ; at least it is clear that in that case its history would have been wholly other than that of which its records give evidence. It is the ceaseless conflict with principalities and powers, with the evil in the world and the evil within itself, that makes the story of the Christian society so absorbing, so touching and so inspiring.

It is impossible that an author, in treating of such a subject, should be impartial. I have not aimed at an unattainable impartiality, and have written throughout as a member of that society of which I have been writing. But I have tried not to obtrude the viewpoint of one Christian communion or of one individual. The attentive reader will not find it difficult to discover that I have strong convictions as to the nature of the Church, its life, its ministry and its sacraments. But I have tried to understand those with whom I do not agree, and to be fair to those of whom I cannot approve. I hope that I have not been wholly unsuccessful.

No one who has not tried to deal in a single volume with the whole history of the Christian society from the time of Christ till the present day can have any idea of the difficulty of the task. Any other writer would have chosen a different set of facts and set those facts in other perspectives. No single mind can hold the whole of Church history, or do justice to every part of this tangled and complex story. Most of my working life has been spent far from libraries and from ready access to books. I venture to hope that twenty years of service as a missionary in a non-Christian environment may have served to afford some insights less easily obtained in lands which have had a long Christian history, and that I may have been able to convey to the reader something of my own sense of the grandeur and the glory of the Christian enterprise. I acknowledge with gratitude permission granted by Sheed & Ward, Ltd., for the use of a quotation from Christopher Dawson's *Religion and Culture* on pp. 225–9.

S. N.

CONTENTS

THE CHRISTIAN SOCIETY

CHAPTER I

JESUS AND HIS SOCIETY

DID Jesus of Nazareth intend to found a Church ? In most epochs of the history of the Christian Church, this question would have appeared too paradoxical to be even raised. It was taken for granted that the Church took its origin from the intention, the words and the express commands of Jesus Christ the Son of God ; by this, it was held, its divine character was guaranteed ; on this ground it claimed the obedience of all men.

In the nineteenth century and after, however, modern critical scholarship has raised the question in emphatic terms. For a considerable period, a negative answer was returned by many scholars ; the concern of Jesus was with the Gospel, the Church was a human afterthought, unconnected with anything in the purpose of the One whom it claimed as its founder. This view was maintained by various arguments. One school, stressing the eschatological element in the Gospels, and holding that Jesus looked forward to a divine intervention very shortly to take place and to establish on earth the Kingdom of God, affirmed that there could be no place in His scheme for organisation, or for a body of believers charged with the carrying on of His work on earth. Another school, emphasising the ethical teaching of Jesus concerning the fatherhood of God and the brotherhood of man, expounded His message as concerning itself only with the relationship between God and the individual, and

1

regarded all Church organisation as an intrusion into the
simplicity of the original Gospel.

Such views are still held. But in the course of this
century, something like a revolution has taken place in
theological thought. It is widely recognised that the
Church, so far from being a later addition made by men,
is itself an integral part of the original Gospel, and that,
indeed, that Gospel cannot be rightly understood, unless
due weight is given to the place occupied in it by the
redeemed people of God, the people of the new covenant.

It is true that the question from which we started needs
to be more accurately framed. If the question is to be
interpreted as asking whether Jesus of Nazareth can be
held responsible for all the developments that the Church
has undergone in its long pilgrimage through time, even those
who believe most firmly in the divine constitution and
vocation of the Church may well be willing to admit that,
since it has a human as well as a divine aspect, it has at
least in its outward organisation and activity suffered
much admixture of human frailty and aberration. But if
the question is set in its more precise form, and asks whether
Jesus Himself regarded it as His vocation to bring into being
a new community, which should carry forward His work on
earth until the end of time, the great majority of scholars
today would return an affirmative answer. The Christian
Church of the ages cannot be understood without reference
to the historic work and mission of Jesus ; the historic work
of Jesus cannot be rightly interpreted, unless it is seen in
relation to the society which, in His own intent and purpose,
was to spring from it.

The theological argument cannot be determined by
reference to single texts or passages of the Gospels. It is
true that the word *Church* occurs only in two passages, in
sections which many critics would ascribe not to the original
traditions but to those secondary strata which have been
deposited upon the earlier foundations. " Thou art Peter, and

upon this rock I will build my church ; and the gates of Hades shall not prevail against it." [1] " And if he refuse to hear them, tell it unto the church : and if he refuse to hear the church also, let him be unto thee as the Gentile and the publican." [2]

Even if it could be conclusively proved that these words were not spoken by Jesus, and that the word *Church* was never on His lips, the theological argument concerning His purpose in the formation of His new society would not be seriously affected.

The most sober criticism of the Gospels now accepts it as unmistakable that, even in what are recognisable as the earliest parts of the tradition concerning Jesus, there is an element of interpretation. The method called Form Criticism has shewn that the Gospels in their present form have been in part at least shaped by the living experiences of the earliest groups of believers, and present not so much precise historical data as the data refashioned in the consciousness of those who were living within the Christian fellowship. This type of criticism, in certain hands, has been pushed to such a point as to suggest that in the Gospels we have scarcely anything that can be regarded as a historical picture of Jesus as He was, and that we have to be content with no more than the broken refractions of His likeness mediated through minds that unconsciously distorted much that they believed themselves to have remembered. Even when all allowance has been made for the exaggerations of individual critics, it is impossible to disregard the element of truth in this approach. We do well to remind ourselves of the insecurity of doctrines based only on individual sayings, the validity of which as direct evidence may be open to question.

But a frank recognition of the need for caution in handling the evidence of the Gospels by no means makes impossible an attempt at theological interpretation. In the end, this

[1] Matthew xvi, 18. [2] Matthew xviii. 17.

very caution will be found to strengthen the modern view of the relationship between Jesus and His Church, since that view is based not on isolated sayings, but on a total conception of the mission and purpose of Jesus, derived from a consideration of the Gospels as a whole, and finding corroboration in the most varied elements of His teaching.

The starting point of the investigation must be the attitude of Jesus to the Old Testament, and to the revelation of God, which was believed by all devout Jews to be contained in the ancient Scriptures of their race. If there is one conviction more patent than any other in the Old Testament, it is that concerning a purpose of God in and for a chosen people, a purpose which works itself out in the historical vicissitudes of the fortunes of that people. It seems clear that Jesus accepted the Old Testament interpretation of the history of His people, and carried out His own mission within the framework of that interpretation.

The people of Israel, indeed, had never as a whole proved faithful to the greatness of their vocation. The prophets had had ceaselessly to bewail their dereliction and to pronounce the judgment of God against them. But judgment had never issued in final destruction. There had always been a faithful remnant, through whom the purpose of God had been carried forward. It might even appear at times that the faithful remnant had shrunk to a single individual. In days of unfaithfulness in the Seventh Century B.C., Jeremiah seemed to stand almost as the sole representative of the cause of Jehovah, and was persecuted by his own people for his faithfulness. Yet the cause did not die ; it went forward, though precariously, into a new stage of God's dealing with men.

It is clear that, in all the Old Testament Scriptures, Jesus had pondered most deeply the passages concerning the Servant of Jehovah in the second Isaiah, and among these most deeply of all the song of the Suffering Servant. It was

in the light of this part of the Old Testament revelation that
He understood most clearly His own mission and His own
duty. The difficulties that beset the interpretation of these
passages are well known. Sometimes the Servant seems
to be the whole people of Israel, sometimes a chosen and
faithful remnant ; but there are other traits which can
scarcely be understood otherwise than in terms of an
individual. This apparent fluctuation of meaning only
makes the Servant Songs more relevant to the work of
Jesus. His first task was to call the whole people to
repentance, in order that the whole people might share with
Him in the redemptive mission of the Servant. As it
became clear that the whole people would not turn to God
in the way that He demanded, He occupied Himself more
and more, like Isaiah of old, with the calling out of a
faithful remnant. But, before the end, it was clear that
the purpose of God might at the last depend on the faithfulness of one single individual, who at that moment would
Himself be Israel, the single link on which the carrying
forward of the purpose of God would depend. And so it
proved. The prophetic vision of Isaiah liii. was fulfilled
to the letter ; only through the suffering and death of the
Servant was the will of God fulfilled.

It is almost certain that in pre-Christian Jewish exegesis
the Servant passages had never been interpreted in a
Messianic sense. The hope of the coming of Messiah,
though undoubtedly existent in the Judaism of the time of
Jesus, was variable and uncertain in its content. It seems
that it was part of the originality of Jesus Himself that He
was the first to understand Messiahship in terms of service
and suffering. If this is so, it becomes clear why He
acted in a way that indicated Messianic claims, and yet
was most careful never to identify Himself with the current
expectations and hopes of His people. He never in the
course of His teaching claimed to be Messiah, though He
did not reject the title when it was freely offered to Him.

Yet He instructed His followers to treat His Messiahship
as a secret to be carefully guarded, and not to be proclaimed
as part of their message during His lifetime.

This caution was carried so far that some scholars have
questioned whether Jesus ever or in any sense claimed to
be the Messiah. But, as we have seen in the case of the
word *Church*, we must be careful not to let our theological
picture be too largely determined by the use or absence of
one particular word. Though Jesus avoided the actual
word Messiah, He did make use of another term that, in
the light of Old Testament usage, could hardly be interpreted in anything but a Messianic sense. *I am the good
shepherd.* Caution demands that we should not lay stress
on any usage in the Fourth Gospel, unless it is supported
by evidence from the Synoptists. Here the evidence is
forthcoming. " Fear not, little flock, for it is your Father's
good pleasure to give you the Kingdom."[1] " It is written,
I will smite the shepherd, and the sheep shall be scattered
abroad."[2] Our understanding of such passages tends to be
distorted by somewhat sentimental representations of Jesus
as the gentle Shepherd, carrying a lamb. The Old Testament
sense of the word is very different. There, it is God Himself
who is the Shepherd of His people. " Give ear, O Shepherd
of Israel, Thou that leadest Joseph like a flock."[3] And the
shepherds, who serve under God, are the rulers of the people.
In Ezekiel xxxiv. after the denunciation of the false and
evil shepherds, who have despoiled and destroyed the flock,
God gives the Messianic promise : " I will set up one shepherd
over them, and he shall feed them, even my servant David ;
he shall feed them, and he shall be their shepherd."[4] It is
such passages as these that lie behind the use of the word
Shepherd in the mouth of Jesus. If Jesus is the true
Shepherd, what is a shepherd without His flock ? What is
the meaning of His work, if it is not to seek His sheep, and

[1] St. Luke xii. 32.   [2] St. Mark xiv. 27.
[3] Psalm lxxx. 1.   [4] Ezekiel xxxiv. 23.

to deliver them out of all places whither they have been scattered in the cloudy and dark day ?

The centre of the preaching of Jesus was the coming of the Kingdom of God. The phrase is always to be interpreted as the sovereignty of a personal and gracious God, and not as a geographical or local realm. As with so many of the words of Jesus, there has been long debate as to His meaning. What was in His mind when He proclaimed that the Kingdom of God is at hand ? Did He mean, as some interpret, that the Kingdom of God is coming very soon, by a dramatic intervention of God in the history of the world ? Or did He mean that the Kingdom of God is already here ? Almost all the Gospel evidence seems to support the second interpretation. " If I by the finger of God cast out devils, then is the Kingdom of God come upon you."[1] In the person of Jesus, the sovereignty of God is already present in redemptive power. The mighty works done by Him are not mere marvels ; they are *signs*, the powers of the age to come already manifest in the age that now is. The *eschaton*, the last stage in the manifestation of the purpose of God, is already here, and for those who by faith will enter into the Kingdom of God the door is already open.

Again, though it does not appear that He Himself claimed the title King, the inscription set upon His cross *The King of the Jews* did not greatly misrepresent, though it may have misinterpreted, what was present in His teaching. And what is a king without His people ? Sovereignty, in Old and New Testaments alike, is not something exercised in the abstract. It represents the relationship between God and His people, or more generally God's relationship to the world that he has made.

In the Old Testament, the special relationship between God and Israel is conveyed by one word, so constantly repeated as to be in many ways the keyword of the Old

[1] St. Luke xi. 20 cf. also St. Matthew xii. 27.

Testament revelation, the word *covenant*. If, therefore,
Jesus, in circumstances of special solemnity, made use of
the word *covenant*, it is almost certain that He must have
used it, and must have been understood by His hearers to
use it, in the context of ideas which the Old Testament
had made familiar. We have extremely strong evidence
that He did so use it. " This is my blood of the covenant,
which is shed for many."[1]

In the hearing of Jews, and in circumstances calculated
to lend a special solemnity to every word spoken, this
phrase could have one connotation only ; it would direct
their minds back to that overwhelming experience at Mount
Sinai in which Israel became a nation : " And he took
the book of the covenant, and read in the audience of the
people : and they said, All that the Lord hath said will we
do, and be obedient. And Moses took the blood, and
sprinkled it on the people, and said, Behold the blood of the
covenant which the Lord hath made with you concerning
all these words."[2] That the early Christians did so interpret
the reference is not a matter merely of inference. The
writer of the First Epistle of Peter, recalling to his readers
the nature of their vocation, tells them that " ye are an elect
race, a royal priesthood, an holy nation, a people for God's
own possession ; that ye may shew forth the praises of him
who called you out of darkness into his marvellous light."[3]
The words are an almost exact quotation from the Book
of Exodus, and apply to the Christian society the very
words which were the proud boast of Israel as the chosen
people of God.

In the Matthaean form of the words, " This is my blood
of the covenant, which is shed for many unto remission of
sins,"[4] the additions are probably glosses rather than parts
of the words as originally spoken by Jesus. But as so often

---

[1] St. Mark xiv. 24. The Pauline form of the saying, " This cup is the
new covenant in my blood," is very strong corroborative evidence for the
actual use of the word *covenant* by Jesus at the Last Supper.
[2] Exodus, xxiv. 7–8. [3] I Peter ii. 9. [4] St. Matthew xxvi. 28.

in Matthew, the gloss is a real interpretation, and not merely a rabbinic expansion. What was the covenant of which Jesus spoke ? The passover, in the context of which He was speaking, was, in one of its aspects, the annual commemoration of the great deliverance, in which the people came out of Egypt, and in which they were constituted a nation. But Jesus could not be concerned either with a mere reminder of what was known from childhood to every Jew, or with a re-enactment of a covenant that He, like every other Jew, assumed to be still valid. If He spoke of a covenant, it could be only a new covenant with a new significance. And for this too there is the unmistakable Old Testament evidence. The great prophecy of Jeremiah looks forward to a time when the old covenant of Sinai will no longer be God's last word to His people, and when the covenant written on tables of stone will lose its primacy. "Behold the days come, saith the Lord, that I will make a new covenant with the house of Israel, and with the house of Judah. . . . This is the covenant that I will make with the house of Israel after those days, saith the Lord ; I will put my law in their inward parts, and in their hearts will I write it ; and I will be their God, and they shall be my people . . . for I will forgive their iniquity, and their sin will I remember no more."[1] Here the two ideas of a new covenant, and of a covenant of which the new feature will be forgiveness, are already joined together. And in each case, the covenant is not between God and an individual, or between God and a group of individuals, but between God and a people. The long exposition of this passage in the Epistle to the Hebrews again makes it clear that this association of ideas was a commonplace among the earliest Christians.

The emphasis on Israel as the recipient of the new covenant, as of the old, might suggest that the aim of Jesus was no more than the resuscitation or revival of the historic Israel, a task to which the prophets of the Old Testament had in succession

[1] Jeremiah xxxi. 31, 33, & 34.

dedicated themselves. There are undoubtedly passages in the Gospels, and especially in the Matthaean record, which suggests a strict limitation of the work of Jesus to the Jewish milieu. The Gentiles who figure in the narratives are exceptions, and are brought in, as it were, almost apologetically. Later Christian interpretation was almost unanimous in holding that this limitation was only temporary, a strategic necessity in view of the immediate task of creating the nucleus of the new community, a condition of the life of the incarnate Lord prior to the resurrection. There are sufficient hints in the words and acts of Jesus Himself to make it probable that this Christian interpretation was more than an invention of the second generation of believers. In the first place, as we have seen, the second Isaiah was that part of the prophetic Scriptures on which the mind of Jesus dwelt with special intentness. That is also the part of the Old Testament in which the doctrine of God as universal Lord, and the destiny of Israel as the instrument in the hand of God to achieve a universal redemption, are emphasised as nowhere else. It would be strange indeed if Jesus had gone back from this wider vision to the parochialism of Judaism as it existed in its narrower forms.

Apart, however, from inference, there is one piece of evidence, which, though indirect, is of striking significance. The one occasion on which Jesus seems in some measure to have identified Himself with the Messiah of Jewish expectation, and to have claimed royal dignity, was the triumphal entry into Jerusalem. It is clear that this episode did not arise from a sudden inspiration, but had been carefully planned. It was intended to serve as a challenge, both to the believers to realise the nature of the Kingdom which they were called to serve, and to the authorities in Jerusalem to make up their minds whether they would or would not accept the coming King. The event was a fulfilment, apparently a deliberate and conscious fulfilment, of the prophecy of Zechariah : " Rejoice greatly, O daughter of Zion ; shout, O daughter of Jerusalem : behold, thy King cometh unto thee : he is just, and having salvation ; lowly, and riding upon an ass, even upon a colt the foal of an ass."[1] This is familiar enough. But not infrequently readers fail to notice the words in which the prophecy culminates : " He shall speak peace unto the nations : and his dominion shall be from sea to sea, and from the river to the ends of the earth."[2] This passage is directly linked with the seventy-second Psalm, the great Psalm of the Kingdom, in which precisely the same words occur. Since the date both of Psalm and of prophecy is quite uncertain, it is not possible to say which is quoting from the other. It is difficult to imagine that Jesus acted on the first part of the prophecy, and was at the same time unaware of the second part, with all the implications of world-wide dominion in which it has been set.

It must be admitted that most of the phrases in the Gospels which refer to a world-wide proclamation of the Gospel belong to those strata which criticism would ascribe to the development of interpretation rather than to a record of the original words of Jesus. The conclusion of Matthew's Gospel with its explicit command, " Go ye therefore, and make disciples of all the nations, baptizing them in the name of the Father, and of the Son, and of the Holy Ghost,"[3] is a passage which we shall be well advised to use with caution. But this saying is not unique. The utterance, " I say unto you, that many shall come from the east and the west, and shall sit down with Abraham, and Isaac, and Jacob, in the kingdom of heaven,"[4] is one which even radical critics admit to be authentic ; it looks far beyond the limits of the traditional Israel as the sphere of the operation of the Gospel. And, when we assign certain parts of the Gospel to the interpretative activity of the Christian com-

---

[1] Zechariah ix. 9.   [2] *Ibid.* verse 10.
[3] St. Matthew xxviii. 19.   [4] St. Matthew viii. 11.

munity, we must not forget the possibility that sometimes that community was right in its interpretations, and that, even when it was not recording the exact words of the Master, it had divined correctly His purpose and the direction in which His teaching pointed.

It would be tedious to accumulate further examples. As a general rule, it may be said that, at whatever point the teaching of Jesus is taken in its natural connection of thought and language with the Old Testament, it will be found most readily intelligible if interpreted in the light of the significance of a chosen people for the redemptive purpose of God ; this remains true, whether we are speaking of the natural Israel, or of the faithful within Israel, or of Jesus Himself as the one in whom the destiny of Israel is fulfilled, or of the new Israel, constituted through faith in Him on the basis of the new covenant.

Interpretation of the Gospels through use of their Jewish background is the correct method of exegesis. Yet, even if this method be not followed, there is still enough material in the Gospels to make plain the integral part which the new community plays in the mission and message of Jesus.

When He said to the disciples " But it is not so among you,"[1] His words imply the existence of a society recognising special responsibilities and governed by special laws. At that moment, that society was represented only by the Twelve, but there is no reason to suppose that the command given to them was intended to be limited in its application only to them. The occasion was one of deep significance. A dispute had broken out among the Twelve, after the request of the sons of Zebedee that they might be given a position of special privilege in the coming Kingdom. Jesus took the opportunity to lay down emphatically not merely the law by which that Kingdom was to be governed, that principle, so often repeated, that whosoever will be the chiefest shall be the servant of all, but also precisely

[1] St. Mark x. 4"

the differentiation between that Kingdom and the kingdoms of the world. There is another type of society, and there is another type of greatness ; this is found in the kingdoms of the Gentiles, where their great ones exercise authority upon them ; the same was found even in the kingdom of Israel. If the disciples are hankering after that kind of eminence, their desire must be accounted natural ; and yet it is condemned, since by this time they ought to have realised that the Kingdom to the service of which, by following Jesus, they had committed themselves was to be governed in a wholly different way. A new society was already in being, and the law of that society had already been revealed.

This principle is already implicit in what is widely re-cognised as the most characteristic feature in the teaching of Jesus, His association of the two great commandments, found in separation in the Old Testament, that men should love God with all their hearts, and their neighbour as them-selves. When the word *love* is taken seriously, in the full extension of meaning given to it in the teaching of Jesus, it is clear that it is no mere emotion or attitude of the mind, but rather a governing principle, which determines all relationships, and must find its expression in redemptive service. But, as relationships come to be determined by this principle, a new society does in fact come into being. The Johannine saying, " A new command-ment I give unto you, That ye love one another ; even as I have loved you, that ye also love one another. By this shall all men know that ye are my disciples, if ye have love one to another,"[1] is an explication of something which is already present in the synoptic tradition. And when the writer of II Peter bids his readers practice first love of the brethren and then love,[2] the order in which he places these virtues must be judged to be historically and psychologically correct. It is only from within a society determined by the

---

[1] St. John xiii. 34, 35.   [2] II Peter i. 7.

principle laid down by Jesus that the Christian can go forth
to exercise in the world outside the redemptive ministry of
love. The redeemed society is indispensable for the fulfilment
of the commandment.

We return to consider again the original society of
the Twelve. In the synoptic account, the choice of this
company is represented as a turning point in the ministry
of Jesus. It comes at the point at which it has already
become clear that the nation as a whole will not accept
the teaching and therefore cannot be reborn into the new
community. The Pharisees have taken counsel against
Him with the Herodians how they may destroy Him. Then,
after the whole night has been spent in prayer, Jesus " calleth
unto him whom he would . . . and he appointed twelve, that
they might be with him, and that he might send them forth
to preach."[1] From that moment onwards, more and more
time is given to the training and preparation of this small
and intimate company, on whose faith and understanding
the continuation of the work of Jesus will depend.

A different number might have been chosen. The number
twelve cannot be understood otherwise than in relation to
the old Israel, and the twelve patriarchs from whom,
according to Old Testament tradition, the nation took its
origin. If there were any doubt as to this, it would be
dissipated by the remarkable saying that in the Kingdom
which Jesus had appointed unto them, they shall eat and
drink at His table, and " shall sit on thrones judging the
twelve tribes of Israel."[2] It may well be that in this saying,
as in so many others in the crisis of the Passion, there is an
element of gentle irony. Yet, even so, the relationship
between the old society and the new is unmistakable ; and
from the beginning of the Church as a recognisable society.
the unique position of the Twelve was never for a moment
in question. The term *apostle* fluctuated in meaning. Saul
of Tarsus, who certainly was not one of the original Twelve,

---

[1] St. Mark iii. 1–19.   [2] St. Luke xxii. 29–30.

was able to make good his claim to that title. But *the twelve* meant one thing and one only. Far on in the New Testament tradition, we read in the vision of the new Jerusalem that " The wall of the city had twelve foundations, and on them twelve names of the twelve apostles of the Lamb."[1] The Christian community recognised that a special gift and special authority had been committed to the Twelve. The whole structure of the synoptic tradition suggests that, in so doing, the community was accepting and following the intention of its Founder.

Even if these various contentions and arguments are accepted, we are left with the question as to the extent to which Jesus foresaw the historical development of His new community, and to which He attempted to determine that development by specific injunctions and rules of organisation.

Of organisation in the strict sense of the term we find scarcely anything at all. The group of Christian disciples in Jerusalem began from the first to practise the two rites of baptism and the supper of the Lord, and the biblical tradition traces both of these back to the institution of Jesus Himself.

This tradition is not, indeed, uncontested. The direct command to baptize is found only, as we have noted, in a section of the Gospels which most scholars would hesitate to accept in its present form as representing the words of Jesus Himself.[2] The command to continue the observance of the Last Supper " in remembrance of me " is found only in the Lucan and Pauline records of the institution. But this measure of uncertainty in the tradition does not justify us in reaching at once a negative conclusion with regard to the institution of the Christian sacraments.

The earliest disciples were familiar with the baptism of

---

[1] Revelation xxi. 14.
[2] The references to baptism in John iii. 22–26, iv. 1–2, are interesting and important. But the context makes it clear that the reference is to an extension by Jesus and His disciples of the baptism of *John,* and not to Christian baptism, as it was later understood.

John. They were clear that what they were bestowing in the name of Jesus was not the same baptism, but something so essentially different that those who had already received the baptism of John must be baptized again in the name of Jesus.[1] For them, baptism was no longer proleptic, a profession of faith in a kingdom yet to be revealed ; it was eschatological, a sealing into a kingdom already revealed and still to be revealed in its eternal fulness. It was associated with the death and resurrection of Jesus Christ, and with the coming of that Spirit foretold, as the record now stands, both by John and by Jesus. How did the disciples come to associate baptism in water with all this new complex of ideas ? How was it that from the first they regarded this rite as the indispensable form of entry into the new society and into the kingdom of which that society was the historical manifestation ? Recent investigation of the sources confirms the view that the explanation which most readily covers all the facts is that here, as elsewhere, the disciples had correctly interpreted the mind of Christ. Actual phrases in the Gospels, even though they may not be precise transcriptions of His words, represent a genuine element in the tradition. Because Jesus himself had associated baptism with the new gift that He came to bring, over and above that which had been brought by John the Baptist, the disciples at once put into practice what they had understood to be His intention.[2]

Many scholars would accept the same type of argument with regard to the institution of the Lord's Supper. The character of the Gospel tradition is well exemplified by the combination of historical certainty concerning the fact of the Last Supper eaten by Jesus with His disciples, with a large measure of uncertainty concerning almost all the details. There is no agreement as to the nature of the meal thus taken. Older tradition identified it with the

[1] See Acts xix. 1–7.
[2] This has been fully worked out by W. F. Flemington in *The New Testament Doctrine of Baptism* (London, S.P.C.K., 1948) pp. 117–129.

supper of the Passover. In this view many difficulties seem
to be involved.[1] Others have held that it was an ordinary
evening meal, to which Jesus, knowing that He would not
live to eat the Passover with His disciples, deliberately gave
much of the solemnity of the actual Passover. Yet others
argue strongly that this was the *Kiddush*, such a meal as was
regularly held in preparation for the Sabbath, and that its
special solemnity derived only from Jesus' knowledge that
it was the last. The argument will doubtless continue. On
one point we can speak with considerable confidence. Jesus
must often have taken supper with His disciples. At such
meals, as the head of the company, He must often have
said the words of blessing over the bread and over the cup.
What gave this last occasion its special significance was the
identification of the bread with His Body, and the association
of the cup with the Blood of the covenant. And His words
did associate this solemnity with the coming of the kingdom
of God in power. When the disciples, after the resurrection,
met without the visible presence of their Lord, they met
in the assurance that the new age of the world, of which
the new covenant was the starting point, had already come,
and that they were both living in that new age and awaiting
the fulness of its manifestation. Then only was it possible
for them fully to understand the significance of what their
Master had done and said on the night on which He was
betrayed. Every time that they met to break bread, their
thoughts would go back to that last occasion, and forward
to the fulfilment to which it pointed. Whether they could
recall actual words of the Master bidding them continue
the observance in memory of Him or not, they were assured
that in doing so they were acting according to His mind.
The later history of the Church and of Christian worship
gives, if not demonstrative proof, at least a strong indication

[1] Though it has lately been revived and strongly defended by Professor J.
Jeremias, cf. his article in the Journal of Theological Studies, Vol. L, Jan.–
Ap. 1949 (No. 197–8), pp. 1–10, and his book *Die Abendmahlworte Jesu* (2nd
ed. revised, Göttingen 1949).

that they were right in their understanding of what Jesus
had intended.

Of positive and detailed instruction, Jesus seems to have
left little. He claimed to be the new Moses, revising and
correcting the earlier law by the sole authority of His " I
say unto you." But it would be hard to imagine a greater
contrast than that between the detailed ritual and even
sanitary prescriptions of the Mosaic law and the generalised
injunctions of the new law as set forth by Jesus. To the
new society, this was an incalculable advantage. The
atmosphere of Arabia in the Seventh Century is indelibly
impressed on the legislation of Muhammad and the institutions of Islam. The Gospel suffers under no such local
and temporal attachments, and enjoys therefore the freedom
necessary for any system that is to become the foundation
of a universal society. Jesus dealt almost wholly in
ultimates, in those supreme principles of the relationship
between God and man and man and man, which underlie
every specific injunction or ordinance or application. It
is true, indeed, that the Christian society has often been
perplexed as to the way in which it should interpret and
apply the sayings of the Master ; it has not yet been able
to make up its mind whether divorce is in all circumstances
excluded from the Christian scheme, and whether there are
situations in which a Christian may rightly bear arms
in war. But such perplexities are inevitable in a world
where the word of Christ has only a limited sovereignty,
and where so much of even Christian action bears the
character of compromise between unlimited obligation and
the limited applicability of principles in a refractory situation
largely conditioned by other and non-Christian concepts.
It is probable that Jesus both foresaw and was prepared
for this perplexity. The promise, recorded in the Fourth
Gospel, that the Holy Spirit would guide the believers into
all the truth, takes up and generalises the hint in the synoptic
tradition that immediate guidance would be given in times

of perplexity and persecution : " For it is not ye that speak, but the Spirit of your Father that speaketh in you."[1]

There is, however, yet a further reason for this apparent indefiniteness in the constitution of the new society. The purpose for which it was called into being was not simply to bear witness to what God had done in Jesus, to carry out His commands or to keep alive the memory of His teaching. The Christian Society was, in its measure and in its place in the divine order, to be the Christ. When Paul spoke of the Church as the body of Christ, so far from inventing a new concept or adding to the Gospel something which was not already present in it, he was making explicit a basic idea, which is implicit throughout. The Christian community, as the Messianic society, is to continue the work of Messiah, by being what He was, and by expressing in its life as a society that which He was representatively, as the One in whom alone the true idea of Israel had been visibly wrought out.

If the Church is to be Messianic, as well as bearing witness to the historical Messiah, there are three principles which at all times must be manifest in its life.

The basis of its life must be that supreme respect for human personality which was characteristic at all times of the ministry of Jesus. He showed this respect by His attitude to all, even the most degraded ; He made it plain that He regarded every individual as of infinite value, just because each was potentially a son of God. But this respect for personality excludes from the divine society every element of coercion ; it is the foundation for the liberty of a society which can exist only through the willing service of all its members. Jesus called men to follow Him. He was at pains to make clear the terms on which they must follow Him ; the Son of Man hath not where to lay His head, and those who come after Him must accept the like conditions. Yet He never makes the least attempt to compel any to

[1] St. Matthew x. 20.

follow, and would rather discourage than coerce the half-hearted. Even when men had committed themselves to Him, they were free at any time to withdraw, if they would. When at a crisis of the ministry, following on His failure to conform to the accepted pattern of Messianic expectation, He turned to the Twelve and asked, "Would ye also go away ? "[1], the words must be taken not as an emotional appeal but as a genuine question. If they wished to go away, they were free to do so ; in this society, loyalty must be unconstrained, and service must be whole-hearted, or it cannot be accepted.

In the second place, balancing this respect for individual freedom, and closely connected with it, is the inexorable demand that those who yield themselves to the service of the new society should do so without reservations and without compromise. Jesus had the right to make such a claim, because of his own perfect and uncompromising submission to the Will of His Father in Heaven. To receive Him was to receive Him that had sent Him. The only way to receive Him was to yield Him just such obedience as He had yielded to God. Never in history has any leader made so absolute a claim on the loyalty of His followers. They must be willing, if need be, to hate father and mother for His sake ; they must let the dead bury their dead and forsake all things. Nothing must come between them and their loyalty to the cause. There is something terrifying in the hardness and sternness with which this demand is reiterated. But, as history has shown, there is no way in which the new society can be held together other than the repetition, in every generation, of just this unconditional surrender of individual selves to Christ. It is through those who have fully accepted the conditions that the Church lives on.

Thirdly, Jesus made no secret of the irreconcilable opposition which must exist between His society and all societies organised on other foundations. The crisis of His own cross

[1] St. John vi: 67.

and passion was not to be taken merely as an individual occurrence, precipitated by certain historical accidents. It was the type and pattern of the life of His society. Secular societies exist to fulfil limited and temporal exigencies. They are based on calculation, on a balance of authorities, on coercive power ; the aims which they consecrate are success, security and worldly prosperity. The society of Jesus abandons all these bases of social living. By its very existence, and precisely in proportion as it is true to its own nature, it constitutes a criticism and at times a condemnation of every other society. And, this being so, it must expect recurrently the hostility of those with whom it cannot finally make a compromise. It has a loyalty beyond all human loyalties ; when any state or community arrogates to itself the right to demand the ultimate loyalty, then the Christian society must challenge its claim to the heart, and in doing so will almost certainly bring upon itself the very same hatred and will to destroy that fastened upon Jesus of Nazareth and hounded Him to His death. Shall the servant be above his Lord ? The new society may have its times of prosperity and of amicable adjustment with the other types of society that condition the life of men ; the inner opposition is ineradicable, and makes impossible a final reconciliation between the new society and the old. The society of the Crucified must be neither surprised nor dismayed, if it finds itself perennially called to bear the cross.

So much concerning the nature of the Christian society may perhaps be safely inferred from the earliest records as we have them.[1] In a historical study, we are right to use the methods of historical criticism, and as far as possible to eliminate considerations of religious faith and of theology. This approach may yield results considerably vaguer and

[1] It will be plain to the reader that, at every point, I have made a minimum rather than a maximum statement. But a sound foundation is best laid by taking only those materials that can be most confidently relied on to stand the strain of criticism.

less confident than those of theological assertion, but not perhaps for that reason any less valuable. But it must be remembered that the earliest believers in Jesus were not critics or historians. They were men still staggering under the impact of an overwhelming experience ; they were convinced that upon them the end of the world, that is, the decisive intervention of God, in which all the issues of human history had been settled, had come, and that they were already living in the new age of the world. However imperfectly they worked it out in the business of daily living, this was their conviction. We shall not be in a position to understand the nature of the Christian society, unless we enter, either imaginatively or by actual participation, into the faith and experience of those to whom Jesus of Nazareth was the Word of God, the author and finisher of their faith, and who had accepted Him as the sole foundation of that eternal city of God, which must assuredly be built.

CHAPTER II

GROWTH AND PERSECUTION

THE new society was launched in Jerusalem as a group of
Jews, who, to the generally accepted tenets of Judaism,
added the affirmation that Jesus of Nazareth was the Messiah,
and the paradoxical assertion that One whom everybody
knew to be dead was in fact alive.[1] Within the customary
framework of Jewish life, this society worked out for itself
certain rules such as have at all times characterised
particular societies within larger religious bodies. There
was the teaching of the Apostles, presumably the beginnings
of that oral recollection and systematisation of the words
and works of Jesus that modern criticism recognises as
underlying the structure of our actual Gospels. There were
the prayers, the specifically Christian prayers, made very
soon or even from the start in the name of Jesus Messiah.
In addition to the public worship of temple and synagogue,
there was the breaking of bread at home, almost certainly
the primitive beginning of what gradually developed into the
elaborated Christian Eucharist. There was a simple communism, in which goods and possessions were shared. This last
was probably connected with the eschatological expectation
that Jesus of Nazareth would return from heaven very soon
and bring in a state of society in which wealth and property
were no longer needed. This reckless dissipation of capital
soon reduced the Jerusalem community to extreme poverty,
and communism in its more radical form was given up ;
but the fellowship and sense of mutual responsibility of

[1] Cf. Acts xxv. 19, *One Jesus, who was dead, whom Paul affirmed to be alive.*

23

which it had been an expression remained a permanent characteristic of the Christian body.

Had life continued peacefully, the new society might have remained for ever a reforming sect within the Jewish fold. It was greatly to its advantage that, within two generations, it had to encounter three major crises.

The first of these concerned the terms on which non-Jews could be admitted to the Christian fellowship. From Antioch came the startling tidings that Gentiles had been admitted to the Church without the preliminary stages of proselytism to the Jewish faith and circumcision, that an attempt to set up two separate Eucharists, one for Jews and one for Gentiles, had been frustrated by the strong action of Saul of Tarsus,[1] and that Jews and Gentiles were living as Christians on equal terms. Many pages of the New Testament bear witness to the violence of the controversy that these events evoked.

The issue was not primarily one of racial narrowness and exclusiveness. It is true that, in the ancient as in the modern world, the Jews had proved an unassimilable element. The picture given, for example by Juvenal, is of a morose and surly people, holding aloof from normal life, and unmoved by the obligations of ordinary courtesy. Yet this aloofness had not prevented a wide dissemination of interest in the Jewish faith. Almost every synagogue in the Levant had its group of " godfearers," men, and particularly women, attracted by the Jewish doctrine of God, of history and of the moral law. Some became proselytes ; the majority were deterred by the obligation of circumcision, a rite which profoundly offended the sensibilities of both Greeks and Romans. It would have been possible for the Christian community also to continue, as it has in many times and places, with its inner group of adherents and its outer group of hearers. The problem, as Saul of Tarsus, apparently at first alone, perceived, was neither racial nor ritual, but theo-

[1] This seems the most probable interpretation of Gal ii. 11–15.

logical. What is the basis of salvation, and therefore of membership in the new society ? Is it single or dual ? Does it include both circumcision and baptism ? Or is faith in Jesus as Messiah, with its corollary in baptism, inclusive of all the privileges of both the old covenant and the new ? When at the council held in Jerusalem Peter stood up and said of Gentile believers : " God . . . bare them witness, giving them the Holy Ghost, even as he did unto us ; And he made no distinction between us and them, cleansing their hearts by faith,"[1] the battle was in fact won. Faith in Jesus was accepted as the one and only requisite. Circumcision might continue as the sign of a special vocation for some within the Christian society ; it was recognised to have no eternal significance, but to be a part of that provisional covenant which was now growing old and passing away.

The abandonment of circumcision as a condition of membership was undoubtedly helpful to the growth of the new society. But it was not this that made the victory of the Pauline party all-important. Since there was now one single door to salvation, universal in its appeal to all men without distinction, a universal society had at last become possible. It was this new discovery or revelation that inspired Paul to heights of lyrical jubilation. This was the secret hidden from all previous ages, but now at last revealed ; this made possible the accomplishment of the divine purpose to sum up all things in Christ.

The ancient world was a world of divisions. The Stoics had arrived at a noble concept of the brotherhood of man, but their ideas remained ineffective except in the world of the philosophers. Not for another century and a half was the Roman Empire to rise to the height of the idea of universal citizenship for all free men who dwelt within it.[2]

[1] Acts.xv. 8-9.
[2] In A.D. 212 Caracalla conferred Roman citizenship on all the free inhabitants of the Empire (with apparently, some insignificant exceptions). Dio Cassius suggests that the real purpose underlying this enlightened measure was the replenishment of the treasury by increasing the number of those liable to pay the duty on inheritances (lxxviii, 9. 4–5),

In the meantime, men were graded in sharply distinguished categories of privilege. The Greek was still conscious of his superiority to the barbarian. The rigid division between Jew and Gentile continued. Not till many centuries had passed was the odious division between slave and free done away. But within the new society the true principle of universality was affirmed, and in a wonderful measure realised. " There can be neither Jew nor Greek, there can be neither bond nor free, there can be no male and female : for ye all are one man in Christ Jesus."[1] It might be maintained by some that the Christian society has not yet realised all the implications of this charter of freedom. It is certain that, in the matters of race and colour and class privilege, it has often failed grievously to live up to its own nature. But no one within the society has ever dared to deny in principle the truth as set forth by Paul. Only as a universal society can this society exist at all ; only so can it maintain the reality of its fellowship with Christ the universal Saviour.

The second crisis was brought about through the capture of Jerusalem by the Romans, and the dissolution of the Jewish nation.

Until A.D. 70, Jerusalem had been for the Christians as for the Jews the centre of their world. James, the brother of the Lord, held, as head of the Jerusalem community, a unique position within the Christian society. The elders at Jerusalem seem to have been regarded, in some way not perhaps very clearly defined, as the great Sanhedrin of the Christian Church. Some seem even to have thought that until the return of Jesus in glory a kind of caliphate should continue in the family to which as a man He had belonged.[2] The destruction of Jerusalem put an end to all such ideas.

---

[1] Gal. iii. 28.

[2] On the death of James, Simeon was chosen as his successor. According to Hegesippus (quoted by Eusebius H. E. IV, 22, 4), " All preferred him because he was the cousin of the Lord." Simeon lived till A.D. 107, but never exercised in the Church an influence comparable to that of James.

From that time forward, the Christian society was to be free from all local and temporal associations. The minds of Christians have always turned with deep interest and affection to the scenes of the earthly life and ministry and death of the Lord. At an early date, pilgrimage to the sacred sites became, and has continued ever since to be, a characteristic form of Christian devotion. But Jerusalem has never been to the Christian what Mecca is to the Muslim. If access to Jerusalem were for ever denied him, he would be grieved, but would have lost nothing that touched the essentials of his faith.

The loss of a local centre appears to have had one consequence of lasting import both for Judaism and for the Christian body. Judaism had relied greatly on oral tradition maintained in the chief Rabbinic schools. Hard on the loss of Jerusalem followed the final determination of the canon of the Hebrew Scriptures,[1] and, apparently, the beginning of the writing down of traditions previously current only in oral tradition. It seems likely that the Christians were influenced by this Jewish example. As long as they believed that the Lord would soon return, as long as Jerusalem maintained in detail the remembrance and the verbal tradition of all that He had said and done, there seemed no strong reason for writing down the traditions of the community about Him. When Jerusalem was lost and the scribal tradition could no longer be assured, it seemed an urgent necessity to commit to writing and so to maintain for future generations all those things the loss of which would imperil the future of the community. The Christians had been from the beginning the people of a book ; they had taken over from their Jewish past the Scriptures of the Old Testament, which bore witness to the Messiah. The process by which they became the people of two books, and added

---

[1] " The precise number and precise text of the Books ranked as sacred was determined authoritatively by the discussions of Jewish scholars about A.D. 150." W. A. L. Elmslie : *How Came Our Faith* (C.U.P., 1948), p. 57.

a new canon to the old, is very obscure. It seems probable
however that we should ascribe to the period between 70
and 95 the writing of three, if not of all, of our canonical
Gospels, and the beginning of that collection of apostolic
writings, which gradually developed into our New Testament in its present form. A society which has a fixed
and unalterable charter has taken a long step away from its
initial fluidity towards becoming itself fixed and unalterable
in its form.

The third crisis was associated with the death of the last
of those witnesses who had been with Jesus and had known
Him in the flesh. " This saying therefore went forth among
the brethren, that that disciple should not die : yet Jesus
said not unto him, that he should not die ; but, If I will that
he tarry till I come, what *is that* to thee ? "[1] These words
could not have been written, unless there had been, among
the believers at the end of the first Century, an expectation
that the Parousia would take place before the death of the
last of the original witnesses. The writer of the Fourth
Gospel is anxious to shew that such a tradition has no
foundation, and to guard against the disappointment that
must ensue, if that last disciple died, and still the Lord had
not come. Early Christian tradition identified the last
survivor with the Apostle John, and affirmed that he
had lived on to extreme old age in Ephesus. Modern
criticism has cast certain doubts on that tradition. Yet it
seems clear that there was in Ephesus, at the end of the
century, one leader who held a position of unique authority
and influence in the Church. It is also clear that on his death
the Church would be faced by a serious problem. When he
died, was his authority to continue in the Church, and if so,
in what form ; or was it to disappear as something belonging
to a historic past that could never be reproduced ? It is
possible to believe both that the Lord Himself had given
no precise instructions to cover this eventuality, and also

[1] John xxi. 23.

that the solution gradually arrived at by the Church was reached under the guidance of the Spirit of the Master.[1]

The origin of the episcopate is still obscure. The evidence, like all our evidence of what happened between the end of the apostolic period and the middle of the second century, is fragmentary and uncertain. It cannot be said that recent studies have succeeded in dissipating the uncertainty. Most scholars reject as unhistorical the tradition that the Apostle Peter was, and was recognised as being, the first Bishop of Rome. We are justified in giving great weight, though cautiously, to the strong tradition that associates the episcopate in its origins with the Apostle John and with Asia Minor. As long as the apostles survived, (and here the word must be taken in its wide sense, to include such men as Paul and Barnabas), they were the living manifestation of the unity of the Church. Each Christian group was the concern of some apostle ; over it he exercised immense though probably undefined authority. Under him was the local ministry of presbyters and deacons, chosen from among the members of the local community. When the apostles died, was the apostolic office to cease, or was it to be continued, as the focus of the authority of Christ in His Church, and as the visible manifestation of its unity ? By the middle of the Second Century, the episcopate had been accepted throughout the Church as the answer to this question. The local ministry had been strengthened by the absorption into it of whatever was transferable of the original apostolic authority. The bishop was entrusted with the dual task of maintaining the unity of the Church through his fellowship with all the other members of the episcopal order, and of keeping the continuity of the Church with its foundation through the maintenance of apostolic doctrine,

---

[1] Dr. B. H. Streeter (*The Four Gospels*, London, 1936, p. 477) very aptly compared the dismay which arose in the ranks of the Irvingites when it became clear that the last of the twelve " apostles " appointed by their founder, or by his associates in 1835, would die. Edward Irving had given no authority to his followers to replace any of the original twelve who died. The last of them died on 3 Feb., 1901.

and the ordination of new recruits to the presbyterate.

It seems probable that the acceptance of this solution was only gradual. The passionate emphasis in the letters of Ignatius[1] on the necessity of fellowship with the bishop as the mark of a true Church seems to be more readily explicable as the defence of something that was being questioned than as the assertion of what was already universally accepted. In later times episcopacy was taken so much as a matter of course that only dim memories survived of a time when a different organisation of the churches was thought possible, or had in fact existed.

From the beginning, the expansion of the new society had been extremely rapid. Of the details, little is recorded. The Acts of the Apostles concerns itself almost exclusively with the ministry of St. Paul, and with the growth of the Church in the countries north of the Mediterranean. But this was only one part of the development of the new society. Before the end of the First Century, it was strongly established in Alexandria, and had begun to take hold in other parts of Egypt. The legend of the correspondence between King Abgar of Edessa and Jesus Himself, like most ancient legends, had a substratum of truth. It points to the fact that Edessa was one of the earliest strongholds of the faith to the East of Palestine ; it may be taken as almost certain that the Gospel had reached that area, and was being proclaimed in Syriac, before the end of the First Century. The statement of Tertullian that there were in his time Christians in Scotland, beyond the limits of the Roman Empire, may be rhetorical rather than a strict statement of fact ; but, if it contains an element of exaggeration, probably it does not go very far beyond the truth.

By the Third Century, the belief that St. Thomas had

---

[1] Ignatius of Antioch was martyred in Rome, almost certainly in A.D. 107. The genuineness of his epistles was long contested ; the establishment (by J. B. Lightfoot in 1885) of the authenticity of the seven main epistles, is one of the outstanding contributions of scholarship to our understanding of the early Church.

reached India and established the Church there was firmly
rooted in Christian tradition. Some scholars incline to
the view that the tradition was well founded in fact. In
the present state of the evidence, and unless new evidence
from an earlier date than that now available is brought to
light, it is not possible to say more than that the tradition
is by no means incredible. There is no doubt that in the
First Century there was close commercial connection between
the Roman Empire and India, both from Alexandria by way
of the Red Sea, and by the land route from Mesopotamia.
Our earliest actual evidence of the existence of churches in
India is associated with the sea-coast, and suggests the
presence of Christian merchant communities in the port
towns. There is nothing intrinsically improbable in the
view that some of these communities, whether founded by
an apostle or not, took their origin as early as the first
century of Christian expansion.[1]

While most of the early evidence points to the growth of
the Christian community primarily in the great cities, the
invaluable testimony of the younger Pliny shows that in
one part at least of the ancient world, Bithynia, the Church
was spreading out into the countryside, and winning
adherents so fast as to cause the ancient shrines to be
almost deserted.[2]

Nothing is more impressive than the anonymity of these
early developments of missionary work. Although all the
great churches of antiquity claimed apostolic foundation,
it is possible to say with certainty of the three greatest
churches of all, Antioch, Alexandria, and Rome, that the
first foundations were laid by unknown and unnamed
Christians ; when the apostles came, they found the
Christian groups in being, and built upon foundations that

---

[1] For a careful study of the available evidence, see two pamphlets by
J. N. Farquhar, *The Apostle Thomas in North India* and *The Apostle Thomas
in South India*, and A. Mingana : *The Early Spread of Christianity in
India* (Manchester, 1926).

[2] Pliny : Epistle XCVI, written in, or shortly after A.D. 111.

others had laid. Many of the earliest Christians seem to have been traders, slaves or soldiers. As they travelled, of necessity, or on their own concerns, they carried the word with them ; where they went, a community came into being. Doubtless most of those who bore witness were simple and undistinguished people. We must not forget, indeed, that the earliest Christian fellowship had within it astonishing and anonymous gifts of intellectual power. If we think only of the writer to the Hebrews, the unknown compiler of the first Gospel in its present form, and the writer or editor of the Pastoral Epistles, we must recognise that, beyond the narrow circle of those whose work is identifiable from the New Testament record, the Church was rich in a diversity of outstanding talents. Yet it remains true that the first movement of Christian expansion was due in the main to the dynamic quality of a whole community, and not to the work of a small number of outstanding individuals.

What was the secret of this expansion, which, in spite of its remarkable rapidity, was lasting in its results, and brought into being an abiding Christian fellowship ?

We are tantalised by the poverty of the evidence for just that period of which we would most gladly have full information. We are left to make what inferences we may from hints and indications in documents written for very different purposes. It is well known that the literature of the post-apostolic age marks a sharp descent from the inspiration of even the later parts of the New Testament. For a time, such works as the First Epistle of Clement, the Epistle of Barnabas and the Shepherd of Hermas were read in churches as part of the collection of canonical Christian Scripture. It is not likely that anyone would now question the rightness of the judgment which gradually excluded them, or would suggest their restoration to canonical rank.

The mind of man seems to be incurably legalistic in tendency. What started as the Gospel of the free grace of God soon began to be changed into a new law, more exacting

than the old, though with the offer of fuller grace than in
the old dispensation to enable man to fulfil it. This
legalising tendency was offset by a somewhat crude eschatological fancy, as we find it in the millenarianism of Papias.[1]
And before long the Christians began to manifest that
addiction to the art of fiction, which was to find its expression
in the apocryphal Gospels, and at a slightly later date in
the legends of the saints. There is little sign in the earliest
Christian writers outside the Canon of any deep understanding of either the Pauline or the Johannine insights
into the meaning of the Gospel. And yet, with all the defects
in their understanding, all these Christians did believe in
Jesus of Nazareth as the One through whom salvation and
life had come to men. Their vision of Him may have been
wavering and uncertain ; but whoso touches Christ touches
life, and the life that was in them was sufficient to bring
into being new life in those that heard them.

The Gospel continued to be, as it had been in the time of
Paul, to the Greeks foolishness and to the Jews a stumbling-
block. But there was much in its message that proved
immediately attractive to the ordinary man, weighed down
by the pressure of this intolerable world. From the time
of Gibbon, there has been a tendency to idealise the age of
the Antonines as a period of peace, happiness and prosperity
for men. There is a measure of truth in this judgment.
But there is also evidence that the time was one of deepening
anxiety, and of the breaking down of the inner powers of
resistance of the human spirit. The Second Century was
more religious than the First. Outward difficulties and inner
poverty were driving men to seek new sources of spiritual
power.

The ancient world was always burdened by the sense of
inscrutable fate. Even behind the power of Olympian Zeus

---

[1] Papias wrote probably about A.D. 130. Eusebius (H.E. III, 39) quotes
him as teaching that, after the resurrection, the Kingdom of Christ would
be visibly manifest on earth for a thousand years, and adds the comment
that he " was a man of very poor understanding, as his writings shew."

stood the dim, dread figure of Anangke, that hard Necessity against which not even the gods could stand. The corollary of belief in Fate is usually belief also in luck.[1] The two great gods of the declining Roman Empire were Fate and Tyche, the lucky chance, which might for a moment set a man free from the iron bands of necessity that in the end would certainly catch him and hold him fast. The increasing recourse of men and particularly of women, in all classes of society, to soothsayers and astrologers is evidence of a failure of nerve in the face of a life that became daily more problematic. In such a society, the attraction of Judaism for many thoughtful men had been its doctrine of the sovereignty of God, a rational sovereignty, exercised not by a distant figure, inapprehensible by the minds of men, but by a Person, whose attributes were faithfulness and mercy, and who was guiding all things according to a purpose. The Christians inherited the assets of the Jews, and could increase them. The figure of the Jewish Jehovah was now made yet more easily intelligible to men, and yet more lovable, since clothed in the grace of the Lord Jesus, who only the other day had been manifest on earth. The Christians could point to a purpose which had become actual at the central point of history in the Incarnation, the summing up, as Irenaeus expressed it, of the whole history of the human race. History was no longer a meaningless recurrence of cycles, infinitely repeated without significance, but a series which one day would be summed up in the gathering together of all things in Christ. And that summing up was looked for not in some unimaginably distant future, but in the return of the Exalted, who might be coming again very soon.

The men of the Second Century longed for an assurance of immortality. To the ancient world death had always been an intolerable mystery. In brighter days, the Athenian

---

[1] See C. N. Cochrane, *Christianity and Classical Culture* (Oxford, 1944) pp. 478–9.

had been able to meet it with the immensely dignified resignation manifest in the sculptures of the earlier sepulchres. As the vital impulse diminished, hope and courage grew less. To read the later inscriptions collected by Erwin Rohde in the twelfth chapter of *Psyche*[1] is to feel an increasing sense of desolation, as the coldness and isolation of the tomb creep in upon the warmth of the human day. The saddest literature in the world is the memorial epigrams in the Greek anthology. It was a passionate desire for the assurance of life that drove men and women in their thousands to the ritual purification and mystic insights of the mysteries. These provided an anodyne. But they offered more than they were able to perform. They had in them no power of genuine ethical renewal, and, while they might offer a certain hope, they could give no clear assurance. The failure of the mysteries is disclosed by the number of those who sought initiation after initiation. Had they found once for all that which they sought, they would have had no need so painfully to seek yet further. What they sought the Gospel offered, in the revelation of the One who had been dead and was alive, and in whom man had the assurance of his eternity. The Christians lived as they preached. The early inscriptions in the catacombs breathe a spirit of quiet and expectant triumph. The Christian society offered a peace which nothing else in that troubled world could give.

But, more than anything else, it was perhaps the ethical emphasis in early Christian preaching that drew men to the Gospel. This emphasis begins to be noticeable in the later epistles in the New Testament. It is increasingly apparent in what remains to us of early Christian preaching. The pagan philosopher preached the doctrine of Apatheia, superiority to passion, as the mark of the wise man. The conscience of the ancient world approved. But in that

---

[1] Rohde, *Psyche : The Cult of Souls and Belief in Immortality among the Greeks* (E Tr. London, 1925).

disordered world, man seemed to be swept away helplessly
by the torrent of his raging inner passions. Was there, in
truth, any society in which mastery over life and inner peace
were attainable ?

The impression left on the mind of a thoughtful pagan
by his first contact with Christians has been imaginatively,
and perhaps accurately, set forth by Walter Pater in *Marius
the Epicurean*. Marius finds himself among people " upon
whom some all-subduing experience had wrought heroically,
and who still remembered, on this bland afternoon, the hour
of a great deliverance."[1] He is impressed by the order and
quietness of the house of Cecilia, by the attention paid to
children, by the constant singing, by gravity tempered by
joy that welled up constantly from some invisible source.
Perhaps there were few houses that so fully expressed the
ethos of the new society ; the new society could not have
grown as it did, unless there were many that in part
incorporated it.

The Church has been criticised for making chastity the
first of all the virtues. It is unlikely that this criticism
would have been made by anyone in the decaying Roman
Empire. Later Christian variations on the theme may
have been pathological and prejudicial to the future of the
human race ; in earlier days the Christians were face to
face with a society that seemed to be involving itself in
race suicide through its own excesses. The evidence for
this is overwhelming. It is not necessary to look to the
deliberately pornographic writers, or to take too seriously
the venom of the satirists. A writer like Apuleius, who
depicts with painful faithfulness society in the Roman
Empire as seen from below, gives evidence of what was
taken for granted with no more than cursory condemnation.
The universal curse of slavery wrought constantly as a
canker in society. The person of the slave, whether male
or female, was always at the disposal of the masters, for

 [1] Walter Pater, *Marius the Epicurean* (London, edition of 1927), p. 256.

the worst of uses, without the possibility of objection or escape. And the slave avenged himself on his oppressor by the growth of a corruption that seemed and in the end became irremediable. We shall see that many Christians were unfaithful to their trust ; but the uncompromising condemnation of every form of unchastity, the Pauline doctrine that the body is the temple of the Holy Spirit had their effects in a new attitude towards women, in a recovery of the sanctity of family life, and in the creation of a society based on mutual respect and on the pursuit of holiness. Pagans took note of these things and were not uninfluenced by them.

It is difficult to assess precisely the part played by the persecutions in the progress of the Church. Undoubtedly the persecutors gave to the Christians advertisement without which the existence of the new society would have been less widely known than it was.

From their own point of view, the Roman authorities were right to persecute the Christians. It is hard for modern man to understand sympathetically the worship of the Genius of the Emperor. But that custom was the outward expression of something fundamental in the Roman conception of society. Religion was the cement of the state. It was the Tyche, the luck, first of Julius Caesar and then of Augustus, that had delivered the world from chaos and brought peace and order. Only by that Tyche could the mastery of reason over chaos be secured, and the always precarious reign of civilisation be maintained. From the Roman point of view, the assertion of a rule higher than that of the emperor and of a loyalty which could conflict with loyalty to him was the insertion into the structure of the empire of a principle which, if allowed to maintain itself, could not but end in the disintegration of order, and would let in again the floods of chaos and dark night. It seems clear that the Roman authorities were not eager to persecute, and for the most part took action only under the pressure of popular clamour. Nevertheless, it remained the fact that by Roman standards the Christians were the enemies of the human race, and that the law was succinctly expressed in the phrase " non licet esse vos." The Gospel, with its claim to total obedience to Jesus Christ, was making its first encounter with the totalitarianisms of men—an experience to be often repeated through the centuries down to the present day.

Those who have never experienced persecution tend to overestimate its advantages. It does indeed test and sift a community. But the threat of persecution, continued over generations, even though intermittent and mitigated by long periods of quiescence, tends to produce an over-strained and even hysterical mentality. Evidence of this is not lacking in the later records. The Church would not have found it necessary to order that none should be accounted as martyrs who had deliberately courted martyr-dom,[1] unless there had been a tendency for some unnecessarily to seek the martyr's crown ; and such a running upon suffering is always evidence of a certain pathological instability. In the earlier days, except perhaps in Ignatius, there is no trace of this hysteria. There are no more moving records in the literature of the race than the letter of the Churches of Lyons and Vienne (A.D. 177) and the artless narrative of the Passion of St. Perpetua and St. Felicitas (c. A.D. 200). Through these breathes a quiet serenity, a spirit of forgiveness and of confident hope in God that still have power to move the heart of the reader. It can hardly be doubted that a deep impression was made on the minds of those who actually saw the horrors and the way in which the Christians endured. Some in the very moment of persecution were impelled to take their stand with the

---

[1] E.g. in Canon 60 of the Council of Elvira, shortly after A.D. 300. The example of the Spanish maiden Eulalia who, to ensure her condemnation, spat in the face of the judge who wished to acquit her, though extolled in popular hagiography, was not commended by the Church at large. See Prudentius : *Peristephanon* III, 121.

Christians ; doubtless many others pondered what they had seen and heard, and so were pointed to the way that they should follow.

As the society grew and expanded, the maintenance of its unity became an increasing problem.

The sense of unity was present from the start. The view, held by some scholars, that originally each Christian group thought of itself as a wholly independent unit, and that later, under the pressure of circumstances, these units gradually coalesced to form the catholic Church, is now generally abandoned as unhistorical. It is enough to point to the Jewish origin of the Christian community. Jews in the diaspora never ceased to think of themselves as part of the one People of God ; each Jewish community *was* the Israel of God manifest at that particular point of space. Since the Church thought of itself as the new Israel, and inherited precisely that sense of unity, the oneness of the Body of Christ was the starting point of thought, and not the goal of conscious endeavour.

But this was not to deny a considerable measure of independence in the local units, and the possibility of wide variations between them. Even in the New Testament, within the general pattern of unity, there seem to have been real differences between the mother church at Jerusalem and such mainly Gentile communities as that of Corinth. The immense vitality of the earliest groups was bound to manifest itself in experiment and differentiation.

Experiments could not but be made in the fields both of organisation and of doctrine. The earliest Church had no settled creeds, it had no developed canon of Scripture. As it came into contact with different types of non-Christian society, it tended, by way either of adaptation or of conflict, to take on varying forms of expression.

The contacts between the Christian community and the thought-world of its environment were inevitably disturbing. Living as it does by the principle of incarnation, the Christian society cannot affect the world around it except by entering into it and undergoing its influence.   The history of Christian thought is that of the effort, permanently necessary and never finally successful, to stand on the central line of the Christian tradition, without being allured away by the aberrations which may result from the admixture of alien types of thought.   In the earliest days, when Christian doctrine was still largely unformulated, the danger was at its greatest. As the moral pessimism of the East came into contact with the metaphysical pessimism of the Levant, the stage was set for the development of Gnosticism.   As a modicum of Christian thought was thrown into the mixture, the various forms of Christian Gnosticism arose to dazzle the eyes of some Christians and to perplex the minds of all.   The brilliant imaginings of Basilides and Valentinus might well serve better than the simplicities of the Gospel to satisfy that craving for the grandiose and the exotic which was one of the characteristics of the aging Hellenistic civilisation.

In one sense, all these varied experiments were legitimate and necessary.   But to admit the rightness of Christian speculation is not to deny the possibility that there may be in fact a central tradition of Christian thought, to which the roving mind must always return, if it is not to abandon some of the treasures of the Gospel.   The early Christian republics were assured that there was such a central tradition, and that in that alone could their unity and permanence be secured.

The first great expression of this sense of doctrinal unity is to be found in the writings of Irenaeus.[1]   Part of the value of Irenaeus for later ages lies just in the fact that he had not to any large extent an originative mind.   He believed himself to be expressing the mind of the Church as it had formed itself in five generations of Christian living ; he laid down the principles by which the Church of the future should determine

---

[1] Irenaeus became bishop of Lyons in A.D. 177.   He was born, probably about A.D. 130, in Asia Minor.

its own orthodoxy. It is noteworthy that Irenaeus quotes from every book of the canonical New Testament except the Epistle to Philemon. There is as yet no question of an authorised and finally determined canon, but his use of the New Testament text is prophetic, in that it is the first clear example of that appeal to New Testament Scripture as the decisive norm and standard of the Church's doctrine, which was characteristic of the whole patristic period. But for Irenaeus the apostolic word does not stand alone ; it is supported and made effective by the apostolic succession. Each great Christian bishopric can trace its origin to the work of an apostle ; each can trace the succession of bishops in order due, who have held the office and with it the responsibility of guarding the true tradition of the Church. There is no emphasis on tactual succession as the means by which authority is conveyed. It is succession in office, in authority and in responsibility, which to Irenaeus is the essential factor in the unity of the Church in space and time, a unity which is grounded in the truth and can be preserved only as the Church maintains undiminished the original deposit of truth.

It is easy to exaggerate the isolation of the small Christian republics from one another. Doubtless there were backward areas, lying apart from the main stream of Christian tradition. Whatever the exact date and provenance of that mysterious tract the *Didache*, it seems clear that it springs from some such backward, indeed archaic if not archaising, community. But the career of Irenaeus himself is a truer indication of the nature of life in that early Christian society. Born in Asia Minor, he served for many years as bishop of the Church of Lyons in the south of France ; throughout that period he was in close touch, by correspondence and by actual travel, with the leaders of the Church in Rome and elsewhere. As has been justly remarked, travel was safer and more rapid in the Empire of the Antonines than at any subsequent period in history until the Nine-

teenth Century. Christians took full advantage of this fact.
Orthodox writers were apt to complain of the mobility of
heretics, and of the rapidity with which their ideas were
disseminated. Already in the time of Cyprian, the assem-
bling of local councils of bishops was a regular feature of
Church life.[1] As early as the First Epistle to the Corinthians,
we find reference to the commendatory letter by means of
which a Christian was passed on from one Christian group
to another. In the days of persecution, the Christians
developed their own secret language and passwords, through
which they were safeguarded against misuse of the evangelic
precept of hospitality. The letter of the Churches of Lyons
and Vienne was sent out widely, in order that those in other
churches might share in the sufferings and triumphs of their
brethren in the fires of persecution.

To maintain the inner unity of the fellowship,[2] the
Christian group had one instrument by far more potent than
any other, the regular celebration of the Eucharist. In
many respects, Christian worship appears to have developed out of that of the synagogue ; this, the Eucharistic
feast, was the one unique and irreplaceable element.
Participation in it was the sign of Christian fellowship ;
exclusion from it was the most serious penalty that could
be imposed on the erring brother. Whatever the peril,
whatever the difficulty, and for slaves the difficulty must
sometimes have been almost unsurmountable, it was
regarded as obligatory for the Christian to be present and
to receive the Bread of Life.[3] In private houses, in cata-

---

[1] Cyprian became bishop of Carthage in A.D. 248, and died as a
martyr in the persecution under Valerian in A.D. 258.

[2] " Une église chrétienne est tout autre chose qu'une société de secours
mutuels, qu'un collège funéraire, qu'un groupement corporatif d'intérêts,
car on a tour à tour comparé les églises à des associations de ce genre pour
expliquer tout bien que mal, leur condition juridique dans l'empire romain.
Une Eglise est un amour : même si le mot n'a pas été employé en ce sens
par S. Ignace, il peut être retenu, car il exprime l'aspect le plus fonda-
mental, semble-t-il, d'une chrétienté." G. BARDY : *La Théologie de l'Eglise*
(Paris, Ed. du Cerf 1945), p. 53.

[3] This is impressively set forth by Dom. Gregory Dix in *The Shape of the
Liturgy* (Westminster N.D.) pp. 147–154.

combs, often before the break of day, the Christians assembled, to do what the Lord had appointed, to be fashioned anew into one bread, one body, to be set again firmly within that eternal redemption which God was accomplishing through His risen Christ. So essential was it that every member should be partaker of the " medicine of immortality " that portions from the one Loaf were sent to those who were sick, and in time of persecution to those in prison.

In the earliest days, the form of the ordinance must have been of the simplest. By the middle of the Second Century, a liturgical pattern was beginning to establish itself. In the famous account in the writings of Justin Martyr (*c.* 150), we find already the reading from the Gospel, the long Eucharistic prayer of the " president," and the Amen of the faithful. So many doubts attach to the work known as the Apostolic Tradition of Hippolytus that it is difficult to use it with any confidence.[1] But if Hippolytus, writing as an old man about A.D. 217, is really setting down the use of the Church as he had known it in his youth, we find, not much more than a century from the apostolic age, in a form still laconic and austere, all the principal elements of the later liturgy—thanksgiving to God for the blessings of creation and redemption, the repetition of the words of Christ, the offering of the natural gifts to God, the prayer for the descent of the Holy Spirit. Such a development at so early a date, though not certain, is by no means improbable.

It is difficult to determine what meaning the early Christians attached to the Eucharist. Most of them, even the ministers, were very simple people, and experienced much more than they could express or define. Some theologians have tried to find in such fragments of early eucharistic teaching as we possess the germ of the fully

---

[1] The text is conveniently to be found in B. S. Easton, *The Apostolic Tradition of Hippolytus* (Cambridge, 1934) or in Gregory Dix: *The Apostolic Tradition of St. Hippolytus of Rome* (London, 1937).

developed doctrine of the later Church ; others have denied
that any such indications are to be found. It is almost
certain that, in early days, the eschatological element was
strongly marked ; the Eucharist was the earthly anticipation of the Messianic banquet, of the final triumph of
Christ. It is probable that the minds of the early Christians
were strongly realist. In this ordinance, they felt themselves incorporate into Christ the Vine, the Head of the
body. When to be in Christ was literally a matter of life
and death, there was little time for speculation. It is
unlikely that we shall find in their testimony answers to
questions which had not yet been asked.

Later generations have always looked back to the days of
the persecutions as the golden age of the Church. Our fathers
in the faith have suffered from this idealisation. In point of
fact, from the beginning the Christian fellowship has been
a strange amalgam of good and evil. Paul addresses his
friends in Corinth as saints, and thanks God that they are
lacking neither in faith nor in knowledge.[1] Yet the whole
of his first Epistle deals with the grave disorders, moral, social
and liturgical from which the Church suffered. It seems
that he had to face a grave crisis through the desire of one
party to repudiate his own apostolic authority. The Third
Epistle of John reflects a situation of tension within the
Church, and perhaps the beginnings of ecclesiastical auto-
cracy. It is unlikely that the succeeding generations were
better than the first. Legislation is not passed against evils
which do not exist. As soon as councils begin to record
their acts, we get sidelights on the standards and practice
of the Christians of the period. The date of the Council of
Elvira in Spain has not been exactly determined, but it may
be ascribed with great probability to a period shortly before
the last great persecution under Diocletian (A.D. 303), and
therefore before the granting of peace to the Church by the
so-called Edict of Milan. The regulations there laid down

[1] I Cor. i. 4–9.

indicate just that mixture of sincere piety and very imperfect ethical observance, which have been characteristic of the Church in all ages.[1] Even the records of the persecutions are mixed in character. Some stood fast, and sealed their witness with their blood. Others failed in the day of temptation. When the persecutions died down, the doors of the churches were besieged by the throngs of the *Lapsi*, the pitiable people who had denied Christ through fear or through an unworthy spirit of compromise. Cases were not unknown in which even bishops denied the faith, and surrendered the sacred vessels and the treasures of the Church to the inquisitors.[2]

" We have this treasure in earthen vessels." To recognise the frailty of God's human instruments is not to deny the reality of His working, but rather, by acknowledging the manner of His working, more truly to glorify Him If it were the case that the Church had started with a perfection never afterwards attained, its history would take the form of a most depressing paradox. If, on the other hand, God was pleased through such very human persons and through so mixed a society to carry out the miracle of the subjugation of the ancient world to the faith, there is no need for any later generation in the Church to despair. Human imperfection may hinder and delay the action of God. It is not a sign that God has deserted His Church, or that He will fail to renew it and to use it for His glory.

Yet when all has been said, the later attitude towards the early Church is not without its justification. The men of that period were nearer than we to the historic event of the Resurrection. They bore perhaps more clearly than later generations the marks of that gigantic revolution in the

---

[1] Harnack's judgment was that the Canons of Elvira reveal " a combination of coarse worldliness and fanatical severity such as has been characteristic of the Spanish Church in every age ". The most startling of the Canons is No. 5 which fixed the penalty of perpetual excommunication for women who beat their slaves to death.

[2] See a vivid description based on original sources, in Dix. *The Shape of the Liturgy*, pp. 24–26.

history of the world.   The power of that revelation of life out of death, and the joy unspeakable and full of glory that followed on it, thrill in the pages of the New Testament. That first level could not be maintained.   And yet those who followed, though their testimony was pitched in a lower key, were still the near inheritors of the original victory.   They knew that God had overcome all the powers of the world, and that the apparently impossible task of winning the world for Christ was not beyond the strength of those whom He had called.   They sinned but they endured. Against inner weakness, against the confusions of many doctrines, against the viciousness and perversity of pagan society, against fire and torment, they held on.   And when, in the providence of God, the ancient world crumbled and passed away, the Church was ready to gather up the best of its treasures, sacred and profane, and to go forward as the messenger of God into a world changed beyond recognition by the unimagined revolutions of the ages that were yet to come.

CHAPTER III

THE CHURCH OF THE EMPIRE

IN A.D. 313, by the so-called Edict of Milan, the Christian society was brought out of the obscurity and peril of the days of persecution into a position of security and privilege.[1]

The motives which swayed the mind of Constantine in making this selection for his favour have perplexed and still perplex the learned. Some have placed his conversion, though not his baptism, early in his career. Others have regarded his decision to patronise the Christians as an act of no more than political calculation. It may be that the truth is inclusive of both these explanations. Constantine did regard himself as the favourite of the God of the Christians, and yet his actions may have been determined more by shrewd political calculation than by anything else.

Whatever judgment be passed on this tangled issue, it is impossible not to be astonished at the temerity of Constantine's action. The Christians were a small minority in his dominions. Unfortunately, the evidence, as it has survived, is insufficient to serve as a basis for even an approximate calculation of the population of the Roman Empire at the

---

[1] Lactantius, *De Mort. Pers.* 48 gives the Latin text of a letter published by the emperor Licinius, no doubt in agreement with Constantine, in June 313, in which the terms of the new freedom are set forth. Complete translation in *Camb. Anc. Hist.* Vol. XII (Cambridge 1939) pp. 689–90 by N. H. Baynes. The operative clauses read : " To each man's judgment and will the right should be given to care for sacred things according to each man's free choice . . . to no one whatsoever should we deny liberty to follow either the religion of the Christians or any other cult which of his own free choice he has thought to be best adapted for himself."

beginning of the Fourth Century, or of the proportion of that population that had accepted the Christian way. Nothing more is possible than somewhat precarious guesswork on the basis of very scanty indications. The most generous estimate of the Christian population would probably not go beyond fifteen per cent of the whole. Even this may be a considerable over-estimate.[1] The distribution of the Christians was very uneven. In parts of Egypt, of Asia Minor, of Italy and of southern France, they were so numerous as to be the dominating element in society. Elsewhere Christians were fewer and much less influential. Even in Asia Minor there were mountain areas that remained wholly pagan until more than two centuries after the time of Constantine.

And yet there were indications, such as could not escape the eye of the prudent statesman, that the future lay with the Christians. The power of a well disciplined and well organised minority is far greater than mere numbers would suggest. The Christians had successfully withstood the attempts of their enemies to destroy them. They were bound together by a strong and self-conscious loyalty. Already they shewed signs of being, far more than the degenerate Romans, the true heirs of the ancient civilisation. Among pagan philosophers, one only, Plotinus, could be compared for penetration and originality with the Christian Platonists of Alexandria. Tertullian for all his eccentricities wrote with greater vigour than any of his contemporaries. The Christians alone were finding new things to say, and working out new forms of language and literature to express them. The supreme genius of Augustine was yet in the future ; but Augustine inherited a great tradition of Christian Latin literature on which to build.

Of all this Constantine could not be unaware. But he had need of more than allies. He had need of a religious sanction for the new Empire which it was his aim to create

[1] For a variety of estimates see K. S. Latourette : *History of the Expansion of Christianity*, Vol. I (London, 1939), pp. 108–9.

[handwritten annotation: RATIONAL ORDER ON CHAOS — TO SET WORLD RYM]

on the ruins of the old.[1]   The worship of the emperors no
longer called forth the right response in the minds of men.
Deeper religious needs called for a deeper answer.   In the
God of the Christians, the Most High, with His universal
sovereignty, Constantine found the answer to what was
primarily a political need.   The Church should be the
faithful servant of the emperor, in supplying that factor of
religious sanction without which no ancient society had
ever held together.

Constantine was right in his judgment of the future.   But
the time had already passed in which a restoration of the
empire on the ancient basis could be accomplished.   His
mind was still working within the framework of the classical
solution of the problem of man's life, the imposition of a
rational order upon chaos, and the safeguarding of a narrow
area of civilisation against the forces of barbarism that
perpetually threatened to overthrow it.   But this involved
always a turning to the past, an attempt to restore the
Roman order as it had been in the days of the republic, or
in the great age of Augustus.   And this proved no longer
possible.   Even with the help of the Christians and of the
new faith, the old order could not be restored.   The efforts
of Constantine and his Christian successors, notably Theodosius, to set the world to rights by legislation proved
abortive.   An inner decay in the substance of life in the
Empire thwarted all their efforts.   Law is effective only if
it proceeds from within the life of a people, registering their
best convictions, and commending itself as coherent with
the actual pattern of their existence.   Paradoxically, the
period in which Roman law was codified and its principles
most fully worked out was that in which its power to control
the life of society most rapidly waned.

---

[1] How deeply this sense of need for a religious sanction had penetrated
the mind of the ancient world is shewn in the preamble to the *Constitutio
Antoniniana* of Caracalla, in which the Emperor asserts that his motive in
passing the decree is to provide the gods with new worshippers on a scale
worthy of the divine majesty.

By choosing the Christians as his allies, Constantine put them in a position from which they could exercise to the full their influence on the future of the world. But it was not within their power to renew the past. In little more than a century, Augustine had written the epitaph of the classical tradition, with its limited concept of the meaning of history and the destiny of man. Constantine himself stood, all unconsciously on the threshold of the Middle Ages. The ancient world was already in dissolution ; it was the Christian society alone which was to survive its downfall.[1]

The inevitable consequence of the " Edict of Milan " was a vast increase in the number of those who professed and called themselves Christians. For a time, indeed, there was at least in outward form, equality between Christian and pagan. It is only in the time of Justinian that we find what can properly be called persecution of non-Christians. The last great historian of the Roman world, Ammianus Marcellinus, was a pagan. The ancient Roman families maintained their paganism until far on in the Fifth Century. Relations between those who adhered to different religions could be friendly, as we learn from the touching story in Jerome of the pagan patrician, who would take his Christian grand-daughter on his knee, and listen to her telling him Bible stories. But it is only a short step from official approval of one religion to discrimination against another. It was not long before men began to see their advantage in acceptance of that form of religion which was approved by the state, and in expression of loyalty to the emperor by worship of the emperor's God.

With increase in numbers came increase in corruption.

---

[1] According to Sir Samuel Dill (*Roman Society in the Last Century of the Western Empire*, London 1898, p. 234), Theodosius was faced with a situation " in which . . . the claims of fancied omnipotence ended in a humiliating paralysis of administration : in which determined efforts to remedy social evils only aggravated them until they became unendurable ; in which the best intentions of the central power . . . were mocked and defeated alike by the irresistible laws of human nature and by hopeless perfidy and corruption in the servants of government."

Dante, looking back over the centuries, saw in the fatal (and legendary) Donation of Constantine, the beginning of all the misfortunes of the Church. Others, not accepting his interpretation of history, would yet agree with him that after A.D. 313 the Church was never again what it had been in the apparently less favourable situation of the days of persecution and of inner growth.

The immediate and most remarkable change was the transformation of the Christian society from an intimate fellowship of those who were pledged, if need be, to die together, into a loose association, many of the members of which had never taken the initial pledge of loyalty. The Church had always had its hearers and its catechumens, as it has in the mission field today ; but it had always been taken for granted that these would either go forward to baptism or fall away. The development of a class of life-long catechumens was a wholly unforeseen contingency. The situation was of the nature of a vicious circle. The Church, to preserve its own purity, had always made a sharp distinction between pre-baptismal and post-baptismal sin, and, although the extreme rigorism of some schools of thought had come to be modified, imposed severe and even lifelong penance on offenders.[1] In such circumstances, only those of the most heroic temper were prepared to increase their responsibilities by taking on themselves the yoke of baptism ; the rest preferred to sin within the less exacting framework of the catechumenate, and baptism was transformed from the eschatological sealing of those who by the grace of God were being saved into an almost magical viaticum for those who in this world would no longer have any need of salvation. Baptism in the last moments of life came to be almost normal practice. And when, as in the case of Augustine's friend, one who had been baptised *in*

---

[1] In the judgment of the Early Church the three capital sins were murder, idolatry and unchastity. Augustine (Sermon LVI, 12) extends this list to include, among other vices, astrology and magic.

117567

extremis unexpectedly recovered,[1] he was likely to view his recovery with a certain rueful anxiety.

The gradual but steady spread of the practice of infant baptism within the Church in time produced another and equally melancholy revolution. The celebration of the Eucharist continued to be the central manifestation of the life of the Christian society. As before, catechumens were required to withdraw before the prayers of the faithful began. But gradually the number of communicants decreased. The majority of the Christians became onlookers and not participants in the sacrament. The Eucharist became not *esca viatorum*, the daily bread of travellers through the wilderness of this world, but a solemnity vicariously enjoyed, except on occasions of special obligation. By the Sixth Century, the established custom of habitual communion had almost disappeared, its place being taken by the medieval rule of communion three times, or it might be only once, a year.

No efforts of reformers have availed to restore the true Christian order. In England this was the point at which the good intentions of the Reformers most seriously failed to take effect ; the people were so wedded to the customs of the Middle Ages that they refused to be led back to the practice of earlier and better days. In the Roman Catholic and Orthodox Churches, worshippers at Mass are very many, but only a small proportion of them are regular communicants. Some of the new Christian bodies which arose in the Nineteenth Century, such as the Brethren and the Disciples of Christ, have alone been successful in restoring the Breaking of Bread to its true and central place in the order of Christian worship ; but among them the ordinance is observed with so little liturgical order, and with so different a theological emphasis from that of earlier days, that it can hardly be regarded as falling within the main tradition of

---

[1] Augustine : Confessions, Bk. IV. c 4 § 8 : Cum enim labonaret ille febribus, iacuit diu sine sensu sudore letali, et cum desperaretur, baptizatus est nescius.

the Christian Eucharist. It is lamentably true that no Church at the present time presents the spectacle of normal Christian living as it would have been understood by the Christian society in the days of its development.

With increase in numbers came increase in wealth. This is a recurrent perplexity to the Church, and to every movement within it. The Christian society has here no rest ; it is always a stranger and pilgrim in this passing world ; it ought therefore to have as its marks the staff and scrip and simple habit of the pilgrim. Yet the moment that it attains to numerical strength and a measure of stability, it begins to make a compromise with the world. It is almost impossible that a regularly worshipping community should continue without the possession of some property. Even those communities that are pledged to individual poverty have found themselves becoming, through the generosity of the faithful, burdened with an increasing weight of corporate wealth. And with the increase of worldly goods comes always the tendency to lose the pilgrim spirit, to make the transitory world more homelike, and so to become confused as to the relative value of temporal and eternal goods. Already by the middle of the Fourth Century, the Church in the great centres was beginning to become rich. Possession of sees could present itself as an object of worldly as well as of spiritual ambition. Hence such disgraceful scenes as those which accompanied the election of Damasus to the bishopric of Rome in 366, when the floor of the Basilica of Liberius (now the Church of St. Maria Maggiore), was strewn with more than a hundred corpses.[1] Praetextatus, the pagan prefect of the city, is reported to have observed to Damasus, " Make me bishop of Rome, and I will turn Christian at once."

[1] The pagan historian Ammianus Marcellinus, who gives the number of the dead as 137 (Bk. 27.3.13), contrasts the ambition and secular splendour of the great prelates with the simple bishops in country places whose " frugality of habits, humility and simplicity of bearing recommended them as men of pure and modest character to the everlasting Deity and His true worshippers." (Quoted by W. Bright, *The Age of the Fathers* (London, 1903) Vol. I, p. 363).

The increasing identification of the Church with the world resulted in an almost inevitable reaction. Those who despaired both of the Church and of the world fled from both to seek salvation in the wilderness. The roots of monachism in its early days were complex. There was an element of Manichean hatred of the body and all its works. There was an element of pathological despair. But the movement which drove thousands of men and women out from the amenities of ordinary life, until the deserts of the Thebais were crowded with multitudes of anchorites and hermits, cannot be understood at all, unless we recognise within it a deep and genuine striving after the perfection of Christian holiness. The Christian world saw from time to time with horror the invasion of the great centres of Christian life by hordes of savage and undisciplined ascetics, who, mistaking fanaticism for sanctity, were prepared for any act of violence in defence of what they believed to be the cause of God. The bitter invectives of Gibbon, who saw in the triumph of monasticism the return of the world to the darkness of barbarism and ignorance, were not without foundation.[1] That is one side of the picture. The other is given in the *Lives of the Desert Fathers*, where we find the attractiveness of extreme simplicity, and that penetration into the realities of the unseen world that is sometimes given to simple and single-hearted men.

The drawing up of the rule of St. Benedict, and the organisation of the community at Monte Cassino are turning points of Christian history.[2] The Roman genius for order and organisation came to impose itself on the chaos

---

[1] The similar outburst of Lecky is perhaps less well-known : " A hideous, sordid and emaciated maniac, without knowledge, without patriotism, without natural affection, passing his life in a long routine of useless and atrocious self-torture and quailing before the ghastly fantoms of his delirious brain, had become the ideal of the nations which had known the writings of Plato and Cicero, and the lives of Socrates and Cato." (*History of European Morals* (ed. 7) Vol. II., p. 107).

[2] The date appears to have been A.D. 529. It is interesting to note that at this very time Justinian was engaged in closing the schools of the philosophers in Athens and abolishing the consulate.

of primitive monasticism. Benedict was not a pioneer with no precursors. Pachomius in Egypt and Basil in Asia Minor had gone before him in providing the framework of discipline for the life and worship of monks living together in community. What Benedict added was a profound understanding of human nature, the tempering of austerity with gentleness, and that balance between work, worship and study which has been characteristic of monasticism at its best in all subsequent ages.

The services of monasticism in later days, in preserving so much of value from the ruins of the ancient world, in spreading the Gospel, in carrying civilisation to barbarous peoples have placed the Church for ever and immeasurably in its debt. But it must not be forgotten that all these things were by-products of monasticism and not part of its original intention. In the Benedictine scheme, the abbot was the father of a family of men, who had withdrawn from the corruption of the world to work out their own salvation. That withdrawal was absolute and final. The task of the monk was to make an island of salvation in the midst of a world doomed to destruction. His purpose was to save himself and not to save the world.[1]

Where monasticism is regarded as a special vocation within a Christian society which in its totality is redemptive, the integrity of the Church is preserved. If, however, the ascetic vocation is regarded as essentially higher than the vocation of the Christian in the world, still more if it is regarded as the only effective means of salvation, the Church

[1] See the admirable chapter on the Rule of Saint Benedict in Dom David Knowles : *The Monastic Order in England* (Cambridge, 1941), pp. 3–15 ; and the important comment on p. 20 of the same work : " It cannot be too often repeated that in St. Benedict's conception a monastery existed for the service of God and the spiritual welfare of its inmates, and for no other reason. . . . Those who attribute to the legislator farsighted designs of regenerating a crumbling society or reasserting the nobility of work and communal service not only fail to see St. Benedict and the Rule in true historical perspective, but fail also to see that he was concerned solely with the monastic life as a spiritual discipline for the service of God, and not at all with works, however necessary, of religion and charity undertaken for the world outside the walls of the monastery."

outside the cloister is in danger of losing its sense of obligation to be salt and leaven, the community of God living
redemptively within the world in order that the whole
life of man in all its avocations and activities may be
delivered out of the bondage of corruption into the glorious
liberty of the children of God. The Church in the world
has never entirely lost this sense of obligation. Yet
monasticism did introduce a principle of duality, a
dangerous division within a society that can be effective
only if it is one in spirit and in body. That danger has
not yet passed away. To be in the world and yet not
of it is a complex and perilous task, and one with which
the Christian society in every generation is called to wrestle
anew.

A small society can be content with very simple organisation. The Church even in the days of persecution had,
as we have seen, maintained a strong sense of corporate
unity, expressed in the episcopate, and in periodical
consultation between the bishops of larger or smaller
areas. There had been considerable local variation in the
development. It appears that, till the last quarter of
the Third Century, there had been only one bishop in
Egypt, whereas in North Africa every place of importance
(and many places of no importance at all) had each its own
bishop. The period after 313 was marked by increasing
uniformity and rigidity of organisation ; in consequence
of the close connection between the Church and the State,
the development was along the lines of the organisation of
the Roman Empire, with its dioceses, its provinces, and its
tendency to centralisation in the government of the emperor
himself.

In A.D. 325, the Council of Nicaea laid it down that a bishop
was to be consecrated by the other bishops of the province in
which his see was located. Technically, all bishops were
equal. As Jerome truly remarked, the Bishop of Gubbio, as
bishop, was equal to the Bishop of Rome, just as in more

modern times the Bishop of St. Helena is equal to the Archbishop of Canterbury. But in practice, equality of status has never been found to mean equality of influence. Great sees tend to be filled by great bishops. Great bishops tend to add lustre and authority to the church of the cities in which they have exercised their ministry. On the one hand, Alexandria could not but be a great centre of influence in the whole Christian world; but part of the eminence of Alexandria was due to the fame of Athanasius and his almost single-handed championship of the orthodox cause in the days of the Arian controversy. On the other hand, it may be that Athanasius would not have attained to equal distinction, if he had happened to be not Patriarch of Alexandria but Bishop of Gubbio. Gradually the distinction between sees according to their relative importance came to be formalised in the superior authority of the Metropolitan, the bishop of the central see, over the other bishops in his province. The process was neither clear nor uniform; in France it seems to have advanced considerably more slowly than elsewhere. The powers of the Metropolitan were never very clearly defined, and in the Ninth Century were to become a matter of violent controversy. But the principle once accepted gained ground. As a matter of convenience, if of nothing else, the regional grouping of Churches commended itself as a solution of many problems.

Above the Metropolitan stood the Patriarch. In the ancient world, three sees stood out above all others as pre-eminent in apostolic foundation, in strength of tradition, and in championship of the orthodox faith—Antioch, Alexandria and Rome. From the Fourth Century, these were recognised as the patriarchal sees, to the occupants of which were attributed great, though as yet largely undefined, authority over all their peers. In the course of the Fourth Century Jerusalem was added, not because of any special eminence in its Christian community, which had in fact long been under the metropolitical authority of

Caesarea, but because of the sacred associations of the name. In the Fifth Century, Byzantium, though a new city, and undistinguished in its Christian history, was added as a fifth pillar, but as second in precedence after Rome. The reason given by the Council of Constantinople, in A.D. 381 for this decision is characteristic of the temper of the age ; the honour was conferred " seeing that Constantinople is the New Rome." It is the presence of the Christian emperor that makes it necessary that the city of his residence should be given dignity in the Church corresponding to its import-ance in the state.

The Church might have gone a step further in its imitation of the order of the Roman Empire. It might have been led to the conviction that, just as all authority in the state culminated in one single head, the emperor, so all authority in the Church culminated in one single sovereign ruler of the Christian society. This step was never taken by the society as a whole. It was only rarely that there was one single emperor ; usually the empire was ruled by a group of three or four, with one Augustus as the chief among colleagues of equal or nearly equal rank. It was to this pattern that the Church conformed itself. It is true that at the Council of Sardica in A.D. 343 the bishops agreed that, in any unsettled dispute involving a bishop, an appeal might be made by the contending parties to Julius Bishop of Rome ; but this was not regarded as recognising any independent right inherent in the Pope to exercise jurisdiction outside his own patriarchate, still less as accepting him as supreme judge and ruler of the universal church. The Council of Chalcedon, by affirming in its twenty-eighth Canon the equality of the Pope and the Patriarch of Byzantium, saving for the honorary precedence of Rome, denied the existence of one supreme authority in the Church. This Canon was never accepted in the west. From the time of Siricius in the Fourth Century, the Popes had begun to issue decretals, which in the west were regarded as having the force of law.[1] Such authority was never accorded to them in the east, and the western decretals have no place in the foundations of eastern canon law, which rests only on the formal decisions of the great councils.

It was not the Church but the emperor who set the coping stone on the organisation of the Christian society in that most characteristic feature of the patristic age, the General Council. Constantine had chosen the Christians to be the cement, the principle of unity in his new empire ; it was intolerable to him that the Christians should be themselves divided. His first experience of bitter disappointment was in the matter of the Donatist schism in North Africa. All attempts at conciliation having failed, the emperor summoned the western bishops to meet in council at Arles in 317 and to settle the matter once for all. But almost at once a graver peril loomed up. The Arian controversy threatened to rend the Church in twain and to make its unity for ever impossible.

Gibbon's gibe that the Christians fought one another over a single letter, Homoousians against Homoiousians, characteristically misses the immense import of what was at issue in the debate. Sooner or later, the Church had to decide whether Jesus the Christ stands on the side of the Creator or on the side of the created universe. In the end, the answer must be a simple Yes or No without compromise. If Jesus is a created being, however eminent, to worship Him is idolatry. If He is not, then the Christian doctrine of God must be thought out in terms of His essential deity. It may be admitted that much of the controversy was trivial and wearisome. It is true that many devout Arians were

---

[1] What is generally regarded as the first unmistakably genuine decretal ever issued by a Bishop of Rome is dated " iii. Id. Febr. Arcadio et Bautone vv. cc. coss "—that is 11 February, 385. It is a reply to questions posed on certain disciplinary actions by Himerius, Bishop of Tarragona in Spain. Siricius answers it in the tone of one conscious of possessing full authority to legislate on all questions for the whole Church. " We bear the burdens of all who are heavy-laden; nay, rather the blessed apostle Peter bears them in us, who, as we trust, in all things protects and guards us, the heirs of his administration."

concerned to guard against the perils of tritheism. But later Christian history has pronounced on the side of Athanasius and his friends. They were standing for a truth, without which the Church could not be the Church. Their victory assured the continuance in the world of the Christian society as the body of the everlasting Son of God.

Constantine summoned the episcopate of the whole world to meet in council at Nicaea.[1] It was the emperor's council. When he entered it, he was received with almost extravagant adulation. In his absence the chair was taken by Hosius of Cordova as the emperor's representative. Without the emperor's permission and authority the meeting could not have taken place.

For all that, it would be a mistake to think of the assembly as primarily political. It was a spiritual event of the first magnitude. For the first time in history, the whole Church, with representatives from the shores of the Atlantic, and with John of Persia and Great India from the farthest East, was present in a single corporate body, to decide an issue on which its whole future depended. It was, as no subsequent council could be, the council of the confessors. All the bishops had lived through days of persecution, and some of them bore in their bodies the marks of the Lord Jesus. As in all such assemblies of later years, the formal discussions and decisions were only a part of what took place. Personal contacts, friendships and antagonisms, sent the bishops back to their sees changed men, with a new sense of the greatness of the Church, of the perils that beset it, and of the spiritual resources available within it, as the organ through which the Holy Spirit was

[1] One of the reasons Constantine gives in his letter for the selection of Nicaea as the place of the Council is that it had a pleasant and healthy climate. The " beautiful town lay on an eminence in the midst of well-wooded, flower-embellished country, with the clear bright waters of the Ascanian lake at its foot," (J. H. Newman). The 4th Century was, apparently, as sensitive to such points as the 20th. The fathers of Ephesus and Trent, however, complained bitterly of the climate of the places in which respectively they were compelled to sojourn so long.

pleased to do His work among men. Later generations of
men were to idealise the Council of Nicaea, and to regard
it as endowed with almost plenary inspiration. In this
they erred. It was a very human assembly, swayed by
passion and prejudice, as all human assemblies are. Yet
this later estimate was not wholly wrong. The first ecumenical council marked the coming of age of the Church.

For centuries, the conciliar method was followed by the
Church, as it strove with the controversies and divisions
that have always accompanied it on its journey through
time. Not that this method commended itself to everyone.
The pagan historian Ammianus Marcellinus complained
bitterly that the imperial posts were utterly disorganised by
the multitudes of bishops hurrying here and there on their
way to councils, fortified by imperial privileges of travel.
The gentle Gregory of Nazianzus was of the opinion that
no good thing ever came out of a council, but only an
increase of evil, with " contention and strivings for dominion
beyond what words can describe." Some Christian assemblies
were neither dignified nor orderly. The first council of
Ephesus was marred by disgraceful scenes of violence. A
conciliar decision did not always bring peace to the Church,
since pressure by the government, chicanery and successful
party management might provide a temporary majority
in favour of a decision subsequently rejected by the Church
as heretical. After the Council of Ariminum, in the words
of Jerome, " the Church awoke and was astonished to find
itself Arian."[1]

Nor was it immediately evident which councils were
ecumenical and which were not. Roman Catholic historians
take the simple view that what gave ecumenical status
to a council was acceptance of its canons as authoritative
by the Pope. This view rests on dogmatic presuppositions and not on historical evidence. The Orthodox view
is nearer to the truth—that ultimately every decision is

[1] W. Bright, *op. cit.* pp. 277–8.

tried and tested by the common sense of the Church, and that that is ecumenical which proves itself to be so by universal acceptance. The age of great councils, with many aberrations, did define the doctrine of the Church. By that doctrine the Church has lived ever since. It has had to face many problems unknown in the Fourth and Fifth Centuries ; but the answers have been found to lie within the limits marked out, with the inevitable imperfections of Greek philosophy and human terminology, by the great councils from Nicaea to Chalcedon.

In that age, between 325 and 451, the Christian society enjoyed an outward unity such as it had never had before, and such as it has never since attained.[1] But it is important not to exaggerate the extent of that unity. Even when all the forces of imperial authority were employed to enforce that particular form of doctrine which the emperor himself accepted, what was defined as heresy showed an unexpected vitality. Arianism was finally overcome within the Roman Empire. It took on a new lease of life among the barbarians. The great missionary Ulfilas converted the Goths to this form of Christianity. The Visigothic and Vandal kingdoms were Arian ; in their domains, persecution of the Catholics went on well into the Sixth Century. It is recorded that in A.D. 378 there were still four churches of the Novatianists in Byzantium. At one period in the Fourth Century there were six bishops of Antioch, all claiming to be in the true succession from the Apostles. Montanism, that curious Pentecostal Puritanism of the early Church, maintained itself in the highlands of Asia Minor, until finally exterminated by persecution in the reign of Justinian.

----

[1] I find myself in agreement with the judgment of F Heiler: *Urkirche und Osktirche* (München, Reinhardt 1937), p. 132 : " The *Undivided ecumenical Church* was of extraordinarily short duration, and the claim of the Orthodox Church to full ecumenicity is from the beginning of the 5th Century a fiction. The full unity and catholicity of the Church of Christ have been so rarely seen in history and have lasted so short a time that we can apply to them the words used by Bernard of Clairvaux of the rarity and shortness of the experience of ecstasy : *Heu rara hora et parva mora.*"

It can, however, be said that for the most part controversy led to division within the Church, rather than to separation from the Church. At one moment a diocese might have an Arian bishop, at another a Catholic. But there was little setting up of throne against throne and bishop against bishop. The unity of the Church was still felt to be a reality, in spite of the wounds and rents which threatened it. Where bishop was set up against bishop, as was the practice of the Donatists in North Africa, reconciliation became so difficult as to be almost impossible.

In the Fourth Century, the Christian society went far to identify itself with the state. It also went far to identify itself with the prevailing culture of the Roman world. In its early days, it had felt conscious of nothing so much as of its radical hostility to the world that surrounded it ; Tertullian (*c.* 155–*c.* 222), for example, was the implacable foe of any reconciliation between Christ and the tradition of an older world.[1] When Clement of Alexandria (born *c.* 150) began to claim that God had not revealed himself only through Scripture, but that Greek philosophy and culture also had been in their measure a *praeparatio evangelica*, he was met by the strong opposition of the fundamentalists of the day. Why should a man who had all that is needed in the Bible wish to occupy himself with the chaff and dross of the days of ignorance ? In the Fourth Century the atmosphere was quite different. The leaders of the Church were the intellectual peers of the most thoughtful pagans, and in some cases were their friends. Basil[2] and Gregory of Nazianzus had been fellow-students of the

[1] Some of his words are famous: "What has Athens to do with Jerusalem, the Academy with the Church ? " (*de Praescriptione*, c. 7.) " What is there in common between the philosopher and the Christian, the pupil of Hellas and the pupil of heaven, the worker for reputation and for salvation, the manufacturer of words and of deeds, the builder and the destroyer, the interpolator of error and the artificer of truth, the thief of truth and its custodian ? " (*Apology*, c. 46) ; quoted by Cochrane *op. cit.* pp. 222–223.

[2] Basil, born in 329, was Bishop of Caesarea in Cappadocia from 370 to 379. Gregory of Nazianzus, born about 325, was Bishop of Sasima, " a frightful and detestable little village," 370–379 and Constantinople, 379–381.

Emperor Julian at Athens. They had mastered the best that contemporary civilization could offer them, and believed it to be their duty to use this knowledge in the service of the Church.

The culture, to which the Fathers both Greek and Latin directed the attention of their fellow Christians, and which they desired to impress into the service of Christ, was not so much the living and growing expression of a contemporary civilization as a return to the great achievements of an age that was already classical. We can form some estimate of their world of thought by a consideration of the writers from whom they quote. The favourites of the Greeks are Homer and Plato, the latter especially in the *Republic* and the *Timaeus*—that dangerous and heady material for later speculators. Doubtless the Christian scholars were familiar with the writings of the neo-Platonic schools and had come under the influence of the later Stoic philosophy. But there is little trace of a direct influence of Plotinus ; it is to the fountain-head in Plato that they continually return. Among the Latins, we find few references to Tacitus or Juvenal or Lucan. Again the return is to the Classical Age, and among the writers of the brief golden age of Latin letters the favourites are Virgil and Cicero, the latter especially in his moral and philosophical writings. In this, the Christians were following the tradition of contemporary pagan scholarship ; with the diminution of the inner force of living, literature became less original, and increasingly depended on imitation or repetition of classical forms and themes.

But there was a difference. Latin was still a more living and adaptable medium than Greek. Greek was already beginning to be fixed in what later became the artificial Byzantine tradition, and literature moved steadily away from the forms of contemporary speech. The liturgies, and especially that of St. Mark, are full of remarkable and learned words, evidence of a kind of nostalgic turning back to a classical tradition of utterance. The Latin writers were nearer to the spoken language of the people, and to that alternative tradition of Latin rhythm that is found in the secondary and less classical writers. The language of the Vulgate is not that of the Augustan epoch. The reader is likely to find in it, and sometimes in Augustine, expressions and turns of phrase that remind him of Apuleius and the *Pervigilium Veneris* rather than of the forms and rhythms of the Virgilian age. This dual tradition was to continue through the Middle Ages, until at last Latin, like Greek, ceased to be a language in which men set down their ordinary thoughts and desires and hopes.

The immense Christian literature of the Fourth and Fifth Centuries is mainly theological—acts of councils, doctrinal treatises, sermons and commentaries on Scripture. From these it is difficult to form an impression of the life of the average believer. This is always the difficulty of the historian of the Church ; the ordinary man leaves little record of his faith and his experience, but these are the real stuff of the life of the Church, and the Christian society cannot in any age rise much higher than the level of its ordinary members. But we are not left wholly without information. We can form a picture of the crowds in the great church of Antioch hanging on the words of Chrysostom, and applauding as some point was specially well taken.[1] We encounter, in the pages of the same writer, the familiar difficulties of unemployment as the seasonal occupations of the summer came to an end. Many collections of letters have survived. Some of these deal at length with ecclesiastical perplexities. But in others, in a more personal strain, the theologians lay aside the doctor's gown and write in the simple strain of Christian shepherds dealing with the

---

[1] Chrysostom (347–407 ; Bishop of Constantinople from 398) did not like this habit and frequently rebuked it. " Pickpockets found so favourable a field in these crowded congregations, rapt in admiration of the eloquent preacher, that C. had occasion to recommend his auditors to leave their purses behind them." D.C.B., Vol. I., p. 521.

problems of ordinary people, birth and marriage and death, comfort in bereavement and the Christian hope. We are introduced to that delightful retreat on the banks of the river Iris—and this is one of the few passages in the literature of the time that breathes the spirit of appreciation of natural beauty—where Basil and Gregory of Nazianzus desired to escape from the worldliness and sordidness of much of the Christian life that they knew and to taste the joys of retirement and of the life of prayer and contemplation.[1]

A happy accident has preserved to us, out of so much of antiquity that has been lost, the letters of Synesius of Cyrene, and here we are admitted into a very different type of Christian life. Synesius comes before us as a typical country gentleman, fond of his wife, devoted to his horses and his dogs, but withal an esteemed friend of the great Christian leaders of the day. It seemed unlikely that such a man would ever be called to the episcopate. But so it came about ; and Synesius, though humbly conscious of his own inadequacy, and distressed by the sacrifice of so much in his comfortable easy-going life that would be demanded of him, yet felt it right to accept the call. The later letters show him as diligent and efficient in the exercise of his office, yet, like the much greater Origen in an earlier day, still retaining in the exercise of the priesthood no small share of the spirit of the Christian layman.[2]

We have yet to consider what is in some ways the most remarkable monument of this creative age in the history of the Christian society, the classical liturgies.

Then, as now, the Eucharist was the centre of the life of the unknown worshipping Christian. In an earlier period, the form of the Eucharistic service was already moving

---

[1] This retreat is described in the 14th of Basil's extant letters. He was so charmed by its ravines and torrents, the purity and coolness of the air, the abundance of flowers and the multitudes of singing birds that he was inclined to give to the place the name of Calypso's isle. Cf. also the 20th Letter of Gregory of Nyssa (Basil's younger brother, c. 335–395), for similar delight in the beauty of natural surroundings.

[2] Synesius was born c. 370, consecrated bishop in 410 and died c. 414.

towards / definition. Though many problems are as yet
unsolved, it is possible to identify some of the stages of
development. In the days of Justin Martyr, the central
part of the liturgy was left to the gifts in extemporisation
of the president. Hippolytus gives an outline which the
celebrant should follow. The prayer book of Sarapion of
Thmuis, a friend of Athanasius, appears to be a bishop's
private manual of the forms of prayer that he would
use on different occasions. By the end of the Fourth
Century, the main types of liturgy are already becoming
fixed in writing.

The most remarkable feature of all in this process is its
anonymity ; we do not know for certain the name of one
single writer of the period who has left his mark on the
worship of the Church. The earliest complete liturgy that
we possess, that in the eighth book of the *Apostolic Constitutions*, dating from the third quarter of the Fourth
Century, seems to be a composition of the study, its
enormous length making it unsuitable for use in Church.
But it contains all the main elements of classical Eucharistic
worship. It may be that Antioch, the centre in which this
anonymous work was written, was the focal point in
liturgical development. In all the classical liturgies—of
the Syrians, the Armenians, the Greeks, the Copts—we
find the same general structure. Here is the Mass of the
Catechumens, with the readings from Scripture, at least
three in number, sometimes more. Here is the massive
anaphora, invariable in general outline, with its complex
interweaving of praise and adoration, of recollection and
oblation, of prayer for the descent of the Holy Spirit on the
elements and for a worthy reception of the Sacrament,
leading up, as to a climax, to the solemn repetition of the
Lord's Prayer. Here is the beginning of elaboration and
splendour, as the Church moves out of the obscurity of the
catacombs into the magnificence of the early basilicas. The
liturgy of Rome alone belongs to a markedly different type,

the origin of which is as yet undetermined.[1] Whereas the
Eastern liturgies tend to long prayers and a cyclical movement, the Latin genius has already begun to find its
characteristic expression in the collect, the maximum of
meaning in the smallest number of words, and in a more
direct movement towards the goal of worship.

More than all the writings of the theologians, these ancient
prayers lead us into an understanding of the profound
Christian experience that underlay the petty bickerings and
unedifying quarrels of the age, and of that continuity of
devotion that makes the Christian society at worship today
one with the first gathering of the disciples in the Upper
Room on the night that the Lord was betrayed.

No age is perfect. The age of the Fathers, with all its
great achievements, failed conspicuously in two cardinal
matters of Christian faith and practice.

The Church gained in outward strength from its association
with the state, but it fell into grievous peril of losing its own
soul. Each party in the great controversies was too ready to
call in the aid of the emperors, and to rely on the civil arm
for the establishment of what it believed to be the truth. All
too soon the persecuted were prepared in their turn to
become the persecutors. A long step on the downward road
was taken when for the first time the blood of Christians
was shed by Christians.

A good deal of obscurity attaches to the story of Pris-
cillian the Spanish heretic. As is so often the case, our
knowledge of him is derived mainly from the evidence of
his enemies. There may have been a Manichaean strain
in his tenets.[2] He is depicted as a sorcerer, and the usual

---

[1] On all matters referred to in this paragraph, see the admirable *Early
History of the Liturgy* by J. H. Srawley (Cambridge, 1947, a second edition
prepared by the author himself thirty-four years after the publication of
the first). Some scholars, including Lietzmann, hold it possible that the
Apostolic Constitutions were written not at Antioch, but at Byzantium.
[2] But, as Lietzmann remarks in his *History of the Ancient Church*, Vol.
IV (Fr. Trans., Paris, Payot 1949), " in the history of the Church, endless
use has been made of this method of pillorying an uncomfortable critic."

charge of immorality is brought against him. When, in
A.D. 385, he was condemned and executed by the Emperor
Maximus, those who had permitted the appeal of Pris-
cillian to Maximus, and had thus sanctioned the transference
of a purely ecclesiastical cause to a secular tribunal, might
claim that they were innocent of his death, and that the
Church had not shed his blood. But Martin of Tours, the
greatest of the bishops of Gaul, and one who was no doubt
perfectly informed of all that had happened, expressed his
disapproval by refusing to receive communion with the
bishops who had been involved in the proceedings. A
disastrous precedent had been set. The Church has never
succeeded in freeing itself completely from the false idea
that violence and persecution can in some way help in the
establishment of Christian truth.

In spite of all striving after unity, the Fifth Century saw a
great and irreparable division within the Christian society.
The occasion of the division was the Eutychian and
Nestorian heresies. While the Church within the Empire
accepted the Chalcedonian formula, the marginal churches
of the East in Egypt, in Syria, in Persia, and in Armenia,
refused allegiance, and remained firmly fixed in what
Chalcedon had condemned as heretical traditions. But
behind this doctrinal division, we can see the working of
profound differences, psychological, national and linguistic.

The Syriac-speaking churches had their own traditions,
going back to the mysticism of Bardaisan and the *Hymn of
the Soul*.[1] They were wont bitterly to criticise the Greeks,
the disputers, who had introduced confusion into the faith
through trying to settle by human logic and argument the
profound mysteries of the divine nature. The oriental mind
sets less store by logic than that of the west. It proceeds
rather by the simplicities of intuition. When the west tried
to enforce submission to its doctrine by the arm of the

[1] A full translation of this, in some ways the most remarkable early
Christian document outside the New Testament, is given in F. C. Burkitt's
Early Eastern Christianity (London, 1904), pp. 218ff.

state, the east retaliated by withdrawing into its own world, and set up a rival and independent structure of its own.

The Nestorians, escaping from the coercion of the Roman arms, found their home in Persia, and established their catholicate at Ctesiphon. From here, Nestorian missionaries carried their version of the Gospel throughout a vast tract of territory in central Asia. They maintained connection with the Christians of India. In course of time, they penetrated China, and made the first beginnings of an indigenous Chinese Christianity.

The story of the Church in Armenia is specially illuminating. Its beginnings are obscured by a mass of legends. Nevertheless Armenia can claim to be the first Christian kingdom in the world ; by the end of the Third Century or a little later it was a Christian country under its own Christian ruler. The reduction of the Armenian language to writing, and the translation of the Scriptures and the liturgy in the course of the Fifth Century, gave a new cohesion and distinctiveness to the Armenian Church.[1] The union of race, state and language was so close and so exclusive, that Greeks and Syrians living in Armenia were not reckoned part of the Armenian Church, but had their own bishops on a linguistic basis, and were subject respectively to the Metropolitans of Caesarea in Cappadocia and of Antioch in Syria.[2] The adherence of Armenia to the monophysite or pre-Chalcedonian faith added only one more element of distinctiveness to those which already existed.[3] Many attempts have been made in history to bring the Armenian Church back into the orbit of the great churches of Byzantine orthodoxy. Every effort in turn has failed. The Armenian Church remains in

---

[1] The translation of the Scriptures is attributed to the Catholicos Isaac, who was deposed in A.D. 440, and who worked with the help of Mesrob. To the latter is attributed the invention of the Armenian alphabet in A.D. 406. The first translation of the Liturgy is affirmed to have been made by St. Gregory the Illuminator himself in the 4th Century.

[2] F. Dvornik : *National Churches and the Church Universal*. (London, 1944).

[3] The Armenian Church anathematised the Council of Chalcedon in A.D. 491, and has never withdrawn the anathema.

the Twentieth Century what it was in the Fifth, the Church of the Armenian race and of the Armenian language.

In their isolation, these marginal churches have contributed little to the development of Christian thought and theology.[1] Today they have preserved only fragments of their great traditions of the past. But they serve to remind the Christian world that its unity was early lost and has never been recovered, unless, indeed, we are to interpret unity in so narrow a way as to exclude from the Christian society those who claim the Christian name, and have maintained themselves as Christian communities for centuries in the face of overwhelming difficulties and conflicts.

The last great utterance of the classical period of Christian theology is the *De Civitate Dei* (413–426) of St. Augustine. The classical ideal was the maintenance, against a surrounding menace of barbarism, of an island of civilisation, within which the true life of man in society could be developed by the exercise of reason ; and many Christians had so far adopted the classical thesis as to identify the security of the Church with the survival of the Roman Empire. Augustine, denying the identity of the City of God with any human society, the foundation of which could only be *superbia*, the principle of rebellion against God, was moved by prophetic insight to realise that the vocation of the Church might be not to maintain a fence against barbarism, but to enter into a world in which for the time being barbarism was triumphant and to remake it from within. With the downfall of the empire of the west, the perils that were to face the Church were far greater than those she had endured in the days of persecution. But the classical age had done

---

[1] If scholars come generally to accept the view, maintained and systematically developed by Dr. Egon Wellesz in his *Byzantine Music* (Oxford, 1949), that Byzantine ecclesiastical music derives from the chants and melodies of the Syriac-speaking Churches, which themselves were in close relation with the ancient Hebrew musical systems, it will be necessary to hold that these isolated churches of the East have made one contribution of immense value to the life of the greater churches, for which in the past due credit has not been given to them.

its work well in providing the Christian society with its instruments of survival. That society was now armed with a canon of Scripture defined and closed, with creeds and canons affirming and limiting the faith, with a ministry universally recognised and honoured, and with a liturgy tested and consecrated by time. If it had not been provided with all of these, or if it had suffered the loss of any of them, it might well have failed to survive the testing of the Dark Ages. As it was, for a thousand years, the destinies of Europe in East and West were to be more closely linked than ever before or since with the fortunes and the development of the Christian society.

CHAPTER IV

GAIN AND LOSS

TO an observer at the beginning of the Seventh Century, it might have seemed that the Christian society was destined to spread in majestic progress throughout the inhabited earth.

The collapse of the western empire had brought great hardship and a measure of disruption. But the Church had found a way to make terms with the barbarians and by degrees to convert them. The impulse of missionary expansion had not died down. Ireland was already well on the way to becoming the Island of the Saints and the last repository of western culture. The conversion of England from north and south had begun. A spearhead had been thrust deep into Africa through the conversion of Ethiopia. The Nestorians continued to spread eastwards into the heart of Central Asia. The sage observer would have been wrong. The sudden appearance of Muhammad and of the Islamic power was one of those unexpected and utterly unpredictable happenings, which upset the calculations of statesmen, and make wise men cautious in the exercise of prophecy.

Scholarly research has not yet said the last word on the early career of Muhammad, and particularly on the question of his relationships with Judaism and Christianity. Certainly there were both Christians and Jews in the Arabia of his day. Certainly Muhammad had some acquaintance with the doctrines and traditions of both religions, though the evidence of the Qur'an suggests that what he knew had come to him by oral tradition rather than through reading, and had been profoundly modified within his mind. The thesis, persuasively worked out by Bishop Andrae, that Muhammad had heard the revivalist preaching of wandering Syrian preachers, and had derived from that source most of his aquaintance with Christian doctrine, seems to have much to commend it.[1] But, from the earlier days of his sojourn in Medina (622–32), Muhammad had turned against both Christians and Jews. The system which he committed to his followers combined extreme simplicity in its essential outlines with determined hostility towards the professors of every other creed.

The success of the Muslim armies is one phase in the eternal conflict between east and west, between the desert and the sown. Just as the children of Israel, fresh from their sojourn in the wilderness, were able to overthrow the civilisation of the Canaanites, so the Muslim warriors, emerging from the same deserts, found the armies both of the Persians and of the Romans easy prey. But the advance of the Muslims differed in one essential respect from the spilling over of the nomad peoples of Central Asia, which threatened the northern borders of the Empire. Those barbarians were seeking only living room and fertile fields. They were awed and subdued by the civilisation which they conquered. The Arabs despised the effete civilisation of the west. They were inspired by a clear and fanatical faith. They sought not only to conquer kingdoms, but to establish their own kingdom of God ; but the Lord whose kingdom they set out to establish was not the God of the Christians, the Father of our Lord Jesus Christ. Their advance was the gravest menace that has ever befallen the Christian society in all its history.

Even when every allowance has been made for the weakness of the ancient empires, the speed with which the wave of Muslim conquest swept forward is astonishing. Within

---

[1] See Tor Andrae : *Muhammad, the Man and his Work* (Eng. Trans., London, 1936), pp. 124–129.

a century of the death of the Prophet, Muslim armies had
overthrown Persia, occupied Mesopotamia and Palestine and
Egypt, overrun the whole of North Africa, conquered Spain
and crossed the Pyrenees. Their encounter with the army
of Charles Martel outside Tours in 732 did indeed prove
to be one of the decisive battles of the world. The Muslim
arms were never again seen in north-western Europe. But
this was only a check in one direction. Elsewhere, more
slowly but relentlessly, the Muslims beat down Christian
resistance, until at last, with the almost miraculous victory
of John Sobieski before the walls of Vienna in 1683, the tide
turned and the slow retreat of Islam began. Spain was
finally liberated only in 1495. Even Elizabethan England
found it necessary to raise special collections for the ransom
of Christian captives in Barbary. For a thousand years,
the juxtaposition of the rival empires and the rival creeds
was one of the determining factors in the development of
the Christian society.

From the Seventh Century onwards, the life of the Church
must be considered in three separate spheres. These are
distinguished, not by confessional or national determin-
ations, and only in part by factors of geography. Within
the general Christian unity, which was never completely
forgotten, the circumstances of history brought into existence
three markedly different types of society. The description
of these illustrates most relevantly the subject of this book.

I

Over a large part of the Christian world, Christians lived
as the oppressed subjects of Muslim rulers.

The terror inspired by the Muslim arms has tended to
leave behind in Christian tradition a false picture of what
actually happened. No war can take place without loss
and hardship to innocent victims. Doubtless there were

massacres of Christians in many places. But the Muslims were not bent on carrying out a war of extermination. The Prophet himself had made a distinction between infidels and Peoples of the Book. The Christians, as recipients of a revelation, albeit from the Muslim point of view a very imperfect revelation and one which the Christians themselves had perverted, were entitled to a measure of consideration, and could purchase their lives by submission to the conqueror. The invaders were too few to occupy in full the lands which they conquered. They were soldiers, and not farmers or administrators ; they had need of the earlier inhabitants to till the fields, and to carry on the work of society in its day to day existence.

Moreover it is clear that to some at least among the Christians the arrival of the Muslims presented itself as a welcome deliverance. Harried by Heraclius (610–641) and the Byzantine authorities, they were pleased to be under rulers, who though oppressive were even-handed as between the different sects of Christians, and, once the initial turmoils were over, made no attempt to imitate the thoroughness and malevolence of the Christian persecutors. The rich land of Egypt could not have fallen so easily into Muslim hands, if the policy of the Greek emperors had not fatally divided their Christian subjects, and made a large section of them ready to intrigue with the Muslims against a ruler towards whom they had long since ceased to feel any loyalty.

Only in North Africa did the Church completely disappear. For this a number of reasons can be suggested. The long continuing schism of the Donatists and the savage excesses of their robber bands, the Circumcelliones, had drained the Church of life and energy. Strife between Arians and Catholics had lasted longer in that part of the world than anywhere else. But probably there was a deeper reason than this. In other lands, the faith had taken deep root in the vernaculars, and therefore in the native thought of the peoples. The earliest Syriac translations of the Scriptures belong to the Second Century. The Egyptian are not later than the Fourth Century. In North Africa, on the contrary, Latin, though always the language only of an élite, was so much the medium of official business and of education that it seems almost to have monopolised the attention of the Christians. Augustine, indeed, refers to preaching in the Punic language and in his own sermons sometimes uses Punic words. But it does not appear that any part of the Scriptures had been translated. Even Punic would have reached only a section of the people. The inland folk of Berber stock had their own dialects, in which there was neither Christian preaching nor written Scripture. When the dominant power was no longer Christian, the native races of North Africa quickly fell away from the faith, and the traces of Christian civilisation among them disappeared.

In Muslim lands no doubt was allowed to exist as to the difference between the conqueror and the conquered. To the Muslim alone belonged the privileges of citizenship. The Christian, indeed, could at any time change his condition by the simple act of exchanging the faith of Christ for that of Muhammad. If he remained faithful to the old way, he became a *dhimmi*, a member of a subject race, entitled to the protection of the state, but bound to the payment of the *Jizya* or poll tax, from which the Muslims were exempt. It was not unprofitable to Muslim rulers to have a large class of taxpayers to undergird the state financially and to bear its burdens. The conditions were troublesome but not intolerable. The *dhimmi* was required to be distinguished from the Muslim by his dress. He was forbidden to carry weapons or to ride on horseback, though he might ride a mule or an ass. Still more strictly was he prohibited from attempting to turn a Muslim from his faith. On the whole the terms of the agreement were faithfully kept. At times the Christians were harried by over-zealous officials or

by outbreaks of mob violence, such as those which lay behind
some of the persecutions in the days of the Roman Empire.
But massacres were rare ; Ishodad of Merv, commenting
about A.D. 850 on the words, " And the hour cometh that
everyone that killeth you will think that he doeth God
service," could find no episode from recent Christian history
to illustrate his text.

Before long the Christians had been formed almost into
a nation within a nation. The Muslims took over from the
Persians the *melet* system, under which the Christian
churches became separate communities within the nation,
each governed by its own ecclesiastical head. The patriarch
became in some respects the civil as well as the ecclesiastical
ruler of his people, authorised to decide such legal cases as
were to be heard under Christian law, and standing as the
intermediary between his people and the higher powers.
Often abused, this system did assure to the churches a
measure of legal protection. It remained in force in the
Turkish Empire until 1923, when under the Treaty of
Lausanne, the Ecumenical Patriarch of Constantinople
ceased to have any civil responsibility and was limited to
the exercise of purely spiritual functions in relation to his
flock. In the ancient Assyrian Church of Mesopotamia, the
shadowy headship of the hereditary patriarch still persists.[1]

The Muslims had other uses for the Christians than merely
as useful milch kine. They had conquered great empires,
which they were at the start incapable of governing in a
civilised manner. They must needs turn to the conquered
peoples for help in those arts in which they themselves
were still incompetent. Almost all the government account-
ants and tax-collectors were Christians. Some rose to
high position as secretaries and chamberlains of the Muslim

---

[1] The contemporary Mar Shimun, who resides in Chicago, still claims to
be both civil and ecclesiastical head of this ancient church. But the headship, exercised at so great a distance, cannot be more than nominal, and it
is doubtful whether it is generally accepted by the people whom the
patriarch claims to rule.

rulers. In such offices it was possible for them to exercise considerable political influence, to work for more favourable conditions for their co-religionists, and to secure many appointments for Christians in the minor offices of state. This Christian monopoly of executive and administrative office could not but provoke jealousy among the Muslims. For a time, there was no alternative, since otherwise the offices could not be filled at all ; but later, as the Muslims themselves learned from their Christian subjects, Christian influence waned.

There was nevertheless much more contact between rulers and ruled than might be inferred from the inexorable tension which everywhere exists between the Muslim and the Christian faiths. The records show that religious debate and discussion were by no means uncommon. That such discussion was possible at all indicates at least a measure of tolerance among the Muslim ruling classes. John of Damascus thought it worth while to compose a dialogue between a Christian and a Muslim to aid Christian controversialists in their disputes with the followers of the prophet.[1] Towards the end of the Eighth Century appeared the *Apology of Timothy*, a work that was taken seriously enough by Muslim scholars for refutation of it to be undertaken in detail. In the course of the Ninth Century, Ṭabarī produced a great apology for Islam, in which the traditional weapon of Islamic polemics against Christians, the discovery of prophecies of Muhammad in the Christian Scriptures, is already firmly established. It cannot be said that the method of controversy produced marked results on either side. But the juxtaposition of the two religions was not without its deeper effects.

Islam is a religion that has proved over many centuries its power to satisfy certain deep instincts of the human

[1] John lived *c.* 690–*c.* 760. His short tract *Disputatio Christiani et Saraceni*, which fills only twelve pages in the printed text, naturally ends with the defeat of the Muslim ; and already indicates the lines on which controversy with Muslims was to proceed for centuries.

spirit, and to produce noble and heroic types of character.
In its stricter forms, it can do little to satisfy man's thirst for
the presence and the vision of the living God. It was not
long before a mystical element began to appear in Islam.
To what extent the experiences and the utterances of the
Sufis can be attributed directly to Christian influence is a
matter of controversy. Some recorded sayings are so startlingly Christian in both tone and expression that the connection can hardly be doubted.[1] Even where mysticism in the
strict sense is not to be found, it is possible to distinguish
in Islam two streams, the one more traditional and legalistic, the other more spiritual and more deeply religious.
It is perhaps safe to say that the greatest of all representatives of the spiritual tradition in Islam, 'al Ghazzali of
Bokhara (1058-1111), would never have been able to
accomplish his work, but for the streams of Christian
inspiration that flowed into Islam in the early centuries
of Muslim domination in Mesopotamia.[2] And one who has
most deeply studied the interactions of the two faiths in
those early days has found it possible to write : " On the
other hand Christian life had made a deep impression. . . .
Strangest of all, there was a wistful looking to Jesus to
supply something that was not to be found in Islam. It
was not the Christ of the theologians, but the JESUS of
the common people to whom they looked. . . . One cannot
read the history of this time without real regret; for the wistful
longing of Muslims towards Christ strongly suggests that
they might have responded if Christ had been more truly
presented to them."[3]

Arab civilisation has proved on the whole unoriginative,
but has manifested great power in the adaptation and

[1] See, for example, the remarkable example of Hallāj, quoted by R. A.
Nicholson in the article on Mysticism, *The Legacy of Islam* (Oxford, 1931),
pp. 215–218.

[2] A very clear short account of his thought is to be found in Christopher
Dawson, *Religion and Culture* : Gifford Lectures for 1947 (London, 1948),
pp. 77–81.

[3] L. E. Browne, *The Eclipse of Christianity in Asia* (C.U.P., 1933),
pp. 135–136.

development of materials derived from elsewhere. Before
long the Arabs began to desire information as to the springs
of that higher and more developed civilisation by which
they found themselves surrounded. Again they could not
but turn to the Christians. Nestorian culture had reached
a high level in the great centres of Nisibis, Beth Lapat,
and Merv. Many works had already been translated from
Greek into Syriac. Under the impulse of the Muslims, this
work was carried further, and from the Syriac translations were made into Arabic. In 529 Justinian had closed
the schools of the philosophers in Athens, and the groves
of the Ilissus no longer heard their disputations ; their
ghosts acquired a strange transformation and a new life on
the banks of the Euphrates. Arabs set themselves to
school with the mathematicians, scientists and philosophers
among the Christians, and absorbed in particular the
methods and the doctrines of Aristotle as seen through the
eyes of his later commentators. For two and a half centuries
the Christians seem to have been supreme in the work of
translation and exposition of the ancient writers. By A.D.
900 they had done their work. The Arabs had at their
disposal the raw materials and the methods of study ; they
were ready to launch out on their own independent course.

Those known and unknown scholars of the oppressed
churches of the East were doing a greater thing than they
knew. The Arabic translations of Greek classics spread
throughout the Moslem world. 'Al Ghazzali read them in
Bokhara. In Spain, where Christians, Muslims and Jews
lived and wrought together under conditions unparalleled
except in the strange, brief, beautiful civilisation that
Frederick the Second wrought in his Sicilian kingdom, a
veritable ferment of the human spirit arose. Averroes
(1126–1198) and Avicenna (979–1037) wrote the great works
that were to perplex, and on occasion to lead into heresy,
the Christian scholars of the west. And, most important
of all, Aristotle began to make his way into Latin from the

Arabic, and so to fructify the thought of the Christian west, just when it was beginning to stir itself after the long sleep of the Dark Ages.

But it was the western Church that was to profit and not the east. The life of those eastern Churches was not darkness, it was a long continued and perplexing twilight, that, as yet, has known no second sunrise.

Even where Christians were not persecuted, they were a people of inferior race. The Muslim was not merely a conqueror ; he was a man who despised with all his heart the faith of the people that he had conquered. Secure in the possession of the final revelation of the will of God, he could never find it in his heart, however much he might dispute, ever to meet the Christian on a level of equality. Was not the Christian stamped as an idolator ? Did not every Christian, every time he said the Creed, commit the unpardonable sin of *shirk*, the attributing of a partner to God ? If men are treated over many centuries as hopelessly and irreparably inferior, they develop the passive persistence of a suppressed people, but they develop also the vices and the weaknesses of servitude.

At first the Christian could serve his Muslim master loyally without compromise to his faith. But as time went on there was increasing pressure on him to abjure. To remain a Christian might mean for an ambitious young man a life of endless frustration and disappointment. To make a change of faith, and sometimes it might seem a very little change of faith, would make everything different and open wide the door to success. In the long process of attrition, many of the most promising Christians allowed themselves to be allured in this fashion, and the Church was weakened accordingly. Of those who abjured the Christian faith, many no doubt did so only outwardly, believing that they could inwardly retain their Christian allegiance. The Caliph Ma'mun (813–833) complained bitterly of those " who have not entered into Islam out of earnest desire for our religion, but desiring access to us, and aggrandisement in the power of our realm. They have no inner conviction, and no desire for the truth of the religion into which they enter." But those who desired to lead a double life rarely found it possible to do so ; they could not bring up their children in the Christian way, and so the process of attrition went on. It continues today ; in Egypt, the Coptic Church loses to Islam every year a number of its most promising young men; it has not yet found the means to staunch this ever-bleeding wound.

The continued existence of the ancient churches of the East, after so many centuries of Muslim domination, is one of the miracles of history. It is evidence again of the power of the Christian liturgy to hold a people together, and to keep them in the Christian allegiance, when almost everything else has been taken away. But survival is not the same as life. Captive Greece led captive her Roman conquerors. None of the Eastern churches has ever been able to win into captivity to Christ the Muslim peoples among whom it has dwelt. There was a moment of promise, when it seemed that the Nestorians might convert the Turkish hordes. But Islam prevailed, with fateful consequences for the whole history of the western world. The churches have influenced Islam, and contributed to its development. But in twelve centuries the frontiers have scarcely changed, and Islam remains the great unsolved problem of the Christian society.

II

When Antioch, Alexandria and Jerusalem had fallen before the Muslims, Byzantium alone among the four patriarchates of the eastern world remained erect.

The Christian society in this second zone lived under conditions as different as it is possible to conceive from those which have been described as prevailing just over its frontier in the lands that had become subject to Muslim domination.

The importance of Byzantium in Christian history is not yet fully understood in the west, though more justice is done to its achievements than in even a comparatively recent past. Few would now subscribe in detail to the vehement condemnation of Byzantium and all its ways penned by F. D. Maurice in 1869 :

> " For a whole millennium the question was tried under the most favourable conditions whether a Christian empire is possible ; whether the idea of it does not involve a flagrant contradiction. Every new passage in the story has helped us in the examination of that problem ; here is the final solution of it. Such a revelation of the name and character of God and of His relation to His creatures as the Christian's Creed and the Lord's Prayer take for granted, cannot co-exist with an Empire such as that which Augustus established, which Constantine transferred to a new city and consecrated with new names. All who adhere strongly to the polity which is described in Scripture as the Kingdom of Heaven must be in hostility to this kingdom, must, however little they may aim at that result, be working for its subversion. . . . One should never contemplate without awe the departure of such an Empire from the earth ; but it was an incubus from which men must have been delivered before they could be convinced that Truth and not Falsehood is the Lord of the Universe."[1]

It may well be admitted that the Byzantine was no freer than any other Christian society from those defects which render perpetually impossible the full realisation on earth of the nature of the Christian family. But societies hold together by that in them which is good, and are disintegrated by that which is evil. If Byzantium held together for a thousand years, and again and again, when it seemed on the point of disruption, discovered within itself new sources

[1] F. D. Maurice, *Social Morality* (London, ed. of 1886), pp. 268–9.

of life and recovery, it is certain that there must have been
other forces at work than those of arbitrary authority
and slavish obedience. For eight hundred out of that
thousand years, Byzantium was the chief bulwark of the
Christian west against the forces of Islam ; if Byzantium
had fallen five hundred years earlier, before the recovery of
the west had begun to be well established, the future of the
Christian Church would have been so different that not
even speculation can form an outline of its possible course.
In an age when Christendom is again threatened with
immense and as yet undetermined perils from the east, it
may be possible to assess more fairly than in more comfortable days the value of that long-continued and heroic
service of the empire of the east.

While the west was falling into barbarism, Byzantium
continued in all its wonted splendour. Though the southern
trade-routes through the Mediterranean were increasingly
cut off by Muslim power, access was still possible, by way
of the Black Sea and the great Russian rivers, to the vast
fertile hinterland of northern and central Europe, and to
Asia as far as China. The quays were thronged with ships,
the bazaars were filled with merchandise ; in the words of
Benjamin of Tudela, the city was " a great business centre,
whither merchants come from all the countries of the
world." And when they came, they were dazzled by the
great buildings brilliant with marble and mosaics, and by
the spectacle of the inhabitants of the city, riding forth on
fine horses in such splendid attire as gave them the semblance
of so many princes.

But Byzantium was not only a centre of commerce. It
was also the greatest centre of Christian culture in the
world. This was, in truth, a backward-looking culture ;
to the Byzantines, it was a matter of obligation to write
as nearly as might be in the Greek that had been current
a thousand years before, and thus literature became more
and more divorced from the life of the people—the pastime

of an intellectual élite. But here as in other ways Byzantium was not incapable of renewal. The reconstitution in the Eighth Century of the University of Constantinople, the influence of Photius, the most learned man of his age, and imperial patronage, combined to produce in the Ninth Century a new epoch of literary brilliance and production. When, in the end, the disaster happened, and Byzantium as a Christian city ceased to be, her doctors carried with them to the west the treasures of Hellenic learning, and opened up to ready pupils a vast world of knowledge hitherto known to them scantily and imperfectly through Latin translations.

Byzantine art early became stylised, and the main lines of its traditions were never broken through.[1] Yet even this, to western eyes, stiff and unyielding tradition had within it elements of flexibility and contact with direct experience of life. Nor did it remain childless. Its effects on the western mind can be seen in the splendours of the mosaics of Ravenna and of the Cathedral of St. Mark at Venice. More accurate study of the beginnings of the great traditions of western painting has shewn that there is in Fra Angelico and in the earlier work of Giotto more of direct Byzantine influence than was at one time allowed for.

The people that dwelt in the great city were nimble, quick-witted, mercurial and corrupt ; they were characterised " by prudent cleverness not overburdened with useless scruples."[2] Their annals seem at times to consist of little but the meaningless and incessant warrings of the factions of the Greens and the Blues. Yet with it all the Byzantines, both in the city and elsewhere, were a deeply pious folk. Part of this piety was no more than the love of

---

[1] Dr. Egon Wellesz (*op. cit.*, pp. 120–21), and others have pointed out that stylisation in Byzantine art is a positive and not a negative quality ; it was a method deliberately chosen to secure certain desired effects, and was never so complete as to render impossible individual initiative and self-expression within the limits of traditional style.

[2] Charles Diehl : *Byzantine Civilisation*, in *Cambridge Medieval History*, Vol. IV (C.U.P., 1936) p. 757.

dialectic and theological disputation, natural to an intellectual people for whom religion was still an over-
powering interest. They were not greatly changed from
their ancestors, of whom Gregory of Nyssa had bitterly
written that " if you ask the price of a loaf, you are told
that the Son is subject to the Father ; if you ask whether a
bath is ready, the answer is that the Son was made out of
nothing." But this is not the whole story. The solemn
hieratic character of Byzantine worship gives the clue to
the real nature of Byzantine piety ; life spread itself before
the people as a series of ordinary happenings, punctuated by
immensely solemn divine events which were carried out with
the splendour of perfected ritual, and in which the whole
people was involved. When envoys from Vladimir, great
prince of Kiev, attended Mass in Santa Sophia, they were
so profoundly impressed as to be convinced that this was
the true dwelling place of God upon earth.[1] Legend is often
the expression of the inner experience of a people ; here we
find set forth what was most characteristic of the Byzantines—their profound sense of the interpenetration of all
human things by the presence of the divine, of the sanctification of human splendour by the effulgence of the divine
glory.

In the midst of the people walked the emperor, the
divinely anointed Christian prince. Individual emperors
might be weak, depraved, insignificant. But all this could
never wholly take away the sacred nimbus, the sense of the
divine by which the throne of Constantine was surrounded.
Every outward circumstance of life tended to enhance this
feeling of supernatural awe. The emperor was never seen
except in circumstances of dazzling splendour, moving

---

[1] See *Byzantium* (edited by Norman H. Baynes and H. St. L. B. Moss,
O.U.P., 1948) pp. 390–1 : " The Greeks led us to their edifices where they
worship their God and we knew not whether we were in heaven or earth.
For on earth, there is no such splendour or such beauty, and we are at a
loss how to describe it. We only know that God dwells there among men
and their service is fairer than the ceremonies of other nations. For we
cannot forget that beauty."

always in such hieratic dignity as is depicted in the great
mosaics of the Churches. The whole ordering of his life
was surrounded by religious ritual, emphasising his character
as not merely the civil but also the spiritual head of his
people. His life was "a completely representative and
pontifical life." On every festival of the Church, it was
part of his duty to go in solemn state to one of the Churches
of the capital, there to participate in the appointed ritual
of the day, and to worship not only with but also for his
people.

It has been usual in the west to speak of the complete subjection of the Byzantine Church to the state. Such terms are
natural in countries and in an age in which it has become so
much a part of the furniture of thought to regard Church
and state as separate and possibly conflicting entities that
it is almost impossible to think in any other terms. From
such a standpoint, no understanding of the Byzantine conception of the Christian society is possible. For there
Church and state were not separate entities ; there was only
one body politic under the direct and theocratic rule of
God Himself. The emperor was not the representative of
secular power ; he was the vice-gerent of God. He was
not a layman. This is not to say that he was a priest.
He was set apart to the particular office and function of
the Christian prince, an office and function as necessary to
the welfare and stability of the Christian body as any other,
but distinct from them all. The solemn anointing that
made him emperor set him apart from other men as
decisively as the consecration of a bishop.

It is difficult for the secularised mind of the modern
world to grasp and take seriously that simple unitary conception of human society. But it is, historically, the
original pattern of society, refurbished and given a Christian
colouring. In all primitive societies the king is at the same
time warrior and priest and lawgiver. For all his different
functions he needs and receives divine grace ; for all he is

fortified and protected by *mana* (to use the convenient Melanesian word), the peculiar and terrifying sanctity that hedges his divinity. On the famous black obelisk, King Hammurabi in the second millennium B.C. is depicted as receiving his code of laws from the hand of his god. As king, it is his task to promulgate the code ; but it is the word of God that he sets forth, and not some invention of his own human wisdom. This tradition of kingship had never died out in the Levant ; when Constantine took over from Diocletian the orientalisation of his empire, he took over with it and superficially christianised the primeval tradition of the prince as the central figure on whom the community in all its functions directly depended. If the modern mind finds it hard to adapt itself to this way of regarding things, it is highly important that it should make the effort, since the very same idea of the Christian prince emerged in the west a thousand years later, and vitally influenced the history of the Christian society in another of its crises.

By no one was this idea taken more seriously than by the emperor Justinian (482–565). This astute, diligent, unlikeable man, claimed the right to legislate for his subjects in every part of their being. If the monastic orders shewed signs of disorder, ill-befitting their name, part of the emperor's task was to codify legislation affecting them, to inscribe it in the law books, and to see that it was enforced. Justinian went further. He regarded himself as the keeper of his subjects' conscience, entrusted by God with the task of setting forth and defending the orthodox faith, and seeing that it was everywhere professed and believed throughout his dominions. Just as he had the civil service, completely under his control and dependent on his will, to see to the enforcement of the civil law, so he had the ecclesiastical service, equally under his control and dependent on his will, to see to the carrying out of ecclesiastical law, though Byzantium never recognised such a sharp distinction between civil and canon law as has become traditional in the west.

At the head of the ecclesiastical service stood the patriarchs, great officers capable of exercising at times a predominating influence on the fortunes of the empire. But Justinian had no doubt at all that the patriarchs were his patriarchs. Though he could not and would not himself perform any sacerdotal function, yet he was the divinely appointed head of the Church ; by the special wisdom granted from on high, he would receive the correct answer to all theological, as to all legal, problems ; the task of the patriarchs was to communicate, through the bishops, to the churches all that the divine wisdom had revealed to the Christian prince, and to see that no cavil or murmur was raised against the divine word.[1]

It is clear that this doctrine, to work perfectly, demands the infallibility of the Christian prince. But what if the Christian prince himself should fall into error ? That which Justinian regarded as impossible was deemed by the Church to have taken place. At the end of his life, the emperor adopted the obscure heresy known as Aphthartodocetism, the belief that our Lord's body had had from the moment of His conception the attributes of incorruption, and that His sufferings, though real, were made possible only by a perpetual and miraculous act of His will. As usual the divine wisdom was promulgated in a decree to the churches. To those who believe that the Byzantine Church had wholly lost its fighting spirit and was bound hand and foot to the will of the emperor, it must come as a surprise to learn that Anastasius, Patriarch of Antioch, assembled a synod of a hundred and ninety-five bishops, all of whom declared themselves ready to give up their sees rather than accept the imperial mandate. The crisis was solved only by the opportune death of the emperor.

---

[1] Cf. Louis Bréhier in *Histoire de l'Eglise*, Vol. IV (Paris, Blond et Gay 1937), p. 440. " Justinien est allé plus loin, il a pris parti : dans les débats, il s'est arrogé le pouvoir de définir lui-même le dogme, sans se référer à une autorité ecclésiastique quelconque, et d'imposer ses conclusions à tous ses sujets et à l'église elle-mmeê."

In a far more serious matter, the Iconoclastic controversy (726–843), the Church, strengthened by the implacable opposition of the monks to the puritanical tendencies of the Isaurian emperors, was able, after many vicissitudes and reverses, to win its case, and to make the worship of the holy images for ever a part of the Orthodox doctrine and practice. There are indeed those who think that paradoxically the victory of the Church in this matter was in fact its most signal defeat, and that by once straining to the utmost its capacity for resistance it lost the capacity to resist again. It is at least certain that the Byzantine Church in the days of the failing Empire never showed such independence as it had manifested in times of greater prosperity and power.

Most Byzantine historical writing deals with the history of the city. It moves in the world of emperors and patriarchs, of high politics and intrigues. But the real life of the Christian society is never found exclusively in such places ; the Spirit of Christ dwells also among the obscure and the humble, and these for the most part have no chronicle, so that the historian has to gather up scraps of information here and there, and weave them into such a patchwork as he may. For the life of the humble in the Byzantine world, however, we are not left wholly without information. In the lives of the saints, we have many vivid touches of life from a simpler and more natural world.[1] Here again, it is difficult for the western reader to become adjusted to the atmosphere. Some of the saints found out for themselves strange and unnatural forms of asceticism, such as that of the famous Simeon Stylites and his imitator Daniel, who stood for years on pillars, and came down from them only

---

[1] Until very recently scarcely anything has been available in English on Byzantine hagiography. An excellent start has been made with the publication by Dr. N. H. Baynes and Elizabeth Dawes of *Three Byzantine Saints* (O.U.P., 1948). The writers remark, on page xiii, that "it is through the biographies of East Roman Saints that we can form some picture of the life of the provinces, some understanding of the thought-world of those humble folk who appear so rarely in the works of writers whose interests are urban, who are closely linked with the life of the imperial court."

as corpses to be deeply venerated after their death. The
whole atmosphere is redolent of what the modern mind is
inclined to dismiss as superstition, of a world in which
demons and evil spirits are just as real as and much more
formidable than human beings. But if we find uncouth
such tales as that of the whole village whose inhabitants
were possessed by a host of demons, and as a result went
about burning granaries and breaking up the whole village,
until they were set free by the intercessions of St. Theodore
of Sykeon, we meet also such humane touches as that of
St. John the Almsgiver, who, if he heard of any master
ill-treating his slaves, would reason with him until he was
willing to treat them better, or if he would not listen, would
arrange for the slaves to escape to a place of safety. It
would be a poor imagination which failed to see behind
the not infrequent crudity and even absurdity of the narratives, that same intense and simple-hearted devotion as
was seen in the Desert Fathers, and worked itself out in
the utmost simplicity of a childlike approach to God. The
east has never developed such elaborate techniques of the
spiritual life of the west ; in its spirituality there is always
an attractive manifestation of the spirit of the little child.

The Byzantine church has always laid great stress on the
hierarchy and its unbroken succession. Simple people knew
that there was another apostolic succession. Patriarchs might
come and go ; but always, far or near, there would be the
holy man, in whom the power of the Christian life would
be manifestly present. And if the saint should die, he would
not go away ; the place of his burial would become a shrine
and centre of pilgrimage, at which he would perfect the
miracles that he had begun in his earthly life. This importance of the saint as against the hierarch has been a
continuing feature of the life of the Christian society in the
east until the present day.

There is yet a third factor in the unchanging stability of
the Orthodox Churches—the village priest. Many of these

priests have been men of little culture, and their theological education has hardly gone beyond the minimum necessary to enable them to carry out the solemn rites of the Church. But the presence of the Church in the midst and the ceaseless repetition of its liturgical solemnities have impressed themselves indelibly on the mind and outlook of Orthodox peoples. A curious and interesting parallel and contrast have been drawn between the work of the Chairman of a Methodist circuit and that of an Orthodox Bishop. To the Methodist, the all-important thing is the weekly proclamation of the word of God. If he can find qualified men, he will use them ; if he cannot, he will use the best material he has to ensure that the Gospel is everywhere proclaimed. He will go round as often as he is able to make available to his people the sacrament, without which the proclamation of the word is incomplete. To the Orthodox Bishop, the essential thing is the weekly celebration of the Eucharist. To make this possible, he will ordain the best men that he can find, even though their qualifications may be exiguous by metropolitan standards, and though they may be unqualified to preach the word of God. He will himself go round as often as he is able and preach to his people, in order that the essential sacramental ministry may be completed by the due proclamation of the Gospel, without which the sacrament cannot be fully effective. Each method may be judged incomplete in the light of the full Christian ideal ; history has at least not condemned the Orthodox solution of an intractable problem.

With the slow but in the end irresistible advance of Islam from the east, the Christian society on the Byzantine model was on one side in a perpetual process of contraction. But justice is not done to it, unless we remember that in another direction it was also in process of expansion. Missionary work was less systematically planned and executed than by the western Church. Yet from Byzantium the Gospel went out to the Slavonic peoples of eastern Europe and, when

Byzantium fell, the old tradition was maintained in lands which had never been part of the eastern Roman Empire at its widest extension.

There are certain features in this Byzantine expansion which are worthy of close attention.

The first is the use of the language of the peoples to whom the Gospel was brought. The prestige of the Greek tradition was so great that there was an initial inclination to believe that Greek was the only language in which Christian theology could be worthily expressed. But, with an adaptability that was not imitated in the west, the Church of Byzantium soon came to realise that this could not be insisted on. The first great missionaries among the Slavs, Cyril (*d.* 869) and Methodius (*d.* 885), preached and produced a liturgy in the Slavonic dialect of the people among whom they worked. When in the Eleventh Century the Russian princes accepted the Gospel, Old Slavonic took its place among the great liturgical languages of the world.

In the second place, the independence of local and national Churches was recognised. In part this was due to political rather than to theoretical considerations. The Byzantine government was closely centralised ; it may have desired to maintain as close a centralisation in the affairs of the Church as in those of the state. But increasing political weakness made this impossible. And just because the connection between Church and state was so close in Byzantium itself, it was natural to recognise that in other independent kingdoms such a connection would reproduce itself. At the present time the Orthodox Churches of the world are organised as a number of autocephalous churches, each with its own liturgical language and independent patriarchate, but bound together by a strong sense of inner solidarity, and by a recognition, not closely defined but real, of the primacy of the Byzantine see. This pattern is a natural development from the period of expansion, in which the new Churches in Russia, in Bulgaria and elswhere, were coming into being.

In consequence of this liberty, and of dependence on inner spiritual devotion rather than on juridical unification, the Byzantine Church was able to hold in a special way the affection of the missionary churches. " The Greek Church was able to bring about, among the peoples which were the object of her missionary activity, something that the west might well envy. She made herself really loved by her dependents. The faithful cling to her with tenderness, even with passion."[1] This inward affection has helped to maintain the stability and permanence of the eastern Churches through all the darkest periods of confusion and upheaval.

Yet great as have been the achievements of the Byzantine tradition, it must be admitted that the Christian society in the east early became, and has in the main remained, a static society. There have been spiritual and theological movements, but they have taken place within an established pattern. After the end of the Fifth Century there was no new outburst of creative theological thinking. John of Damascus, the last great dogmatic thinker before the awakening of Russian theological thought in the Nineteenth Century, worked out in detail the implications of the thought of the Greek Fathers, but added little that was new. The eastern Church remained unaffected by the travail that came upon the western world through the writings of Augustine, and again in the period of the Reformation, and has thus found no answer to questions that must be asked, even though no finally satisfactory solution can be found for them.[2]

---

[1] K. Holl : *Gesammelte Aufätze,* Vol. III (Tübingen, Mohr, 1928), p. 126.
[2] This point is stressed by Fr. G. Florovsky in an article published originally in Russian in *The Christian Messenger* (Paris, May, 1949), and quoted in *The Ecumenical Review,* Vol. I., No. 4 (1949) p. 438 : " The problem of the Reformation . . . cannot just be passed by, even though the Protestant solutions of these problems must be decidedly rejected. We must traverse the whole road of these problems with full comprehension and with sympathy, and lead them from within outwards to the clarity of ' Catholic solutions.''
It is probable that Western scholarship has unduly neglected Hesychasm, the mystical movement of the 14th century, in which deep theological as well as spiritual problems were involved. See *Byzantium* (O.U.P., 1948), pp. 114–116, and the bibliography on pp. 400–1

The Christian society, if it is perfectly to fulfil its function in the world, must be a creative influence, fashioning the social and political order, as that changes in response to new factors that come in from age to age from sources outside the control of the Church. On this side the eastern churches have had little to contribute. They grew up and identified themselves with a certain pattern of society, powerful, stable and resistant to change. When that pattern was broken, they were content to give old answers to new questions. As long as there were Christian princes in the Orthodox world, it could be held that these answers were in a measure relevant ; with the final disappearance of the Christian prince, those churches find themselves hesitant and uncertain. It remains to be seen whether, by a return to their own great days of the period before their life was too closely determined by the acceptance of the Constantinian settlement, they can develop new creative vision, and a message for a new society that has broken away at every point from the Christian tradition and from those foundations on which the ancient Christian society was built.

III

If the Byzantines despised the Christians of the west as ignorant barbarians, there were better grounds for their point of view than mere arrogance. The collapse of the classical system in the west was far more complete than in the east ; the west suffered a disruption and breach of continuity such as the east was not to experience until the fall of Constantinople in 1453.

It is impossible to fix a point at which it can be said that the ancient world disappears, and the Dark Ages begin. Augustine still moves within the classical framework, though his own philosophy of history points beyond it,[1] whereas Gregory the Great (*c.* 540–604) is already medieval in his outlook and in the process of his thought. When Rome was sacked by the troops of Alaric the Goth in 410, it seemed to many that the end of the world had come. But the event was far less decisive than it had appeared ; the empire, though only a shadow of itself, did struggle on for a few more years, and only gradually faded into nothingness. In reality, the overwhelming of the ancient world by the barbarians was a slow process, continued over centuries. Long before the empire fell, barbarians had been domesticated within it, and had even, like Stilicho (*c.* 408), held high office. Many of them were already Christians before they came in as invaders. Only the Huns remained exactly what they had been in their primeval home in Central Asia, incurable nomads and pitiless destroyers. All the other peoples had to some extent come under the civilising influence of Rome, and had felt the magic of her name.

In consequence, when the invasions had run their course and the old order had been destroyed, there was much more co-existence of the old and the new than a simplified and summary picture might suggest. What we see, especially in Gaul, is the gradual barbarisation of the Romans, and the gradual Romanisation of the barbarians. The extent to which the two factors influenced ône another, and the character of the resulting synthesis, varied very much from place to place. In every case, it resulted in a society basically different from that of the classical world. Where Romans of the old type, such as Sidonius Apollinaris[2] or

---

[1] See the concluding chapter of Cochrane, *op. cit.*, pp. 456–516, on the contribution of Augustine to the philosophy of history. Classical thought had identified pure Being with the divine ; it was Christianity alone that could claim the world of Becoming, *of process*, also, as the sphere of the operation of the divine. See especially pp. 483 ff.

[2] A.D. 431–82, Bishop of Clermont in A.D 472. See a good account in C. Scott Holmes: *The Christian Church in Gaul* (London, 1911), pp. 409–51; this author notes that " It has been remarked by a learned French historian that the bishops in Gaul in the fifth century were either monks or noblemen."

Paulinus of Nola,[1] were able to maintain themselves on their own great estates, much of the old culture could be maintained. But this became increasingly rare, and by the Eighth Century the transformation from classical to medieval was everywhere almost complete.

As always in history, the economic factor played a major part in the change from one form of social organisation to another. And since the Church does not exist *in vacuo* but in the places where men live, it was impossible for the Church to remain unaffected by the changes. The classical civilisation had been based on the city. The Greek *polis* was the centre of political living and thinking. Rome had been the centre of the empire, and had reproduced herself, in different forms and guises, in innumerable colonies and *municipia* from the Roman Wall in Scotland to the frontiers of India. The country was of importance only in so far as it fed the city and made city existence possible. The characteristic feature in the history of the Dark Ages was the disappearance of the city, and the shifting of life back to the land and to a more primitive economy.

It is not possible to assign this change to any one cause, but it is clear that one great factor was the breakdown in trade. Internal stresses had tended to break up the old economy. At the same time, the advance of the Muslims almost completely closed the Mediterranean to traffic, and cut off the Christian world from what had been its principal highway of commerce. The old gold currency, the stable medium of exchange, tended to disappear. Each country was thrown back on its own resources for production and exchange. The cities dwindled. Even the Romans degenerated into a barbarous rabble, living among the splendour of the monuments of antiquity, which they could no longer maintain, and which they habitually used merely as quarries to secure materials for the erection of their own squalid habitations. It was not until the

[1] Landowner, philanthropist, builder, poet, Paulinus was born in A.D. 353, ordained A.D. 393, bishop of Nola probably from A.D. 409–31.

emergence of Venice in the Tenth Century as the new commercial metropolis that the west had anything to show comparable to the continuing stability and splendour of Byzantium. Even kingdoms could no longer be said to have capitals.[1] At the height of the power of Charlemagne, there was no one city that could bear permanently the weight of the royal residence and the royal court. The emperor must remain in a state of pilgrimage from centre to centre, as economic causes made desirable. Where the emperor led, the ecclesiastic naturally followed ; far on in the Middle Ages, the medieval bishop can be seen, moving about in the same way from manor to manor, in order not to exhaust too completely the resources of one single place of residence.

It is always hard to characterise briefly a long period of history. The use of the term " The Dark Ages," as a general title for the centuries between A.D. 500 and A.D. 1,000, though unkind is not wholly unfair. The old culture was in process of dissolution, and nothing of comparable value had emerged to take its place. Roman society in the last days of the Empire was undoubtedly corrupt ; that which took its place was no more virtuous, though its vices tended to be of a different kind. The barbarian nations brought in with them their own habits and ways of life. They were simpler than the peoples whom they conquered, but they were not innocent. Society, as we find it, represented with artless vividness in the pages of Gregory of Tours (538–594), presents a depressing picture of almost ceaseless war and strife, treachery and malice, drunkenness and reckless violation of every canon of sexual morality.

If this were the whole picture, it might seem inexplicable that the golden Middle Age had ever emerged from such a chaos. But there were other factors also at work. Within this period fall the pure integrity of the Venerable Bede, the humility and personal charm of Cuthbert, the missionary

[1] Cf. H. Pirenne: *Histoire de l'Europe* (Paris: Alcan, ed. of 1939), pp. 59–61.

passion of Boniface. Culture on the whole tended to decline.
Yet the Carolingian Renaissance, with Alcuin of York
(*c.* 735–804) as its greatest representative, was a real revival
of learning. Its permanent memorial is the Carolingian or
Caroline script, that beautiful form of minuscule writing
that has influenced all western handwriting up to the present
time.[1] While Islam was steadily advancing in the East,
the Christian forces were working north and west and east,
until by the end of the Dark Ages the great majority of the
barbarian peoples had been brought within the Christian
fold.

A sharp distinction can be drawn between the missions
of the ancient and those of the medieval Church. In the days
before the Church won imperial favour, progress had been
slow, from individual to individual and from group to group.
When persecution was still a possibility, nothing less than
strong personal conviction would make a man a Christian.
By contrast, the conversion of the northern nations was
almost entirely a matter of mass movements. The simpler
the community, the greater its tendency to act corporately,
without regard to the will or purpose of the individual.
In Kent, Augustine preaches to king Ethelbert ; the king
is converted, and the conversion of his people follows after.
In Scandinavia, the kings take the lead in discussion of the
new faith with their nobles, and are sometimes more effective
as missionaries than the professional representatives of the
Church.[2] In a more democratic society, such as Iceland,
discussion is freer and less subject to authority ; yet there
too, in the end the matter is referred to one single man of

[1] On this see especially E. A. Lowe, in *The Legacy of the Middle Ages*
(Oxford, 1926), pp. 211ff.

[2] The conversion of Norway is typical. Olaf Tryggvason was baptized,
apparently in the Scilly Isles, about A.D. 995. On his return to Norway,
he set himself to secure the conversion of his realm. The combination of
persecution, cajolery, authority and occasionally open and undisguised
violence was so successful, that by the end of his reign, Norway could be
reckoned as among the Christian nations. For a brief account, see
K. S. Latourette, *History of the Expansion of Christianity* (London, 1939),
Vol. II, pp. 120–28, and the references there given.

outstanding ability for decision ; the decision once made, all together throw in their lot with the new way.[1] On some occasions, the introduction of the new faith was accompanied by violence and cruelty. The best known and therefore most harshly judged instance is the conversion of the Saxons by the power of Charlemagne ; though in that instance the records suggest that violence was used rather to suppress repeated attempts by the Saxons to withdraw themselves from the new allegiance, than as the method by which their assent was originally secured.

An individualistic age may be inclined to doubt whether there can be any element of real faith at all, when a mass of people make a decision that would appear to be meaningless on any basis other than that of personal understanding and commitment. The history of Christian mass movements, ancient and modern, suggests that this judgment is superficial. Nevertheless the Church, as it gathered in the multitudes of the hastily converted, was faced with difficulties of a new and formidable kind. When one God is substituted for another, the new God tends to take on all too closely the lineaments of the old. To the Anglo-Saxon, Christ is the young hero, who joyfully ascends the Cross, like a warrior going to some deed of derring-do. But Christ is in truth incommensurable with any other deity ; unless He Himself creates His own dimension, He is no longer the Christ. Hard as was the conflict of the Church to bring the rude tribes into some recognisable relation to accepted Christian rules of conduct, even harder and more prolonged was the effort to disentangle Christian truth from the web of pagan tradition and outlook in which inevitably it became enmeshed. The process took longer than is usually imagined. The baptism of Jagiello, king of the Lithuanians, in 1386 may be taken as the end of official paganism in Europe ; and this

---

[1] The first full account in English of the Church History of Iceland is *Icelandic Church Saga* by J. C. F. Hood (London, 1946). For the events connected with the conversion of Iceland, see especially Chapter II, pp. 26–41.

date lies far on in the high Middle Age. But Karl Holl refers to a case of pagan sacrifice in Prussia as late as 1520 ;[1] and, though this was probably an isolated instance, it is indicative of the survival of a deep level of pagan thinking and acting, even among people who had long been nominally Christian.[2]

Christianity had begun as the new religion of the city. The bishop was bishop of a city, and secondarily of its adjoining countryside. In the Dark Ages, the Church had to change its character so as to become the Church of the countryside, since cities were no longer the centre of the life of men.

For the moment, the change was not apparent. The bishop was still the bishop of a city, in so far as that word continued to apply. In fact, he was almost the most stable factor in society, the guardian of all that could be saved from the ancient world, and the one settled official in a generally peripatetic world. But just his central position and his importance to the new kingdoms that were growing up led to a transformation, as a result of which the office of a bishop in the Church came to be regarded as little more than a part of the apparatus of a secular state.

Most of the barbarian princes were illiterate. They found it easier to conquer realms than to administer them. It was only with the help of churchmen that the secular affairs of the kingdom could be carried on. And, since men cannot work without reward, the churchman had to be endowed with lands and estates, which he held from the king, just like any other landed nobleman. The Christian society came to terms with the feudal system ; the bishop became almost, and sometimes in fact, the secular ruler of an inde-

---

[1] *Gesammelte Aufsätze* (Tübingen, 1928), Vol. II, pp. 127–8.

[2] Many superstitions of pagan origins survived, of course, far later than the 16th Century. Some were harmless ; others, like belief in the existence of witches, led to horrible excesses, even in civilised Europe and America, till the end of the 18th Century. One of the causes for the separation of the Secession Church from the Church of Scotland in 1733 was " the repeal of the act against witchcraft, thereby dethroning God's word." I owe this reference to Silcox, *Church Union in Canada* (New York, 1933), p. 57.

pendent princedom.[1]   But, this being so, and the influence of
the bishop being proportionately great, it was essential to
the prince that the bishop should be his man, and that the
appointment of bishops should be entirely in his hands.
There might be a faint survival of the old right of the laity
to have a voice in elections, but in practice the first and last
word was with the king.   Sometimes the choice might be
excellent.   Often it was not.   If Gregory of Tours is to
be believed, many bishops were far more distinguished
as warriors in the field than as spiritual pastors.   We even
read of two whose habit it was to keep up their carousals
all night, until the sound of Matins being chanted in the
neighbouring Church had begun to be heard.

The supremacy of the crown was most clearly asserted
in the fact that, from 511 onwards, councils were called and
presided over by kings and not by churchmen.[2]   Charlemagne carried as far as Justinian or Henry VIII the idea of
the divine right of kings to rule the Church, and would not
have tolerated for a moment the idea that any bishop or
priest could be above the emperor.   The Bishop of Rome,
like every other bishop, was a landholder ; those lands which
were fiefs of the emperor he held like every other landholder in virtue of doing homage.   To Charlemagne, the
Pope was simply another bishop, subject in certain respects
to his jurisdiction, bound to accept his decisions in ecclesiastical affairs, and under obligation to pray for " the Lord
and Father, King and Priest, the Leader and Guide of all
Christians."[3]

What the king could do on a large scale in relation to
bishops, the local landholder could do in his own sphere in
settling the position of the local clergy.

---

[1] The main facts concerning the feudalisation of the episcopate are set
out with admirable clarity by T. M. Parker in his chapter on Feudal Episcopacy in *The Apostolic Ministry* (ed. K. E. Kirk : Oxford, 1946), pp. 351–
387.

[2] *Cambridge Med. Hist.*, Vol. VI, p. 542.

[3] See E. Amman in *Histoire de l'Englise*, Vol. VI (Paris, 1937), pp. 76–7,
and Seeliger in *Camb. Med. Hist.*, Vol. II, p. 617.

Even in the days when Christianity had been in the main a religion of the cities, there had been some organisation of religion in the countryside. Bishops had founded a number of village churches, dependent directly on themselves, and maintained from funds at their own discretion. With the breakdown of the old order in the west, the initiative in this matter was more and more taken by the owner of the land, or rather, under the feudal system, by the tenant-in-chief. He would build a church, he would choose a minister, and he would set aside that part of the land and its produce from which the minister was to be maintained.[1] The Christian minister so appointed was, in part, an heir of the Christian tradition ; in part he appears to have been the successor of the heathen priest of the tribe or clan in earlier days. He acquired a specific position in society ; certain lands were definitely assigned for his maintenance, usually twice as great in extent as those allotted to ordinary colonists, in return for the enjoyment of which he ·was expected to serve the community by the provision of bull and boar for servicing the herds, or in certain cases, stallion and ram, a custom which survived in the Church for more than a thousand years.[2]

But with this privileged position went certain drawbacks. The parish priest was the lord's man, bound to him, as feudalism developed, by all the onerous and inflexible customs of the manor. He had no remedy against oppression or caprice. If the lay lord, as often happened, chose to regard the revenues of the churches on his land as a profitable speculation, in which he might claim the larger share, there was no court, other than that of the lord himself, in which the priest could hope to claim redress. Belonging, as he often did, to the servile class, attached to the soil, he could not,

[1] On the development of the village Church and the parish in England, see F. M. Stenton: *Anglo-Saxon England* (Oxford 1943), pp. 147–52. Stenton remarks that "the division of a diocese into parishes, each under the spiritual charge of its own priest, was still a remote ideal in the early Eighth Century."

[2] E. W. Watson in *Camb. Med. Hist.*, Vol. VI, pp. 531–32.

without becoming a criminal, find refuge in flight. Bishops
were distant and shadowy figures. They could exercise
greater discipline on their own lands, and on clergy holding
land from them on the same tenure as that by which priests
elsewhere held from lay lords. But diocesan organisation
was only in its infancy; the bishop could claim only a
limited measure of obedience from, just as he could exert
only a limited measure of protection on behalf of, men who
were pledged by allegiance to another lord than himself.

Crude and unsatisfactory as this system may appear, it yet
contained within it the germ of one of the most characteristic and enduring of all the features of the Christian society,
the parish. Europe in the feudal period was thinly populated
by small and scattered groups, living separated by large
tracts of heath or uncleared forest land. Gradually it came
to be taken for granted that every such group would have
its priest and its church. The priest might be ignorant
and inadequate to his spiritual task ; the house of God
might be little more distinguished in appearance than the
huts of the common people by which it was surrounded.
But there in the centre of human habitation was the house
of God, with its ceaseless round of services, closely integrated
with the course of nature and of the life of the village. If,
unlike the eastern Church, the western refused to put the
Gospel and the liturgy into the rough barbaric dialects of
the invaders,[1] that made the worship all the more venerable
in the eyes of simple people, able to apprehend more by
way of inner intuition than they could grasp by intellectual
process.

The village priest began as pastor of a group of people
living huddled close together for protection against the

---

[1] It must not be forgotten that vernacular translations of some portions
of the Scriptures were made in western Europe in the early centuries.
According to the beautiful story, the last act of the Venerable Bede on his
death-bed was to rouse himself to dictate the last verses of his translation
of the Gospel of St. John into his native Anglo-Saxon. W. Bright : *Early
English Church History* (Oxford, 1888), p. 338. But Latin remained everywhere the sole liturgical language.

perils of nature as yet very imperfectly subdued. Gradually he came to be regarded as the spiritual guardian of all the people living within a certain area. As population grew and government became stable, these areas came to be contiguous, until whole countries came to be mapped out in parishes, a civil as well as an ecclesiastical division of the country. In England, this process seems to have reached completion before A.D. 1,000. The boundaries of not a few parishes remain today exactly as they were fixed in the feudal period. The system has been extended by European Christians, to whom the territorial rather than the congregational planning of Christian activity is second nature, to many other parts of the earth. It has endured through all the changes of Reformation and Counter-Reformation, Enlightenment, and French Revolution. It has been extended, often inappropriately, to great cities. Although its usefulness has come to be questioned in an age when the whole structure of society has undergone such radical changes, no one has yet been able to suggest any other system that could satisfactorily take its place. The village church, with its spire and its bells, remains the monument of a great epoch of Christian penetration and progress.

The high days of the feudal system were the period in which the Church was " in the power of the laymen."[1] If nothing had happened to set other currents in motion, the unity and spiritual independence of the western church might have been for ever destroyed. The Holy Roman Empire never succeeded in unifying the western world in more than idea. If the Church had remained the appanage of quarrelling and worldly-minded feudal rulers, without opportunity of rallying its own spiritual forces and speaking to the world in the name of Christ as the only Ruler of

---

[1] The title of Volume VII of the French History of the Church, *Histoire de l'Eglise Depuis Les Origines Jusqu'a Nos Jours*, edited by A. Fliche and V. Martin (Paris, 1940).

princes, its rôle as the maker and mother of nations would have been at an end.　But the other tendencies were there. Periods in Church History do not succeed one another ; the new always grows out of the womb of the old.　Within the feudal dominance, there was growing up quietly and coming to fruition a wholly different conception of the Church, and of the part that the Christian society is destined to play among the nations of the earth.

CHAPTER V

THE MEDIEVAL SYNTHESIS

IF Augustine dominated the strictly theological thinking of the western Church through the whole medieval period and after, the great figure of Ambrose is the starting-point for the development of its thought on the relations between the Church and the state and between the Christian society, and the world. On a famous day in A.D. 390, so men believed, when the Emperor Theodosius, fresh from commanding a massacre of his subjects in Thessalonica, presented himself at the doors of the cathedral in Milan, Ambrose withstood him to the face, refused to admit him to the Church or to Communion, and demanded that he should make by penance such restitution as was within his power.[1] The event was never forgotten. It was not an isolated instance of courageous resistance to worldly authority. Ambrose was taking his stand on a consistent and clearly held view of the relation between the authority of the powers that be, and that of the Church as the bearer of the word of God. There is no area of life, and no power on earth, not even that of government, which can be withdrawn from the judgment of God. It is only as authority submits itself to the ordinances of God that it can be restrained in its inveterate tendency to

[1] This is the event, as it took shape in popular imagination, and as it is set forth in the pages of Theodoret (V, 18). What men believe to have happened is often as important in history as "the undoctored incident that actually occurred," and I have therefore allowed the statements of Theodoret to stand in my text. A more sober account is to be found in the writings of Ambrose himself (Ep. LI and *De Ob. Theod.* 34). It is clear both that Ambrose firmly took the Emperor to task for his sin, and that Theodosius shewed very plainly the sincerity of his repentance, and his recognition of the right of his spiritual father to deal with him as Ambrose had done.

arbitrariness and caprice. But it is only the Church that can declare with authority that word of God, to which the earthly powers are to be subject. In such affirmations, as Hans Lietzmann points out, the medieval idea of government and of the relation between Church and state is in its broad outlines already fully present.[1]

As we have seen, the weakness of the Church in the west and the dominance of strong rulers drove this concept of the relationship of the secular and the ecclesiastical for a long period underground. It was never entirely forgotten. But it could not again become effective, until it was united with another movement of thought, the tendency to find in the Bishop of Rome the living centre of western Christendom, and to ascribe to him an authority with which that of no other bishop in the Christian world could be compared. Such authority was claimed by the bishops of Rome from early times. Gregory the Great, in the circumstances of his time and through his own unique personal qualities, was able to extend the power of the Papacy, and to make it a reality over a large part of the west. But after his time, the Papacy fell again on evil times, and, whatever the theoretical claims may have been, the Popes were utterly unable to check the increasing disruption of the western Church through the power of the lay lords in the Frankish kingdoms.

The first strongly marked movement in the opposite direction came from an unexpected source. England, at least in its southern parts, had owed its Christianity to Rome, and to the direct interest of Gregory the Great.

---

[1] See H. Lietzmann : *History of the Ancient Church* (French Tr.), Vol. IV. (Paris, 1949), pp. 73–5 and 85–6 ; and also Hendrik Berkhof : *Kirche and Kaiser* (Zurich, 1947 : the German translation of a work written in Dutch in 1942), p. 12. Dr. Berkhof works out in great detail the development of the theocratic concept of the Church. He quotes also from Palanque, *St. Ambroise et l'Empire Romain*, p. 403, the statement : " For a long period, he exercised an influence of decisive importance. The thought of Ambrose has left its stamp on the thinkers and Popes of the Middle Ages, from his contemporary Augustine up to Gregory the Great and Gregory VII."

More than any other part of Christendom it felt itself
bound to the Roman See by affection and loyalty.
Consequently, when Anglo-Saxon, as distinct from Irish
and Scottish, Christianity, became a strong missionary
force on the continent of Europe, it brought with it
this tradition, and the conviction that there can be no
real Christianity except in communion with the bishop
of Rome.[1]

The greatest of the English missionaries was Wynfrith
of Credition, better known under his ecclesiastical name
of Boniface (680–754). The outstanding qualities of Boniface as a missionary have remained fairly well known
to his fellow countrymen ; his singular importance at a
turning point in the history of the Church seems to have
been less fully realised. When Boniface went to Rome in
722 to be consecrated bishop, he took an oath of allegiance
to the Pope similar to that taken by bishops of the Roman
province ; by so doing, he set himself and his future work
in Germany directly under the direction of the Pope. From
739, he worked as the Pope's legate and representative
in the Frankish kingdoms. Many new sees were created ;
in every case, the bishop took a similar oath of direct
obedience and loyalty to the Pope. A new or revived idea
of centralisation and unification in the see of Peter was being
brought in, to counteract the fissiparous tendencies of the
Frankish system. Dr. Watson goes so far as to say that
" he thus prepared the downfall of the Frankish system,
which came as soon as the Empire grew weak and the Pope

---

[1] See W. Levison: *England and the Continent in the Eighth Century* (O.U.P.,
1946), pp. 70–94: and especially p. 73: "The Roman origin of the English
Church began to exert an influence overseas through the ideas of ecclesiastical unity which the English missionaries disseminated."
" Through the Anglo-Saxon Mission, a factor of the utmost importance
was introduced into the Christianity of the Continent. The great regard
for the Roman Church, which had characterised the Anglo-Saxon Church
from its foundation on, and its conviction that Christianity can subsist
only in fellowship with the Roman bishop, laid the foundation for the position of the Pope in the Middle Ages. . . . The connection with Rome gave
this mission . . . its great world-encompassing character." Ficker and
Hermelink, *Das Mittelalter* (Tübingen Mohr, 1923), pp. 12–13.

advanced a theory and established a system which displaced the Carolingian."[1]

The work of Boniface was rather a prophecy of things to come, than the actual achievement of a unified Christian society of the west under the direct rule and guidance of the Pope. That unification, as it developed, was to find its theoretical basis in some of the most remarkable forgeries that have ever influenced the history of human thought and of the Church. The Donation of Constantine, that strange legend, according to which the first Christian Emperor, having been cured of leprosy by Pope Sylvester, decided to found his new capital in the east, and to leave undisputed sovereignty in the west to the Pope, to whom all bishops were made subject as all magistrates are subject to the emperor, seems to have had its origin in the Papal chancery at some time towards the end of the Eighth Century. It is probable that the document itself incorporates older legend ; the legal form in which it is drawn up impressed an uncritical age, and the authenticity of the Donation seems never to have been doubted until the beginning of the Renaissance period.[2]

This was followed by the emergence of the more extensive collection of the False Decretals. This body of documents, purporting to include the decisions of the Popes from the earliest times, was almost certainly brought into existence in France in the second half of the Ninth Century.[3] Its primary aim was not so much to glorify the Pope as to protect bishops from the aggressions of their metropolitans

---

[1] See *Camb. Med. Hist.*, Vol. VI, p. 543.

[2] It was first exposed as a forgery by Laurentius Valla in 1440. His work, printed by Ulrich von Hutten in 1517, had a profound effect on the mind of Luther.

[3] A. Villien, in *Dictionnaire de Théologie Catholique* (Paris, 1924), Vol. IV, col. 214, gives 21st April 847 and 1st Nov. 852 as the dates between which the appearance of these collections might lie. The most famous discussion of the forgeries is that published at Geneva in 1620 by the Protestant David Blondel, under the elegant title *Pseudo-Isidorus et Thorianus Vapulantes.*

or of covetous lay lords.   But once completed and accepted
as authentic, it put into the hands of the Popes a weapon of
enormous power.   The first Pope who can be shewn to have
made use of the collection was Nicholas I (858–67), the
greatest champion of the authority of the Papacy after the
days of Gregory the Great.   Whether Nicholas himself knew
the documents to be a forgery is a matter of debate.   His
successors at least accepted them in good faith, and used
them unquestioningly for their own purposes.   Here was
set forth once more the Ambrosian concept.   The whole
Christian society is to be unified under one visible spiritual
head, endowed with all the authority of the prince of the
apostles, supreme lawgiver and ruler of the Church, entitled
to proclaim the law of God with authority even to princes
and to demand their submission.

So great a revolution in thought and practice could not
be put through in a day.   It awaited the man and the
occasion.   But from the moment that the False Decretals
came to be accepted as the basis of Canon Law, the change
was on its way.   The first step was a change in the position
of the clergy.   The Church began to organise itself as a
spiritual society within the world, and to detach itself
from that subordination to the authority of the layman
that had so gravely threatened its unity and its spiritual
independence.   " The clergy tended to become a closed
corporation, the constitution of which inevitably became
feudal.   The relation of the beneficed clergy to the bishop
resembled that of the bishop to the king.   No longer is the
parish priest the man of the lord who appointed him ; he
becomes the bishop's man. . . .   The security of tenure was
actually increased by the obligation laid upon the bishop
of maintaining the rights of his man."[1]   The clerical
revolution was already launched.   The Church was coming
to self-conscious existence as a power independent of the
state.   The clergy were coming to form a body within the

[1] E. W. Watson in *Camb. Med. Hist.*, (C.U.P.) Vol. VI, p. 546.

Church, with interests of their own, separate from and sometimes opposed to those of the laity.

On April 22, 1073, Hildebrand, Archdeacon of Rome, was elected bishop and took the name of Gregory VII.[1] The man had appeared, who was not merely to renew the Ambrosian concept of the duty of the spokesman of the Church in relation to the civil power, but for a time to make his purposes remarkably effective in the affairs of men.

The ideas of Hildebrand were simple and readily expressed. His life was dominated by a passion for righteousness. He saw the western world divided by ceaseless strife, and at the mercy of monarchs who for the most part recognised no rule except self-interest and no limit to their rapacity except that of their power to make the possessions of others their own. He saw a clergy weakened by the still lingering corruptions of the Dark Ages, and therefore ineffective in proclaiming the will of God for the world. In contrast with this, he saw in vision a world united under the rule of God and subject to His law. But since the law of God must be proclaimed in order to be obeyed, and since the world can be unified only if there is one authority by which that law is proclaimed, he saw in the throne of St. Peter the one centre to which all must turn, the one supreme authority, through the recognition of which alone men could find the remedy for the grievous ills of a violent age.

The arrogance of Gregory's pronouncements was compatible with a very real personal humility. For himself he seeks nothing. He has inherited the plenitude of power promised by Christ to Peter. It is only in the name of Peter that he will act. Disobedience to him is direct disobedience to Christ in the person of his representative and therefore an act of rebellion against God Himself. His weapons are only spiritual. He has the dread power of excommunication, and is confident that what he has bound on earth is also bound

[1] Hildebrand was born in 1020 and died in 1085. The date of his great triumph over the Emperor Henry IV was 25–28 January, 1077.

in heaven. From his sentence there is no appeal. No human creature is exempt from his authority.[1] If kings transgress, they too must be made to submit to the yoke of God, since it is only from God that they derive their authority, and there is one on earth who stands above them in the interpretation and expression of the authority of God. To William I of England he writes " As I have to answer for you at the awful judgment, in the interests of your own salvation, ought you, can you avoid immediate obedience to me ? " If the king is recalcitrant and refuses obedience, he is no longer a king appointed by God ; he is a rebel and an adversary. The Biblical precedent for action is clear ; apostate Saul was deposed by Samuel, and his place taken by David the man of God's own choice. The Pope, representative of the risen and victorious Christ, has an authority greater and more extensive than that of an Old Testament prophet ; can he hesitate to use his power to excommunicate and depose a disobedient king, and to release his subjects from all their duties towards him ?

This theocratic concept of the Christian society can be made effective only if the one head of the Church has at his disposal an obedient and thoroughly disciplined spiritual army.

On the ecclesiastical side, Gregory asserted the fullest control over all the bishops of the Church. It is his sole right to appoint them (whatever concessions must be made at times to the claims of secular rulers to nominate to sees within their realms), to excommunicate or to remove them, to learn of the details of their doings, to reprove, rebuke, exhort on every occasion. He is the judge in all important causes in Christendom, but he himself cannot be judged of any, since he stands directly under God with no intermediary.

[1] This claim was made in the most literal sense of the words. Innocent IV (1243–54), a great Canonist who became Pope, declared : " Credimus quod papa qui est Christi vicarius, potestatem habet non tantum super Christianos, sed etiam super omnes *infideles*, cum enim Christus habuerit super omnes potestatem." Quoted by W. Ullmann : *Medieval Papalism* (London, Methuen, 1949), p. 49.

In relation to the other clergy, Gregory tried to put into force in all their stringency the decrees against the marriage of the clergy. The ascetic tendancy in the Church had from an early date led to disapproval of the clergy continuing in the married state. Whereas the East gradually withdrew from this position, and permitted, as it does till the present day, the marriage of all its parochial clergy, the west had maintained the ideal of clerical celibacy, and had fitfully tried to bring about its observance. But success had never been more than partial, and the true celibate, outside the cloister, had been a rarity. It was the aim of Gregory to separate the clergy from the cares and perplexities of life in the world, and to enforce on them a far higher standard of devotion to duty than was either expected or enforced in less strenuous times. The application of the rules was strenuously contested by the clergy in many places, and was never more than superficially successful. It did, however, represent a step forward in the clericalisation of the Church in the west, to which there is no exact parallel in the life of the Christian society in the east.

Gregory felt himself strong enough to try conclusions with the one great rival power in the world, the Holy Roman Empire, and to launch his sentence of excommunication against the Emperor Henry IV. Four centuries and more were to pass before a German monk successfully defied the sentence of excommunication issued by another Pope. Henry IV did not dare so to resist. The world looked on in astonishment, as the heir of Augustus and Charlemagne crossed the Alps in the depth of winter, and stood for three bitter days as a penitent in the courtyard of the castle of Canossa, pleading for restoration and absolution. It may be that the inner reality of the scene was a little different from the outward appearance. Henry's abject approach as a penitent may have been the astutest stroke that he could have made to win men's sympathy to himself and away from his proud assailant. Gregory's delay of three days may have been due to embarrassment and uncertainty rather than to heartlessness. Nevertheless the event was never forgotten ; it lingered on in men's minds as a manifestation of the supremacy of the spiritual over every other power on earth.

There was little that later Popes could add to the Hildebrandine concept of the Christian society, theocratically organised under its visible head, guarded against all possibility of error by the presence of Peter perpetually present in his successor. Innocent III[1] might assert the same claims with even greater vigour, and as in the case of England with even greater temporary success. He might adopt the title Vicar of Christ, not apparently used by his predecessors. Boniface VIII[2] might express the claim that both the swords, the temporal and the spiritual, were at the disposal of the Pope to use as he might see fit, and that it was altogether necessary to the salvation of every human soul that it should be subject to the Roman pontiff. In essence, these add nothing to the claims already made by Hildebrand. In essence, they are the same as the claims put forward by the Bishop of Rome today.

It must not be supposed that this idea of the Christian society met with immediate or universal acceptance. Marsilius of Padua, in the *Defensor Pacis*, (1324), worked out a wholly different idea of the Christian society, as the organised fellowship of the faithful, within which the specific functions of the priestly element are to be carried on as an organ of the whole body, but under the direction of the state, in which the authority of the whole body finds expression. Dante, in the *De Monarchia*, worked out his own theory of Church and Empire as independent spheres of man's existence, each appointed by God, the one with a view to man's temporal, the other to

---

[1] Innocent III was born in 1160, became Pope in 1198 at the age of 37, and reigned till 1216. He was one of the strongest of the long series of Popes, and is reckoned, next to Alexander III, the greatest lawyer who has sat on the Papal throne.

[2] Boniface VIII, Pope 1295–1303. His famous Bull *Unam Sanctam* was promulgated on 18 Nov., 1302.

his eternal beatitude, each with its own sphere of autonomy, within which any aggression by the other would involve rebellion against the ordinance of God.[1] Occam,[2] more anti-papal, seems to hold that the fellowship of all Christians under Christ is the supreme authority over Pope, bishop and Council, and that the Papacy finds its proper place as the culmination of authority in society, only through its rigid restriction to the spiritual spheres of *lectio, oratio, praedicatio, cultus dei.* Opponents of the Papacy were many. Gregory VII did in fact die a defeated man in exile at Salerno, saying with his last breath, if tradition is to be trusted, " I have loved righteousness and hated iniquity, therefore I die in exile." And Boniface VIII lived to see the overthrow of all his plans, and to die in the misery of impotent frustration.

Nevertheless, intolerable though the Papal claims may have appeared in certain respects, the great Popes stood for two principles which to the Christian are incontestable— that in the affairs of men, the spiritual has the primacy over the secular, and that the families of men can be gathered into one only in Christ and in obedience to the law of God.

The medieval synthesis was imperfect. But during that brief and splendid epoch of the high Middle Age, Europe again became conscious of itself as a unity, far beyond the precarious and variable limits of the Holy Roman Empire, and the Church attained a level of power and influence over the lives of men, for the most part used beneficently, such as has never been known before or since.

No precise date can be fixed for the end of the Dark Ages any more than for its beginning. But as the first point at which it began to be apparent that the darkness was beginning to pass away, though some of the worst degrada-tions both of the Papacy and of civilisation came at a

[1] This is the doctrine of Dante, as worked out by M. Etienne Gilson in his outstanding book, *Dante the Philosopher* (London, 1948, trans. David Moore), pp. 162–225.

[2] William of Occam, *doctor invincibilis* (c. 1300–49) was a student of Merton College, Oxford. His principal controversial works were written between 1330 and 1342.

later date, it may be useful to suggest the foundation of the great monastery of Cluny in A.D. 906. Cluny was fortunate in having only six abbots in the first two hundred years of its existence, all outstanding men. All subsequent monastic reforms can be traced back directly or indirectly to the Cluniac spirit. As monasteries spread, they carried with them into remote and barren regions not only the faith, but also the spirit of an active and progressive civilisation. Recent research has shown the great part taken by the monks in the development of high farming, without which an agrarian economy can never escape from the perennial poverty and recurrent famines which are the accompaniments of primitive methods and primitive organisation. Men like John of Taunton and Henry of Eastry (Prior of Christ Church, Canterbury, 1285-1331), may be reckoned among the great creators of European civilisation in the Middle Ages.[1]

As Europe grew out of its disintegration into a new consciousness of its unity, that unity, and with it a new capacity for self-assertion, found remarkable expression in the adventure of the Crusades. Already in Spain the Christian forces had begun very slowly to press back those of Islam. By the end of the Eleventh Century, Christendom was ready to maintain that the future of civilisation and of religion was not to remain in Islamic hands, but that the centre of the life of the world was to shift again to the western Mediterranean and to the lands bordering the Atlantic Ocean. It is easy to criticise the Crusades, both in their general conception and in detail. They permanently embittered the relations between Christians and Moslems, and left a legacy of hatred and suspicion which no subsequent centuries have availed wholly to exorcise. Yet to fail to recognise in the Crusades the stirring of a spiritual ideal would be gravely to miscon-

[1] For an excellent account of this development, see Dom David Knowles: *The Religious Orders in England* (Cambridge, 1948), pp. 32–55 and 64–78.

ceive the spirit of the times. There were base and shameful elements—bickerings between Christian leaders, massacres of captives, treacheries, sheer lust of gain. But these were not the whole story. To the man of the times the Crusades "are a 'holy war'—a war, which, in the theory of the canonists, is not only 'just', but also attains the full measure of consecration ; a war which is *res Christiana*, and unites the Christian commonwealth in common hostilities against the arch-enemy of the Christian faith."[1] The participation in the Crusades of such pure and noble spirits as Godfrey of Bouillon, the first Christian *princeps* of Jerusalem[2], and at a later date, of St. Louis of France (1214–1270), indicates that here we are dealing with something more than the aggressiveness of a military caste. One part of the Christian society has found itself again, and is able to act as a unity in a common cause.

From the east came light. As the darkness of ignorance passed away, men began to recover again the treasures of ancient learning. Aristotle was brought in to teach Christian scholars to think and to re-express the whole compass of the Christian faith. Among the most characteristic features of medieval Christendom was the growth of the medieval university. It was of immense advantage, for the unity of the Christian society, that educated men everywhere in the west thought and spoke in the same language. From Iceland to the furthest outpost of the Crusader kingdoms, Latin was the medium of communication. Not only so, men of education everywhere underwent much the same discipline of thought. The modern university suffers from the fragmentation of knowledge. It is almost impossible for those brought up under the humane disciplines and those who have been fed solely on the strong meat of science, to understand one another and to engage in the fruitful interchange of thought. The medieval scholars

---

[1] Ernest Barker in *The Legacy of Islam* (O.U.P., 1931), p. 44.
[2] More precisely *Advocatus Sancti Sepulchri*. See S. Runciman : *A History of the Crusades*, Vol. I (C.U.P., 1951), pp. 289–314.

laboured under no such difficulty. Every man passed through the discipline of the *trivium* and the *quadrivium*. All had mastered much the same technique for the handling of any problems that might come their way. There might be great differences of opinion. There was in fact much greater variety in scholastic thought than a later age, dazzled by the supreme achievement of St. Thomas Aquinas, has always been ready to recognise.[1] But there was a common world of discourse. The beginnings of new investigation of nature and of the world in which man lives, and with it the enormous extension of modern knowledge, were still in the future.[2] There was an established body of fact, almost the whole of which could be mastered by a single student in a lifetime. It was possible, therefore, to reach a synthesis of all available knowledge, such as, with the development of modern scientific investigation, has become an ever-receding dream. And this knowledge was all subject to theology, the queen of the sciences. It was within a Christian society that the scholar thought and moved ; he saw all things in relation to the Christian revelation, and like Aquinas, found the end of speculation in contemplation, and, if such grace were given, in the mystical vision of God.

Of this great period of Christian thought, Dante (1265–1321) is at the same time the greatest representative, the climax, and the prophet of doom. It seems that he had read almost every book written before his time and available in Latin. His speculation has been refrigerated by an active experience of political life in the intense and turbulent cities of the Italy of his day. And in his work medieval man is seen in the round, in the totality of his being. Here is the perspective of eternity that lends dignity to the meanest life,

---

[1] See Dom David Knowles, *op. cit.*, pp. 205–16 and 233–52.

[2] The blindness of men to the world around them and their apparent incapacity for accurate observation, already fully apparent in the Eighth Century and unchanged till the Fifteenth, are among the most curious of all the phenomena of history. As Dr. Raven correctly notes, when the change did come, it began rather among the artists than among the scientists *de métier*. See C. E. Raven : *English Naturalists from Neckam to Ray* (Cambridge, 1947), pp. 31–32.

the sense of the eternal significance of human action, the judgment and the mercy of God, under which at every moment man stands, the pity and the terror, the pathos and the splendour of human existence. But when Dante, in prose and poetry, turned his back on Latin and produced in Italian the first great Christian classic since the writing of Augustine's *De Civitate Dei* nine hundred years before, he pointed the way both to a new birth of the human spirit, and to the breakdown of that unity of the Christian society to which, at its culminating point, he had himself given the noblest and most lasting expression.

It is easy to delineate the outward factors that determined the life of the Christian society in the Middle Age, much less easy to discern how life within that society presented itself to the ordinary man who was a member of it.

Of one thing he was well aware—that the Church was an institution of immense power, holding him in its hand both in life and in death. It has been reckoned that by the end of the Middle Ages one third of the whole land surface was in the possession of the Church. The ordinary round of daily life was determined by the Church's year. The only relief from endless toil was in the recurrent Holy Days, which meant also holidays, strictly enforced as days on which no work might be done, sometimes to the irritation of the farmer, more concerned with getting in his hay than with the strict observance of the Church's law. To the criminal, or to the man falsely accused, the Church, with its places and rights of sanctuary, so sacred that only in rare cases did lay lords dare to violate them, offered a hope of protection and security. Such was the power of the ecclesiastical arm that the villager might see his own lord put to a painful and humiliating penance in church before the eyes of the congregation. Even kings like Henry II of England, or nobles like Raymond of Provence, could not claim exemption from what the Church saw fit to impose.

Even after the Hildebrandine reforms, the ordinary

church-goer saw little of the chief shepherds to whom his welfare had been committed. Bishops continued to be great magnates, largely concerned with the affairs of the court, and only at rare intervals at leisure to concern themselves with the spiritual needs of the flock. Not all were so continuously absent from their sees as the Italian bishops of Worcester at the end of the Middle Age, not one of whom ever crossed the sea to visit his northern diocese. There were the great exceptions, Grosseeste, Richard of Chichester, and others, who won the reputation of sanctity by their pastoral care for the poor and needy. But for the most part the bishop was a distant figure. With the development of Canon Law, a gradual change had taken place in the nature of the functions that he was expected to fulfil in the Church. He was less a lord of the manor than he had been in earlier times, and more specifically a judge. " The highest officers of the Church exercised powers which were pre-eminently judicial ; their pastoral care was discharged, not in evangelical exhortation and pious encouragement, but in bringing their subjects to book for defaults against the spiritual code, and even their acts of grace were executed with a strictly legal propriety. In the eyes of those subjects they were first and foremost judges ordinary—they might and habitually did perform that office by delegation or deputy, but their powers in any case were corrective and were enforced by pains and penalties."[1]

The association of the office of a father in God with juridical authority is found at an early date in the history of the Church ;[2] it was an association from which the episcopate found it most difficult to free itself. The idea of the bishop as primarily a judge and not a pastor survived the Reformation. It is surprising to find that most unprelatical of

[1] A Hamilton Thompson: *The English Clergy* (O.U.P., 1947), pp. 6–7.
[2] A law of Theodosius, passed in A.D. 412 (Cod. Theod. xvi. 2. 41), exempted all ministers of the Church from trial except in the ecclesiastical courts. Even earlier, the Emperor Constantine had recognised the right of bishops to hear civil cases in which Christians were concerned.

bishops, Hooper of Gloucester (*c.* 1500–1555), spending at times almost half of his days in hearing cases in his own court. When the churches of the Reformation rejected, as many of them did, the episcopal order, what they were repudiating was a sad travesty of the office as it had existed in the primitive and apostolic days of the Church.

In the Middle Ages, as at all other times, the real life of the Church depended more on the ordinary working parson of the village than on any other single factor. It is hard to determine what the average standard may have been. Chaucer's poor parson was probably to some extent an idealisation ; but the picture would have been unreal unless Chaucer could count on most of his readers recognising it as one with which they were already to some extent familiar in individuals whom they had known.

The first thing that strikes a student is the large numbers of the clergy in medieval as contrasted with modern times. In the absence of reliable statistics of population, an exact figure cannot be given ; but it seems probable that one person in every hundred in a country like England was in some sense a clerk, as having been admitted to at least one of the minor orders, and that about one in every hundred of the adult male population was a priest. Even today, there are hundreds of parishes in England with a population of under four hundred ; in earlier days, the number must have been much larger, and each of these cures was at least in theory supplied with the whole-time services of a man. The villager might sometimes resent the demands of the priest upon him for tithe and other dues,[1] and his descent upon

[1] According to M. R. C. Fowler, *Secular Aid for Excommunication* (*Trans. Royal Hist. Soc.*, Third Series VIII, 1914, pp. 113–17), about ten thousand writs of *Significavit* or *de excommunicato capiendo*, issued by the civil powers for the apprehension of excommunicated persons who were contumacious, have been preserved in England, dating from the reign of Henry III to that of George III. In the vast majority of cases where the offence is specified, it is non-payment of tithe. We may remember that Chaucer's poor parson

  " Ful looth were hym to cursen for his tithes,
  But rather wolde he yeven, out of doute,
  Unto his povre parisshens aboute
  Of his offryng and eek of his substaunce."

the house of mourning to claim his heriot from the possessions of the dead man.[1] He could not at any moment be unaware of the presence of the Church in the nearest neighbourhood to himself.

The Middle Ages were a great time of church-building. In many old parish churches, it is possible to trace the stages from the small dark Saxon structure up to the splendour of Early English and Decorated styles. But it was only by the gradual progress of centuries that Europe was covered with the parish churches that remain the noblest monument of the age of faith. For the most part, we are to think of small buildings, sometimes of impermanent materials, bitterly cold in winter, dark even in summer, with no seats except for the rich and well-to-do. Visitation records frequently give a picture of chancels in ruins and letting in the rain, because the rector (who might be a monastery, or the canons of a collegiate church) would not pay the cost of repairs ; of churches equipped only with ragged vestments and imperfect service books. There were few regular places for the training of the clergy ; many of them, doubtless, were almost illiterate, and able only to stumble through the half-unfamiliar words of the Mass.[2] And yet the service of the Church went forward. Every day, the bell would sound out over the village and the fields. Every Sunday at least (and foreigners were impressed by the willingness of the lay people in England to come even

[1] Dr. G. G. Coulton draws attention to the importance of this system, in *Life in the Middle Ages*, Vol. III (C.U.P., 1929), pp. 123–7, where actual texts are given. " On a peasant's death, the lord of the manor had frequently a claim on his best beast or other possession as *mortuary* or *heriot*. Side by side with this grew up a similar claim from the parish priest. It was presumed that the dead man must have failed to some extent in due payment of tithes during his life-time, and that a gift of his second-best possession to the Church would therefore be most salutary to his soul. This claim had admittedly no foundation in law, but was maintained already in 1305 as a custom which, being pious and reasonable, must therefore have the binding force of law."

[2] Describing the state of the clergy in Cornwall at the end of the Reformation, A. L. Rowse writes of the poor village parsons who "lived poorly beside the peasant, sharing his life and in death mingling their dust into his, leaving nothing by which we may remember them." *Tudor Cornwall* (London, 1941), p. 155.

to weekday services), the villager would find himself in Church, subject to the perennial reminder in the Mass of the mysteries of the faith. The words he could not understand ; something of the meaning of what was happening would leave its traces on levels of consciousness deeper than those of intellectual process.

Much controversy has raged over the question whether the medieval Church permitted or encouraged the reading of the Scriptures by ordinary people, and divergent views are held by the experts. To the ordinary man it did not matter either way. Being illiterate, he could not read, even if reading was permitted. His situation in relation to the Word of God was probably not very different from that ascribed by a high authority to his successors in a much later age : " To this day, so far as English-speaking Catholics are concerned, the Bible consists of a handful of fragments read out in Church, two psalms, a remembered phrase here and there in the liturgy, and a few dozen dogmatic texts."[1]

But this was not the whole range of his information. Increasingly, the histories of Scripture looked down at him from glorious stained glass windows, such as the great series in the church of Fairford in Gloucestershire. The walls of his church were adorned with frescoes, perhaps crude in workmanship and colouring, but for that reason all the more able to speak to him of eternal truth. And he was not altogether deprived of the ministry of preaching. It is probable that the local clergy rarely if ever preached ; they were at best ill qualified to do so. But from the Thirteenth Century and the rise of the Friars onwards, preaching became increasingly a normal part of the life of the medieval Church.[2] The whole aim of Francis, in his Christlike simplicity, had been to bring the Gospel to the poor and to bring back joy into the lives of the oppressed and joyless.

[1] Mgr. R. A. Knox, *On Englishing the Bible* (London, 1949), p. 48.
[2] The fullest studies of this subject in England are G. R. Owst, *Preaching in Medieval England* (Cambridge, 1926), and *Literature and Pulpit in Medieval England* (Cambridge, 1933).

" Francis was always clear in his declaration that it was
their vocation as a body to preach to all men, faithful and
heathen alike, both by the example of a life of service lived
among men, and by direct, formal, widespread evangelisation."[1] The preaching of the Dominicans was less
evangelical, more explicitly directed to the extirpation of
heresy and the establishment of the faith ; but it also helped
to bring the spoken word of the Gospel to those who had
long lacked it. It may be that the low-pitched roofs of
some later medieval Churches are to be accounted for
by the need to make a preacher audible, whereas at an
earlier date, when the purpose of the structure was more
exclusively liturgical, the tendency of the builder had been
to give added splendour to his building by making it as
lofty as the nature of his materials would stand.

Medieval man could not doubt for a moment that the
Church was about his path and about his bed. He might be
violent, lustful, unscrupulous. But when he sinned, unless
he was one of the rare sceptics, like the emperor Frederick II
(1194–1500), *stupor mundi*, he did not sin as those without
law ; he knew that a time would come when these things
must be reckoned with. If, improbably, he should wake
long before dawn from sleep in Elysium, he would hear the
bell of the monastery calling the monks to prayer, with its
reminder that every man lives under judgment, that in the
end all earthly gain must turn to loss, and that in truth a
man has no lasting possession other than his participation
in an eternal inheritance.

The medieval Church was the Christian society at perhaps
its highest point of integration and power. But to idealise
it is to distort history. The west was not the whole
Christian society ; and even within its own limits, it was
not successful in keeping all Christians within the unity of
a single family.

The west had never ceased to be aware of the existence

[1] Dom David Knowles, *op. cit.*, p. 120.

of the Church of the east. Even after the decisive separation had taken place in 1054,[1] the hope of union had perhaps never been finally given up. But few greater disasters have ever befallen the Christian society than the attempt made by the Crusaders, in the fourth Crusade, to restore the broken unity by the capture and sack of Byzantium. Just how it came about that a Crusade directed towards Palestine was turned aside to the destruction of the greatest Christian city in the world remains uncertain ; it seems clear that the heaviest part of the blame must be carried by the ingenious and commercially-minded Venetians. However that may be, on 9 April, 1204, Byzantium, so long at bay against Muslim enemies, was assaulted by Christian enemies ; on 12 April, it was captured. Even after its long agony, it was a city of splendour that nothing in the west could match. " You may well know that those who had never seen Constantinople before looked well on it ; for they could not imagine that there could be in all the world so mighty a city, when they saw those lofty walls and rich towers by which it was closely encircled all about, and those rich palaces and lofty churches, so many that a man could not believe them to be so many, if he had not seen them with his own eyes, and the length and the breadth of the city, that was the sovereign over all other cities of the world."[2] So wrote Villehardouin. The great city was spared no single horror of the brutality of war. Even Innocent III who on the whole approved the setting up of a Latin Empire in Byzantium wrote in stern condemnation : " These defenders of Christ, who ought to have turned their swords only against the infidels, have bathed in Christian blood.

[1] In that year, the emissaries of Pope Leo IX laid on the altar of Santa Sophia in Constantinople the Bull of Excommunication against the Patriarch Michael Cerularius. George Every, in *The Byzantine Patriarchate, 451-1204* (London, S.P.C.K. 1947) supports the view that "recent research has reduced the significance of both these crises, and prolonged the period of transition between unity and schism far on into the central period of the Middle Ages," (p. viii, and 153-203).

[2] Villehardouin : *History* §128, cited by Charles Diehl in *Histoire Générale*, Vol. IX (Paris, Presses Universitaires de France 1945), p. 130.

They have spared neither religion, age nor sex. They have committed before the open heaven adulteries, fornications and incests. . . . They have been seen to snatch from the altars ornaments of silver, to break them in pieces, and to fight over them, to violate the sanctuaries, to carry off sacred pictures, crosses and relics."[1]

The tragic episode of the Latin Empire in Byzantium was not of long duration. In the early morning of 25 July, 1261, the city was recaptured by the troops of Michael VIII Palaeologus, " exactly fifty-seven years, three months, and thirteen days after the Greeks had been driven out of it." But recovery was only partial. Byzantium had been driven by Christian hands a long way down the slope that led to the final disaster of 1453. The west was to pay in many strange ways for what may be judged by some to be the most conspicuous crime of recorded history. It is one of the wriest ironies of time that the presence of the Turks in Byzantium and their alliance with Francis I of France made possible the survival of Protestantism in Germany, at a time when it seemed certain that it would be destroyed by the power of the Emperor Charles V.

In western Europe, every individual, except for the tolerated and spasmodically persecuted Jews, and the decreasing Muslim remnants in Spain and elsewhere, was baptized and therefore a member of the holy, catholic, apostolic and Roman Church. But the Church has never at any time been successful in preventing rifts and tensions within its membership.

The definition of heresy is a difficult task. At times, heresy has involved such denial of essential doctrine as would, if successful, have made the Christian Church unrecognisable as the heir of its own past. Sometimes what was called heresy appears to have been no more than legitimate criticism of a Church that had lost its own first love. And heresy has existed in every possible combina-

[1] Letter 133, in Migne, P.L. 215, col. 712.

tion of these two tendencies, and at every point between these two opposing poles. The stricter the orthodoxy demanded from above and the more totalitarian the system of the Church, the more probable it is that every movement towards independence will be stifled and that every divergence from established ways will be stigmatised and persecuted as heretical. It is startling but not unnatural to find that, just at the moment when the Christian society in the west was reaching its most perfect and effective organisation under the one visible head, it was racked by such inner tensions as threatened, in some of its fairest and most prosperous regions, to subvert it altogether.

On the subject of the Albigenses, or the Cathari, as they are more correctly called, in southern and western Europe, the historian must express himself cautiously and must qualify all his statements. To Protestant hagiography the Albigenses have appeared as innocent victims of wicked authority and forerunners of the Protestant martyrs of the Reformation.[1] To their enemies, and most of our information about them, as about all heretics, is derived from the persecutors, they seemed to be monsters of iniquity, deserving of no consideration or pity. The evidence is so perplexed and contradictory that their history cannot yet be written with any certainty.[2]

Whenever the Church waxes high and prosperous, the memory of the evangelical principles of poverty and re-

[1] The English reader can most readily find this type of presentation in Foxe's *Book of Martyrs*.

[2] A great deal of light has recently been thrown on the origin of the Cathari and on their connections with eastern Manicheanism by two books that appeared almost simultaneously, Steven Runciman's *The Medieval Manichee* (C.U.P., 1947), and Dmitri Obolensky's *The Bogomils* (C.U.P., 1948). But on many matters these two books point out the need for further study. As Prince Obolensky puts it: "The problem of the influence of Bogomilism on the development of dualistic heresy in western Europe still awaits a definitive study. Western medievalists for the most part have not investigated the Slavonic Bogomil sources, while Slavonic historians have generally taken the filiation of the Cathars and Patarenes from the Bogomils for granted, but have not attempted a detailed study of Western dualism from the point of view of its connection with Bogomilism." *Op. cit.*, p. 286.

nunciation of the world calls out a puritan reaction. One such reaction was the early Franciscan movement; this the Church, though with some difficulty in adjustment, succeeded in retaining within itself. The movement of the Cathari may have started in just this way. A doctrine of purity, of renunciation and of asceticism was proclaimed. The existing Church was condemned as unfaithful to the Gospel which it professed to teach. As early as 1030, there was an organised community of Cathari in Monteforte.

The movement spread and gained adherents. At the beginning of the Thirteenth Century, the authorities of the Church were horrified to find whole areas honey-combed with heresy that persecutions and burnings had failed to suppress. Two features rendered the heresy particularly dangerous. Whatever its origin, it had before long incorporated dualistic elements, partly perhaps through memories of Manichean doctrine surviving even in the west, partly through the dualistic doctrines that came in from the Bogomil communities in Bosnia and other parts of the east ; and the prevalence of such doctrines tends always towards a policy of race suicide. In the second place, the movement secured the support of the lay lords of the south of France. It is not to be supposed that these laymen were in every case actuated by spiritual motives. They found in the opposition of the Cathari to the established Church something that was, on other grounds, highly con-venient to themselves. " It provided the Southern barons not only with an excuse to rob a Church of which they were desperately jealous, but also with a nationalist creed with which to oppose the Capetians, the Plantagenets and the internationally-minded prelates of Italy."[1]

The west was already familiar with the idea of a Crusade, and with the special privileges and indulgences granted to those who took up the Cross in defence of the Christian world. It was left to Innocent III to declare a Crusade

[1] Runciman, *op. cit.*, p. 147.

within the Christian world itself. All other measures having failed, in 1207 Innocent addressed himself to the chief nobles of the north of France, telling them that, as heretics had proved incorrigible by any spiritual methods, the secular arm must be called in to suppress them, and the miseries of war used to bring them back to the truth. The usual privileges accorded to Crusaders were to be granted to those taking up the Cross against the heretics.[1] The result was repeated devastations of the most fertile provinces of the South of France, with an interminable series of burnings of those identified as heretics. Even so, more than a century was to elapse before the final disappearance of the Cathari as an organised Church. New persecutions were needed between 1304 and 1312. It was not till 1330 that the authorities of the Church were able to rest in peace in the assurance that their work of purification had reached a satisfactory conclusion.

These events, and others like them from other epochs and countries, raise deep and anxious questions in the mind.

What is the nature of the unity of the Christian society ? Is it to be identified with precise acceptance of detailed formulae of doctrine ? If any departure from these formulae is at once regarded as heresy, to be extirpated if necessary by the most violent means, what possibility is there of theological progress in the understanding of the Gospel ? What possibility is there of reform from within the body, without the necessity, sooner or later, of revolution ? The medieval answer to all these questions was quite clear. Heresy was the worst of diseases, within the body politic as well as within the body of the Church. To expel it was the primary duty of the ecclesiastic. To aid him in this task was the responsibility of the civil ruler ; if he shewed himself lukewarm in carrying out this responsibility, he might be deposed from his rule, and dispossessed by other

[1] Epistle 229 in Migne P.L., 215, col. 1545.

more faithful servants of the Lord. This was the fate actually endured by Raymond of Toulouse.

The argument is logical and irrefutable, on its own premisses and within its own sphere. But if the conclusion of an argument is intolerable, it may be doubted whether the premisses are self-evidencing and certain. The Christian is called to judge of the nature of the Christian society from what he learns of Christ and His purpose in the Gospels. Confronted with the spectacle of the official head of the Christian society in the west deliberately giving up whole provinces to fire and slaughter, and proclaiming a crusade in which it was certain that thousands of victims would lose their lives, some of them at least not guilty of the gravest crimes against God and humanity, the question cannot but be raised whether that Christian society, for all the splendour of its achievement in many directions, had not in some way strayed at the central point from the allegiance of Christ, and become so unfaithful to His rule of gentleness and grace as to make inevitable sooner or later such a signal judgment of God upon man as was denounced by the prophets of old against unfaithful Israel.

CHAPTER VI

NATIONALISM AND REFORM

FROM at latest the Third Century, Christians have been accustomed to speak of the Church as the soul of the world, a phrase which occurs already in the Epistle to Diognetus. If the soul were, as the Greeks conceived it, a separable divine entity that has somehow become imprisoned in human flesh, it might go on its way, throughout the whole of a man's earthly pilgrimage, unaffected by any of the accidents that befall the muddy flesh. If the Church were a wholly divine entity, no doubt it too could have traversed the long course of the centuries, without having contracted any defilements or distortions from its contact with the ebb and flow of human vicissitude. In actual fact, the Church is both divine and human. It has always retained a mysterious link with its own past; it has always retained, though fitfully and imperfectly, fellowship with its divine Head. But in the outward expression of its life, it has always been influenced by the changing forms of society about it, on which it has never been able more than imperfectly to imprint the divine image of its own commission.

The end of the Middle Ages introduced a period of revolutionary change. As the old feudal order broke up, its place was taken by the age of nationalism. The *corpus Christianum* was not wholly dissolved, but its effective power to hold the Christian peoples of the west in some kind of unity was gravely weakened. The competing nations tended often to be more conscious of their own individual self-hood than of their responsibilities to a spiritual whole.

Nationalism is one of the strongest forces in the world.

133

It is impossible to define with any precision the meaning of the word *nation*. Switzerland defies all the usual categories of unity of race or language or religious confession, and yet has managed to retain for centuries, within the framework of a system of government that allows for considerable and continuous tensions, such a unity as makes it perhaps the best contemporary example of a civilised nation. It may almost be said that any group of human beings that decides, on the basis of some common and shared traditions or ideals, to be a nation can become one. And nations that have been submerged for centuries, stripped of every vestige of political independence, robbed of their language and of everything except this persistent national consciousness, can come to the surface again, and take up the thread and tradition of independent national life. The Republic of Ireland, artificial as it is in many ways, grows out of an age-long tradition long suppressed. Even more remarkably, the State of Israel has arisen as the creation of a faith that would not surrender to any circumstances of fate or discouragement.

National feeling was of slow growth in Europe. England, naturally, from its insular position, was one of the first countries to experience it. Not too much weight is to be placed on the famous phrase in Magna Carta *Ecclesia Anglicana sit libera*. The words *Ecclesia Anglicana* mean no more than that part of the one Church of the west which happened geographically to be situated in England. Yet the use of such words at all is significant. The development of national feeling, once started, was continuous, though far slower in Germany and Italy than in England or France or the Scandinavian countries.

It is possible that an explosion in the Church might have been avoided, if Rome had taken note of the prevailing tendency, and had gone some way to meet it by decentralisation of machinery and by some regard for the growing sentiment of the countries on the far side of the Alps. But the tendency in Rome was in precisely the contrary direction. The Hildebrandine policy demanded strong centralisation, as a means of securing efficiency and the establishment of that higher standard of administration and moral order without which the Hildebrandine reforms would have wholly failed to take effect. The policy of Gregory's successors increased rather than diminished the tendency. The claim of the Popes to be the lawgivers, and, in the last instance, the judges of all ecclesiastical causes in the western world was not seriously disputed in the Middle Ages. But there is a great difference between a court of first instance and a final court of appeal. The Roman Curia failed to make this distinction, and throughout the medieval period tended more and more to assume the position of a court of first instance, to which any Christians anywhere in the world might have recourse.[1] Whatever the theological concepts underlying this practice, it was one which was to say the least extremely inconvenient, and perplexing to canon lawyer and to layman alike. Not every case could be tried in Rome. Situations might come about, and actually did come about, in which, in a case in which a Metropolitan was involved, the Pope appointed one of the suffragans of the same Metropolitan as his deputy to try the case with full and final rights of decision. Ordinarily, appeal would lie from the court of the suffragan to that of the Metropolitan, with a further right of appeal to the Pope ; now the situation was reversed and the Metropolitan found himself pleading before his own suffragan, with no right of appeal beyond his decision.

This was typical of Roman procedure. The officials of the Roman curia, a vast army, which lived, and for the most part had to live, either from the profits of legal cases or from provision to benefices in lands which they would never see and in which they would never undertake the cure of souls,

---

[1] Innocent IV (1243–1254) had definitely laid it down that "the Pope was the ‘judex ordinarius’ of all and everyone. He could be appealed to without taking the somewhat troublesome and laborious course of obtaining judgment from an inferior court of appeal." W. Ullmann: *Medieval Papalism* (London, Methuen, 1949), p. 158.

had no knowledge or understanding of the resentments which they were creating. When the leaders of the German church and people presented their complaints to the Papacy, they took the form of the *Gravamina* of the German people against the courts of Rome.

Undoubtedly the Reformation sprang from many causes besides national discontent. The Renaissance had opened men's minds to new horizons. Knowledge of the Greek originals behind the Latin translations of Aristotle and his commentators, and of the New Testament itself in Greek, was spreading. Erasmus came to teach Greek in Car..bridge. The uprising of the new merchant class in Holland, in the Hansa towns, in London, was preparing for a rebellion against the tyranny of the old feudal and restrictive methods. The discovery of a new world was opening men's eyes to horizons beyond those of the simple three-storied universe of medieval thought. But not one of these causes, nor all these causes together, would have produced the Reformation or produced it in the form that it actually took, without a Martin Luther.

Recent historical studies have tended so to stress the economic causes and complications of the Reformation as to leave it doubtful whether there was any religious element in it at all. Such lines of interpretation can lead only to a series of intolerable and insoluble enigmas. Men did not give themselves up to be tortured and burned alive in order to transfer wealth from the dying feudal aristocracy into the hands of the rising commercial bourgeoisie. They faced martyrdom, because they believed that they had seen a new religious vision of incomparable significance, for the sake of which it was well worth a man's while to die. To do otherwise appeared in their eyes as the unpardonable sin of treachery against God. Their heirs do ill to question the rightness of their judgment, in the circumstances in which they were called to bear their witness.

Martin Luther was a religious genius of a stature such as appears only rarely in the centuries of Church history. But, for all his compelling spiritual power, the Reformation would hardly have been possible, but for the accident of the invention of the printing-press shortly before its outbreak. Until the end of the Fifteenth Century, books had been rare and generally the possession of a small and wealthy class. With the beginning of the Sixteenth, through the discovery of movable types and the production of small and handy editions, the ordinary man, if he could read at all, was introduced into the movement of world thought. Luther spoke not only to the handful of followers who could hear his lectures, but to the whole of Christendom. His books were produced in edition after edition, translated out of Latin and German into other tongues, and sold with astonishing rapidity in almost every country of Europe, not excluding Spain.[1]

This popularisation of books made possible the development within western Christendom of a new type of Christian worship. For centuries, the lay worshipper had been a spectator in the services of the Church, dimly following words in a language which he did not understand. The purpose of the reformers in all countries was to make the ordinary man again conscious of his priesthood by demanding of him responsible participation in every part of the Church's worship. We must not exaggerate the extent to which before the Reformation Christians had been, or had felt themselves to be, excluded. As every missionary knows, the ideal form of prayer for an illiterate congregation is the Litany, where the suffrages can be infinitely varied, but the congregation can quickly learn the unvarying response. Of such forms of worship, and of books in the vernaculars available to those who could pay for them, there was no

---

[1] This fact, which is of crucial importance for the understanding of Reformation history, is dealt with at some length, and with excellent illustrations, in R. H. Bainton's biography of Luther, *Here I Stand* (New York, 1950).

lack.   But the aim of the reformers was far other than this.
It was that the meanest man in the congregation should
understood the words he heard, should, if possible, have
in his hands Bible and prayer-book and hymn-book in his
own language, and should be restored to an active share in
the life and worship of the Church.   It may be said that,
almost without exception, unreformed churches have worship
in a language not understanded of the people, whereas
reformed Churches use the vernacular to which the congregation is most accustomed.[1]

The Reformation was, in the first place, a recall of the
Church to biblical orthodoxy.   The Bible was far from
being unknown to the Christian of the Middle Ages ; but
the exegesis of it had been submerged under mystical,
allegorical and analogical forms that had tended to obscure
its plain and simple sense.   Luther, one of the greatest
of biblical expositors, cut through the whole of these accretions, and taught men to read the Gospels again as they
were written, as the living word of God to men, the living
centre of which is Christ Himself.

Secondly, the reformers called all men to repentance and
to the actual achievement of godliness.   Even in the dreary
Fifteenth Century, when the Church had striven so hard and
with so little success to reform itself, there had never been
a lack of saints, such as the author of *The Imitation of
Christ*, and the Lady Margaret, the mother of Henry VII of
England.   But for the most part men had left sanctity to
the monk, who might or might not achieve it, and had
supposed that for the ordinary man the Christian standard
of morality was an ideal, the attempt to attain to which he
need not take too seriously.   The Reformers took it for

---

[1] The statement cannot be categorical, since the Old Catholics have now
in every country adopted the local vernacular, and the Malankara (Monophysite) Church of Travancore has taken to Malayalam, interspersed with
some Syriac, as the language of its services.   This Church would not claim
to be in any sense a reformed Church.   It is worth noting that the Book of
Common Prayer of the Church of England or parts of it have been translated into more than 200 languages.

granted that what the New Testament said it said to all ; there was no longer to be a distinction between two standards, one for the seeker after perfection in the monastery, the other for the man of the world. All alike were equally to be called to aim at the highest. It may readily be confessed that the Reformers failed in their high enterprise. The Sixteenth Century was paying for the sins of the most degenerate period of the Middle Age and of the Renaissance. It was a neurotic and hysterical time, so deeply corrupted that Bishop .Creighton once expressed a doubt whether anyone ought to read its history.[1] When Calvin attempted to set up the earthly Zion in Geneva, he found himself unexpectedly frustrated by the inveterate sinfulness and wilfulness of men, who did not want to be good, or to be made to be good. Even in Wittenberg, Luther found the devil actively at work.

From the lamentations of the Reformers, some have concluded that the Reformation actually produced a decline in the level of European morals. It is difficult to judge one age against another. Severe condemnation of sin may be due as much to a more deeply sensitive conscience as to the immediate presence of sin in an inordinate degree. The best evidence for the success of the demand of the Reformation for sanctity is the moral reform achieved within the Roman Church itself. The Councils of the Fifteenth Century, the Renaissance, the teachings of Erasmus and the humanists, had left the Roman Curia unrepentant and a scandal to the whole of Christendom. The morals of Albert of Mainz, the Archbishop with whom Luther had most to do, and to whom he wrote in terms such as one might expect to be used by an angry schoolmaster to a defaulting schoolboy,[2] would have disgraced a feudal nobleman in the worst days of the Dark Ages. But once the

[1] *Life* by his Wife, Vol. I (London, 1904), p. 288.
[2] See his letter of 31 October, 1517, printed in B. J. Kidd's *Documents of the Continental Reformation* (Oxford, 1911), pp. 27-8, and Albert's answer thereto.

Reformation was well and truly launched, serious spirits in the Roman Church realised that, unless an immediate inner reformation were carried through, there was no bulwark that could be raised against the progress of the Protestant rebellion. Since the middle of the Sixteenth Century, there has been no successor on the Papal throne to the vices of Alexander VI.[1] Perhaps the Roman Cardinals have not all been saints. Never again have their vices been a public scandal to the world at large.

In the third place, the Reformation was a serious attempt to claim the whole of life for Christ and the Gospel. The use of the term " religion " to denote the clerical and monastic life invariably involved the connotation that other forms of life were irreligious and secular. The reformation idea of vocation, of that occupation in which a man was engaged, whether secular or clerical, as the sphere in which he was called to glorify God, and in which witness was to be borne to his responsibility as a member of the Christian society, may have been grievously abused. Success in secular life, and particularly in commercial ventures, may have been too closely identified with the favour and blessing of God. Yet the ideal is one without which the Christian society can never reach its perfection. It is still too much the case that the vocation of the missionary or the priest is regarded as being in some sense more religious than that of the layman, a false estimate against which the Protestant doctrine of the priesthood of all believers is a permanent and necessary protest.[2]

It is one of the most melancholy facts of human history that in no country in the world was either the Reformation

---

[1] Alexander VI (Rodrigo Borgia), Pope from 1492 to 1503. Recent attempts to whitewash him have not availed to clear the character of one of the most disreputable villains ever to disgrace an episcopal throne.

[2] Serious theological objection may be taken to the phrase. To be correct, we should speak of the priesthood of the whole Church, derived from the heavenly high priesthood of Christ, in which every believer participates, but in which there is a necessary distinction of function between the layman and the ordained minister.

or the Counter-reformation permanently successful except through the support of the civil power. In each, great spiritual powers were developed, yet nowhere did victory or defeat depend solely on the spiritual factor. Where, as in Italy and Spain, the Inquisition could act unchecked, Protestantism was exterminated in a long and melancholy series of *autos-da-fe*. In the Scandinavian countries, Roman Catholicism banned by the rulers vanished, and remained unrepresented for centuries even by a minority of the population. The stolid and obstinate resistance of the Dutch Protestants eventually secured both political and spiritual independence for their country, but only as a result of fortunate and unpredictable success in war. The forces of the Counter-reformation spread through the Duchy of Austria, and won it back to the Catholic cause, but not through the unaided weapons of persuasion and spiritual zeal. At no time in human history have the intrusion of the world into the affairs of the Church, and the implication of the Church in the affairs of the world, been more lamentably demonstrated.

The political aspect of reformation was clearly discernible first in England. Henry VIII desired a declaration of the nullity of his marriage to the widow of his brother Arthur.[1] As delay followed delay, and it appeared that the Pope was more influenced by political considerations than by a pure regard for justice, men began to ask whether Henry was under any obligation at all to submit his case to the Pope. This raised the whole question of the source and fount of Canon Law. Who had the right to declare law for the Church ? The medieval answer gave

[1] The habit of referring to Henry's *divorce* has become so firmly established that it is perhaps too late to hope that it be given up. What Henry wanted, of course, was not the dissolution of an existing marriage, but a declaration that no marriage had ever taken place. Henry VIII was an unpleasant character, and the natural prejudice against him has tended to obscure the fact that, in Canon Law, he had a strong case ; just as his fantastic series of matrimonial misadventures has obscured the fact that his personal life was much less disreputable than that of Philip II of Spain or Francis I or Henry IV of France.

this right unhesitatingly to the Bishop of Rome. But his claim was based largely on the False Decretals, introduced into England, as it appears, by Lanfranc, but previously unknown. In the meantime, Renaissance scholars had proved the Decretals to be a late forgery; the basis of the Papal claim was shown to be questionable; but the claims were still made in their full rigour. But, also in the meantime, the Fifteenth Century scholars had rediscovered Justinian. The first discovery of the ancient code of laws in the Eleventh Century had set the intellect of Europe in a ferment, and had led to the development of the great law schools of Bologna and Pisa. Commentator followed commentator, and by degrees the original lineaments of the great codes were lost under the weight of glosses and interpretation. Valla and the humanists put on one side all these medieval accretions, and went back to the original texts; and there they discovered, as the fount of all law, both for the state and for the Church, not a bishop but an emperor.[1]

To Henry, then, anxious to get his business quickly dispatched, the question seems to have presented itself more or less in the following terms: If he had a case in the civil courts, no appeal lay beyond his dominions to the Holy Roman Emperor or to any other outside potentate. If he had a case in the ecclesiastical courts, on what ground was it held that an appeal lay outside his dominions to the court of a foreign bishop? His advisers informed him that England had been from ancient times recognised as an empire. An emperor is commanded and empowered by God to declare and maintain the law, both civil and ecclesiastical, for his subjects. He is the final source of law. His judges have the final word in all causes, whether civil or spiritual.

---

[1] "Justinian declared that his codification was to be the sole statement of the law; nothing outside it was to be regarded. In case of need, resort could be had only to the Emperor himself, inasmuch as he was the sole source of the law." Hazeltine, in *Camb. Med. Hist.*, (C.U.P) Vol. V ,p. 717.

The claim of the Bishop of Rome, therefore, to declare the canon law for England and to hear causes under it is a usurped claim, and a diminution of the majesty of the emperor of the farthest west. This supreme jurisdiction of the kings of England had indeed been obscured in the centuries of ignorance ; but, if Henry were to restore it, he would not be guilty of innovation, but only of recovering the true and God-given status of the Christian emperor, as it had existed in the days of Justinian.[1]

Henry's attempt to appear before the world as the new Justinian was an anachronism. But it was a move that had much to commend it to the spirit of the age. After the intolerable disturbances of the Fifteenth Century, in which almost the whole of the old English aristocracy had been blotted out in the senseless carnage of the wars of the Roses, the common people welcomed with relief the strong central-ised government of the Tudors, and were willing to grant almost anything asked of them by the king. The clergy, wearied by the long tale of Roman exactions, opposed little resistance to the new order of things. Henry VIII, savage and unprincipled as he shewed himself, succeeded to the end of his days in keeping the loyalty and affection of the majority of his subjects ; when he died, the virtuous Cranmer allowed his beard to grow in sign of perpetual mourning for

---

[1] In most discussions of the issue, less than due weight seems to have been given to the use of the word *empire* in the Act for Restraint of Appeals of 1534: " In divers old authentic histories and chronicles it is manifestly declared and expressed, that this realm of England is an empire, and so hath been accepted in the world, governed by one supreme head and king, having the dignity and royal estate of the imperial crown of the same: unto whom a body politic, composed of all sorts and degrees of people, divided in terms and by names of spirituality and temporalty, been bounden and owen to bear, next to God, a natural and humble obedience . . . without restraint or provocation to any foreign princes or potentates of the world." Henry was prepared to admit a primacy of the bishop of Rome, and therefore claimed that he was not making any division in the one body of the catholic Church, but he refused to the Pope all jurisdiction, that is the right to declare and administer canon law within the realm of England. Refusal to admit Henry's claim to be *fons utriusque juris* was treated as high treason; for this refusal, men like More and Fisher, who maintained against Henry the medieval tradition, suffered death. One of the main points of con-troversy between Cranmer and Cardinal Pole was just the question whether the Pope could rightly be called a foreign bishop.

his master.[1] At the start, it is probable that Henry lighted on the imperial view of his office as an opportunist solution for the otherwise insoluble problem presented by his own affairs. Once grasped, the concept was firmly and logically held. The evidence for this is the advice repeatedly given by Henry to the German princes that each in his own dominions should grasp the nettle, as he himself had done, and carry through his own reformation, according to his own ideas and on the basis of the authority given him by God.

The one man who did carry out Henry's ideas, even more logically and thoroughly than their originator, was Christian III of Denmark. Christian was a far better man than Henry, and, though less of a theologian, a far more devout and godly Christian. As a lad of eighteen he had been present at the Diet of Worms, and had yielded to the personal magnetism of Luther and to the power of his evangelical witness. He had married a Protestant wife, and, even before acceding to the throne, had been active in propagating Lutheranism in his own duchies of Schleswig and Holstein. After the death of Frederick I in 1533, there was an interregnum of three years. When Christian entered Denmark by force of arms and made himself master of the capital on 29 July, 1536, the doom of the old order was sealed.

From the start, Christian made it clear that he intended to be master in his own country, and that in his view his responsibility as king included the duty to decide what form of the Christian religion his subjects should profess, and what alone they might legitimately be taught. At the first meeting of the Rigsdag after his accession, the king announced through his representative that he proposed to bestow on the country a new civil and ecclesiastical consti-

[1] The epithet has been chosen with care. Even Cranmer's sharpest critics do not, if they have read his writings, fail to recognise the integrity and uprightness of his personal character. And those who accuse him of timidity conveniently forget that, when Thomas Cromwell lay under sentence of death, Cranmer alone ventured to approach the king with an appeal for mercy for the man whose greatest crime was that he had been too faithful in carrying out the commands of his royal master.

tution. This ecclesiastical order, a lengthy document in the form of a Church Ordinance, was drawn up by a number of Lutheran divines, submitted to Luther for his approval, and finally signed by the king on 2 September, 1537. On the same day, on the authority of the king, seven Danish divines were set apart by the laying on of hands for the new office of superintendent. But no attempt was made to preserve the ancient episcopal succession ; in fact this was deliberately avoided. It was to be made clear that the new " bishops " derived their authority from the king as head of the Church, and that they were appointed not to administer the ancient ecclesiastical order but to develop the Church of Denmark from a new beginning. Appropriately the laying on of hands was performed by the German Lutheran reformer Johannes Bugenhagen.[1]

The Reformation in Denmark was in some respects conservative. But it is a remarkably clear example of the identification, in the minds of Sixteenth Century rulers and their subjects, of the civil and ecclesiastical functions of the Christian prince. "The State" as an abstract idea, had not yet clearly appeared ; the state was the prince, a man chosen and appointed by God, solemnly anointed and crowned, and responsible to God for all his acts, and for the temporal and eternal welfare of his subjects.[2]

[1] Appropriately, since it appears that Bugenhagen (1485–1558), a close friend and colleague of Luther from 1521 onwards, was the first to conclude, from his study of the Greek New Testament, that there is no distinction between the office of bishop and that of presbyter, and that everything which is done by a bishop can equally well be done by a presbyter. Having persuaded himself, he then persuaded Luther, who also on occasion performed episcopal consecrations. There was no question of bishops in the historic succession being unavailable ; they were deliberately rejected. By contrast, in Sweden, where Gustavus Vasa thought that the people would be more ready to accept him, if he were crowned by anointed bishops, the historic link with the past was maintained through an unbroken episcopal succession.

[2] Fortunately for English readers the main facts about the Danish Reformation are now accessible in an accurate and reliable book, *The Reformation in Denmark* (London, 1948), by E. H. Dunkley. The following note on the Norwegian Church in the *World Christian Handbook* (London, 1949), p. 17, would be in all essentials true of the Scandinavian Churches today: "The King 'ordains all official divine service' (i.e. liturgical legis-

When the strife between Roman Catholics and Protestants
had worn itself to a standstill, and it was clear that neither
party would be able to destroy the other, the contestants
in sheer weariness fell back on the compromise *cuius regio
eius religio.*[1] This is the *reductio ad absurdum* of the idea
of the Christian prince. If it did at least guarantee to a
number of people the right to worship according to their
consciences, it recognised also the right of the prince to
oppress and persecute those who did not happen to agree
with him. It meant suffering and hardship, and the dis-
placement of innocent people whose only offence was
religious dissent. But if one Christian prince of a small
territory can lay down as the norm for his subjects one
particular variety of Christian faith, and another a dozen
miles away can lay down another, the inviolable sanctity of truth is lost under the perplexities of political
expediency and the very idea of the one Christian society is
dissolved.

No one had found a solution to the old problem of what
is to happen if the Christian prince himself should fall
into heresy. This was the agony of the closing years of
Cranmer. For twenty years, he had been the protagonist in
England of the idea of the supremacy of the prince as the
anointed of God. But when Mary, loyally accepted as the
legitimate successor of her brother, bade Cranmer burn all
that he had adored and adore all that he had burned, he
was placed in a dilemma from which death was the most
comfortable escape. His religio-political philosophy drove
him in the direction of compliance ; his profound and

lation is in his hands), and appoints bishops and ministers. The Church
is administered by a State Department of Church and Education. The
parliament (Stortinget) is the legislative authority and the High Court of
justice is the supreme court in ecclesiastical matters."
    [1] This conclusion was reached at the Peace of Augsburg in 1555. But
the final settlement of the question, and of the frontiers of Roman Catholicism and Protestantism, was to wait for nearly a century, when, after the
frightful devastation of the Thirty Years War, the Peace of Westphalia
(1648) ended the period of religious wars. See C. V. Wedgwood, *The
Thirty Years War* (London, Cape, ed. of, 1947), pp. 381-6 and pp. 525-6.

personal adherence to the reformed doctrines made compliance impossible. In the end, religious conviction triumphed over ecclesiastical theory, and Cranmer's heroic death made its own strong contribution to the final victory of his convictions in the English Church: But if men can be driven by their theories to such intolerable moral entanglements, it is clear that there must be something wrong with the theory.

Most men would hold today that the doctrine *cuius regio eius religio* is flagitious through and through. But it is surprising how strongly and stubbornly it has maintained itself in history. That all the subjects of one ruler should worship according to one pattern—the pattern selected by their prince, is undoubtedly most convenient from the point of view of the ruler. It is a doctrine that the states of the world have found it very hard to abandon. In Sweden, for example, the Roman Catholic religion was prohibited for more than three centuries, not only in the sense that no public preaching or teaching of it was allowed, but to the extent that any Swedish subject converted to the Roman Catholic faith was compelled to leave the country. Many restrictions on religious liberty were withdrawn only in 1873. And even to this day, no one who is not a member of the national Lutheran Church of Sweden can be a member of the government.[1] The Roman Catholic Church, no less logical than the Lutheran, and sometimes even more ruthless, naturally holds that a Church which is in possession of the whole truth of God must use every effort, including, where it can, the coercive power of the state, to prevent the teaching and the spread of heresy. The Waldensian Church, the historic Protestant Church of Italy, received the minimum recognition of the civil rights of its members as recently as 1848. The Roman Church, so zealous a champion of religious liberty in Finland, does not

---

[1] A new law for the removal of religious inequality in Sweden was promulgated on 16 May, 1951.

show itself so zealous a defender of the rights of the small Protestant churches in Spain.

In England various parties contended for religious supremacy. Their convictions differed, but in essence their principles were the same. Each believed that there should be only one Church in the country, and that that Church should be organised on those principles which it accepted as valid and biblical. So in succession, Romans, Elizabethan and Laudian Anglicans, Presbyterians and Independents, strove for the mastery, and, perhaps providentially, none prevailed. Toleration was a virtue, if indeed it is a virtue and not merely another name for religious indifference, which developed slowly, not so much from inner principle, as from the necessity of finding a *modus vivendi* in a country where the different parties had proved too tenacious either to be won over by argument or to be obliterated by force. After Laudians had persecuted dissenters, and dissenters had expelled the Anglican clergy and forbidden the use of the Prayer Book in the parish churches, and James II had engaged on the forlorn hope of trying to restore Roman Catholicism as the religion of the state, in 1689 all parties agreed, albeit unwillingly, in recognising that it was possible for more forms of the Christian faith than one to co-exist permanently and to receive some measure of legal recognition in the same country.

But toleration is very different from full religious and civil equality. It was only by slow degrees that in England all Christians, and even those who were not Christians, obtained the full rights of citizenship. The Roman Catholics had to wait till 1829 for their emancipation. Not till the second half of the Nineteenth Century were non-Anglicans admitted to membership of the ancient universities. To this day, no one professing the Roman Catholic faith can be Lord Chancellor of England.

If the problem of Church and state were susceptible of any simple solution, it would have been solved long ago. The

break up of western Christendom after the Reformation has
resulted in a large number of experiments being tried. There
are states in which one form of Christianity is so strongly
established that other forms exist only as minorities on
sufferance. In some countries, such as England, one Church
is established, but there is almost complete equality for all.
There are secular states in which no preference is accorded
to one religion over another, others in which one Church by
the predominance of numbers does secure a practical
ascendancy. The United States of America is trying the
unique experiment of a state which, though mainly Christian
in conviction, has carried the separation of Church and state
almost to the point of obsession. And recent events in
some formerly Christian countries have brought the Church
back to the not unhealthy position of a persecuted minority.

For centuries the Constantinian conception of a close
connection between Church and state had prevailed, and
was little affected by the main currents of either Reformation or Counter-reformation. But a new or long forgotten
possibility came to life within the Christian society with the
emergence of those who, long persecuted under one name
or another,[1] became known in England as the Independents. These sects, the ancestors of those who now call
themselves Free Churchmen, believed that there should be
no connection between Church and state at all, no dominance
of Church over state, or of state over Church ; they believed
in the " gathered Church," the company of believers brought
together by nothing but their common faith in Christ, and
dependent on no allegiance but their direct allegiance to
Him.

In these small gatherings of believers, something was

[1] The extremer reformers in Germany, the " Enthusiasts," whom Luther
so much disliked, and the Anabaptists, were the forerunners of the
Brownists and other dissentients in England, who took up a position
considerably to the left of that of the orthodox Puritans. But, whereas
the Socinians on the continent were unorthodox, most of the independent
groups in England were strictly orthodox in doctrine, though by the then
prevailing standard highly erratic in Church order and practice.

recovered which had almost disappeared from Christendom, and without which the Christian society can never attain to the fulness of its being. The ordinary layman who believed in Jesus found himself accepted into a real community of the saints. Even though he might be an ignorant and unlearned man, it was taken for granted by all that at any moment he might be that one instrument through whom the Holy Spirit was pleased to speak a word to the whole assembly. So there came into being a genuine Christian equality, such as had perhaps scarcely been seen since the early days of the simplicity of the people of Christ. Students of political science have attributed to these assemblies of the saints immense importance, as rebels against the hierarchial ordering of society based on privilege, and as pioneers of that sense of political equality, which is one of the main roots of modern democracy. Students of Church history may see here a recovery of the vocation of the layman to be a sharer in both the kingship and the priesthood of Christ, which is certainly implicit in any sound doctrine of Holy Baptism, but has tended through many centuries to be obscured through confusion of differentiation of function within the Church with inequality of status.[1]

By 1541, with the failure of the Colloquy of Ratisbon, the hope of doctrinal reconciliation between Protestants and adherents of the old religion had disappeared. By 1555, the main lines of political division were already fixed. Four centuries have not availed either to bring about a reconciliation, or markedly to alter the boundaries then laid down between the Protestant and Roman Catholic worlds. The Roman Catholic Church has carried on able and energetic propaganda in all Protestant lands, but with only limited success. Nowhere has a decisive change in the

---

[1] See an excellent discussion of this point in A. D. Lindsay's *The Modern Democratic State* (London, 1943), Vol. I, pp. 64–7. The remarkable burgeoning of these ideas in America is the principal theme of the first volume of Anton Phelps Stokes' immense study, *Church and State in the United States* (New York, 1950).

balance of religious adherence been brought about.[1]

The unity of western Christendom, never complete or perfect, had been finally shattered ; the broken fragments have continued to live in separation, to the grave detriment of all.

It is important not to exaggerate the extent and depth of the division. Both Reformation and Counter-reformation took place within the western tradition. Luther and Calvin no less than Loyola and Bellarmine were heirs of the medieval tradition, and in particular of that form of Christian thinking which the whole western Church had inherited from St. Augustine. Men were divided by sharp and bitter theological controversy on particular points; but more than they knew they were united by drawing on the same great heritage of Christian thought and living. The differences between Roman Catholic and Protestant remain. Four centuries of division have made them even more intractable than they were. Yet, if western Christendom today is compared with any part of the non-Christian world, the still unbroken unity becomes at once more obvious than the deep and tragic divisions within the profession of a common Christian faith.[2]

It has been acutely pointed out[3] that the word Reformation ought strictly to be used only of that which took place in the Roman Catholic Church in the Sixteenth Century,

---

[1] It is difficult to secure fully reliable figures for any country. Statistics for Germany before the war suggest that the losses of the Roman Church were slightly larger than the gains. The percentage of Roman Catholics in England today is certainly far higher than at the time of Roman Catholic Emancipation in 1829 ; but most of the increase seems to be due rather to immigration from central Europe and Ireland than to changes of allegiance by individuals, though these too have been on a not inconsiderable scale. In Switzerland, the proportions have remained almost unchanged for four centuries. The country in which the advance of Roman Catholicism has been most marked is Holland, but there the progress seems to be almost wholly due to a higher birth-rate among Roman Catholics and not to the success of religious propaganda.

[2] "How enormously more important than the things which divide them is the outstanding belief in which, as against everything outside Christianity, they are one." Edwyn Bevan, *Christianity* (London, Thornton Butterworth 1932), p. 202.

[3] By Lord Eustace Percy in his book, *John Knox* (London, 1937), pp. 105–6.

the movement inaugurated by Luther being more correctly designated as revolution. The Roman Church did in fact undergo as complete a reformation as could be achieved without breaking up the structure of thought and organisation that had developed in the medieval period.

The task of the Council of Trent (1545–1563) was to make precise and to define. This it did, with splendid success, within the limits laid down at its early sessions. In the conflicts launched by the Reformation, the Roman Church was henceforth to be armed with a majestic and ordered system of doctrine, in which many points previously left open for the discussion of theologians were now to be permanently determined. Many others, besides Baron Friedrich von Hügel, who was to the end of his days a loyal Roman Catholic, have regretted this process of codification, and have found themselves much more at home in the freer atmosphere of the Church of the Thirteenth Century. But it may be doubted whether the Roman Church in its present form could have survived without just such a rigid front as was provided by the decrees and canons of the Council of Trent.

The Bishop of Rome claimed as before to be the supreme head and father of all Christians in the world, the universal pastor of every Christian soul, the supreme judge in every Christian cause. He still claimed the right to release Christian subjects from their allegiance to heretical sovereigns. After so many millions of Christians had withdrawn themselves from the Roman allegiance, this claim had less meaning than in earlier days, and could less effectively be brought into play. Yet there was not, and never has been, any mitigation of the claim. And with the consciousness of new enemies and new perils, there has been a steady tendency towards centralisation in Rome, and towards an assertion of the direct control of the Curia over every part of the life of the Church. In theory, a bishop in the Roman Church is still elected by the chapter of his diocese. But, since it is recognised that the Pope has the right to pass over all the persons named by the chapter, and to appoint at his discretion some entirely different person, the liberty of canonical election means little more in the Church of Rome than in the Church of England, where members of a cathedral chapter which refused to accept the king's nominee would be subject to the grave penalties of the Statute of Praemunire. And, if the Pope is in person the universal pastor of all Christians, what is the position of the bishop ? Does he hold his office directly from Christ as the head of the Church, or is he merely the deputy and representative of the Pope ? On this question many of the bishops at the Vatican Council in 1870 pressed for a clear answer. No clear answer was given, though, until it is given, much doubt must exist as to the structure of the Christian society as understood within the Roman world.[1]

One of the first great successes of the Roman reform was the appearance of the post-Tridentine bishop. As we have seen, the pre-Reformation bishop had been a great landed magnate and an ecclesiastical judge. As a result of the work of the Council of Trent, the bishop recovered his function as a pastor.

The most conspicuous example of the new type in the Sixteenth Century was St. Charles Borromeo, Archbishop of Milan (1538–84). This remarkable man, when scarcely out of his teens, had been secretary to his uncle, Pope Pius IV, and had played an outstanding part in the concluding sessions of the Council of Trent. At the age of twenty-eight, he withdrew from high politics, and for the next sixteen years gave himself with outstanding devotion to the work of his archdiocese. When Luther took in hand his Saxon Visitations, he found that there had been no episcopal visitation of that part of Germany within the memory of the oldest living inhabitants. St. Charles set himself to visit in person the eight hundred parishes of his

[1] See Cuthbert Butler's *The Vatican Council* (London, 1930), pp. 71–89.

diocese, preaching in every place, expounding to the people
in simple language their Christian duties, using every means
to bring the clergy to higher standards of devotion and
discipline, himself setting the example by a life of prayer
that, in addition to all his other labours, wore him out and
helped to bring about his early death. When the plague
visited Milan, he went everywhere in the city at the risk
of his own life, caring for the sick and restoring confidence,
until the danger was past. Such a bishop was a portent
in the Sixteenth Century. But Charles was only the
forerunner of an innumerable line of holy and devoted
bishops.

The second triumph of Trent was in the education of the
clergy. It was laid down that there must be diocesan
seminaries for the training of the priesthood.[1] Systematic
training in the Middle Ages had been almost confined to
monks; the ordinary village clergy were left with the bare
minimum of knowledge necessary for the performance of
their tasks. There is little in common between the old
"mumpsimus-priest" of legend and the modern Roman
Catholic priest, with his three years of philosophy and four
years of theology, equipped for controversy as well as for
pastoral duty among the faithful. Yet this reform, admirable and necessary as it was, had its drawbacks. Seminary
training draws men away at a very early age from the normal
pursuits of men and from ordinary contacts with the world.
It has marked a further step in the clericalisation of the
Church, and has made more difficult the realisation in practice
of that common priesthood and common kingship which are

[1] The better training of the clergy was one of the reforms that was almost
forced on the Roman Church by the success of the Reformers. Luther's
greatest work was the training of preachers at Wittenberg. Geneva under
Calvin became a great centre of theological education. In many of the
Swiss cities, the victory of the new movement was brought about by the
complete failure of the Roman Catholic controversialists to meet the reforming preachers in argument. The Church of England alone lagged far behind
in this matter. On the whole the Puritans in the reign of Elizabeth were
better equipped theologically than their opponents. It was only in the
Seventeenth Century that the Church of England developed a preaching
ministry on a large scale.

set forth in the New Testament as characteristics of the
Church as the body of the Risen Christ.

The Roman reformation was accompanied by a great outburst of devotional and mystical fervour. In Spain, St.
John of the Cross (1542–1591), St. Ignatius Loyola (1491–
1556), and St. Teresa (1515–1582) in different ways brought
into the service of the Church that peculiar passion of the
Iberian races, which at its worst turns into narrow fanaticism,
at its best results in an uncalculating and uncompromising
devotion to a spiritual ideal. In France, the Latin genius
in another form found its expression in the *Introduction to
the Devout Life* of St. Francis de Sales (1567–1622), a book
beloved as much by Protestants as by Roman Catholics,
and in the splendid pulpit eloquence of Bossuet (1627–1704)
and his successors.

The post-Tridentine Church has been able, more fully than
any other Christian body, to call out in generation after
generation the passionate devotion of men and women, and
to produce the most varied types of heroic and joyful
sanctity. Its versatility is seen in the continued emergence
of new orders, devoted to the service of the Church for
special needs. The weakness of that Church is that it has
never transcended the traditional distinction between the
two standards of life, and the belief that a higher level of
perfection can be attained in the "religious" life than is
possible in the service of Christ in the world. It is true
that some of the saints, like that Mme. Acarie, of whom P.
Bremond has written so movingly,[1] attained to sanctity
while living in the world and fulfilling the duties of the
home and of society. But for the most part what has been
demanded of the ordinary members of the Church has been
conformity and obedience rather than individual decision
and a high level of sanctity in personal life. The division
between *ecclesia discens* and *ecclesia docens* has always been

[1] *Histoire Littéraire du sentiment religieux en France* (Paris, 1916), Vol. II,
pp. 193–262.

sharply marked. Itself hierarchically organised, the Roman Church has generally found itself more happily at home in countries where traditional forms of government have been maintained than in fully democratic societies. Only in recent times has it developed a social consciousness, and a new apostolate among those oppressed and disinherited by the crises of modern industrial society in the west.[1]

When we turn to the non-Roman world, the first and lasting impression is of the divisiveness and fissiparous nature of Protestantism. This goes so far back in the history of the movement as to seem inseparable from it. When Luther met with representatives of the Swiss Reformation at Marburg in 1529, his mournful conclusion was that "ye are of a different spirit from us." Lutheran and Reformed agreed to go on their separate ways, and by so doing gave the Counter-reformation its opportunity to recover for the old faith great parts of western Europe. There are differences of doctrine and of emphasis between the Lutheran and the Calvinistic traditions. To those who stand outside these traditions, the similarities appear much greater than the differences. Lutheran piety has a more emotional quality, Calvinism is in most of its forms more rigidly intellectual. It would seem that often the barriers to understanding are psychological and emotional rather than theological. Yet even in the Twentieth Century they continue to form a barrier to united action, at a time when the unity of the Christian forces in Europe might be judged essential to the survival of the Christian faith.

The Reformers did not quickly abandon the hope of a united front. Cranmer himself kept constantly in mind the idea of a common Christian council and of some league of Protestant Churches. The persecuted Protestants of the continent looked to England as their natural helper

---

[1] The great series of Papal Encyclicals, beginning with the *Rerum Novarum* of Leo XIII (1891), are justly famous. Such working-class movements as the *Jeunesse Ouvrière Chrétienne* seem to have attained a greater success than any parallel movements of the Protestant Churches.

and protector. Throughout the Seventeenth Century, there was much coming and going. It was not an accident that the English delegates were the first to append their signatures to the decisions of the Synod of Dort in 1618. But the forces of division were stronger than those making for unity. For the most part, the Protestant churches accepted the principle of national division, and sank down into a tame acceptance of separation. The distinction between the visible and the invisible Church made possible a sincere profession of faith in the Holy Catholic Church, without any sense that its visible unity on earth was either important or a necessary part of the fulfilment of the divine purpose on earth.

From the Roman Catholic point of view, the divisions of the Protestants are a perpetual and effective weapon of attack. The majestic unity of the Church of Rome and its rapidity and decisiveness of action are in marked contrast to the divided councils and the ineffective witness of the Protestant bodies. The perpetual proliferation of new sects, until the United States of America counts nearly 250, and the native Churches of South Africa are reckoned at more than 800, cannot but appear ridiculous to one brought up to believe that the Church of Christ must be one body as well as one spirit. From time to time, an earnest group of believers sets out to create a new fellowship in which denominationalism shall be transcended. Such was the purpose of the men who founded the body now commonly known as the Disciples of Christ.[1] The result, as might have been foreseen, was only the addition of one new denomination to the already existing groups.

The Protestant might be inclined to answer that all this, though true, is not the whole truth. The development of

[1] This body, the expressed purpose of which is to overcome denominationalism and to work tirelessly for the union of Christ's Church, was brought into existence by the labours of Thomas (1763–1854) and Alexander (1788–1866) Campbell in the early Nineteenth Century. It now claims 1,189,600 members in the United States and appears to be growing more rapidly than any other Christian body in that country.

new orders within the Roman Church is evidence of the continuing vitality of that Church. In the same way, it is claimed, the development of new sects within Protestantism is a sign of the vitality of the movement and not of its decay. Every division does involve, indeed, a denial, even a denial of doctrines deemed essential by other parts of the Christian family. But to treat Protestantism as merely negative is completely to misunderstand its nature. Division comes ordinarily by way of the affirmation of some truth obscured and neglected in the existing churches, a truth regarded by some as so vital that even the price of division must be paid, if that is the only way by which its full expression can be secured. Most Protestant sects have arisen well within the main framework of Christian orthodoxy. " It might prove that the divided Christian bodies had each stood for some part of the truth which it apprehended more vividly than the rest did, and when that part of the truth was freed from the distortions and errors which now make variety mean conflict, it might prove that each of these bodies had brought its distinctive contribution to the life of the universal Church."[1] Even those who most deplore the abandonment of the Christian sacraments by the Quakers and the Salvation Army, and for that reason find it impossible to accept them as being in any sense within the visible *corpus Christianum*, are fain to recognise the value of the witness of these two bodies in realms where most of the traditional churches have been conspicuously weak.

Just because non-Roman Christendom[2] is so divided, its ethos is much more difficult to identify and to describe than that of Roman Catholicism. Anglicanism, with its strong Catholic sense of continuity with the past, its liturgy

[1] E. Bevan, op. cit., p. 175.
[2] I have occasionally used the words Protestant and Protestantism, as an heir of the traditions of the Church of Ireland is entitled to do, without prejudice as a convenient term for non-Orthodox, non-Roman Christianity. I regret it, if any members of the Church of England object to this classification, but it is notoriously difficult to find any more satisfactory term.

so largely made up of ancient materials and its essential sobriety, stands at some distance from all other types of western Christianity. Even among Lutherans, there are marked differences between the German and the Scandinavian traditions, and even between the Lutheranism of northern and southern Germany. Yet it remains true that non-Roman western Christendom has within it such common elements of tradition as tend to the formation of a recognisable type of Christian society.

It has been said that the most characteristic products of Protestantism are the *Passion according to St. Matthew* of John Sebastian Bach, the portraits of Rembrandt and St. Paul's Cathedral in London.[1] In each of these supreme productions of Christian art, there are the two elements of continuity and difference—continuity with the great stream of the classical Christian tradition, modified but unbroken by the experiences of the Renaissance and the Reformation, with at the same time a new emphasis on the experience of the individual and on personal apprehension of the Christian faith.

The recovery of the doctrine of justification by faith, which was common to all the Churches springing from the Reformation, including the Church of England,[2] could not fail to produce a profound modification in the Christian society. In terms of reformed preaching, each man is called to an individual and personal act of choice. His part is not mere passive acceptance of a tradition handed on to him, but

[1] On the Protestant ethos, see some extremely interesting remarks of Professor Paul Tillich in *The Christian Answer*, p. 29, (ed. H. P. Van Dusen, London, Nisbet 1946). He refers to the portraits of Rembrandt, the best school of all for the study of Protestantism in its greatness and its weakness, in the following terms : " If we study the portraits of Rembrandt, especially in his later period, we confront personalities who are like self-enclosed worlds—strong, lonely, tragic but unbroken, carrying the marks of their unique histories in every line of their faces, expressing the ideas of personality of a humanistic Protestantism."

[2] See Article XI: "We are accounted righteous before God, only for the merit of our Lord and Saviour Jesus Christ by Faith, and not by our own works or deservings: Wherefore, that we are justified by Faith only is a most wholesome Doctrine, and very full of comfort, as more largely is expressed in the Homily of Justification."

decision in the moment of personal confrontation with Jesus Christ as the One who demands the response of personal faith. This confrontation takes place within the Church, through which the Gospel is proclaimed ; there is no absolute new beginning ; yet the Church continues to exist as the living body of Christ only as in each generation those who have been brought into it by baptism accept through the assent of faith the reality of the Christian life.   The fellowship of the Church is the gift of God, but it continues only through the willed and deliberate choice of men, who have heard the voice of God through the Scriptures and the preaching of the Gospel.

From this conviction springs the Protestant emphasis on education.   When John Richard Green wrote that, in the Sixteenth Century, the English people became the people of a book, and that book the Bible,[1] he was not far from the truth.   One of the first great achievements of the Reformation was Luther's translation of the Bible into German. In a surprisingly short time the whole Bible had been translated into every language of Europe.   Edition succeeded edition.   It was the aim of the reformers that every Christian individual should have the word of God in his own hands, and read and study it for himself.   The language and thought of the Bible passed into common speech, became a living part of the tradition of the peoples of northern and western Europe, and exercised a profound influence on the ideas and thoughts of common men.

In general, it may be said that in the Protestant, as contrasted with the Roman, tradition, there has been far more emphasis on personal and conscious adherence to the Christian faith.   This emphasis on individual responsibility and individual choice proved congenial to the new spirit that was coming into European society, as the restrictions of medieval life were done away, and the dominant influence passed to that active energetic middle class that set itself to

[1] *Short History of the English People* London, 1893), Vol. III, p. 935.

the conquest of new worlds and to a new mastery over nature. The weakness which this attitude brought with it was the tendency towards individualism, the exaltation of the individual against the claims of society upon him. Its strength was in a form of society which gave the individual liberty to assert and develop his natural gifts, and which was enriched and diversified by the different and individual contributions of each member in his own occupation, seen as a vocation from God, in the due and faithful exercise of which God was to be glorified.

The sense of the direct and personal responsibility of each individual to God in every part and aspect of his life resulted in a high, though sometimes narrow, standard of Christian morality. Honesty, sobriety and diligence ranked high in the scale of Christian virtues. A serious attempt was made to bring the teaching of the Bible to bear on the affairs of daily life. Generations of children in England were brought up on the Church catechism, in which they learned nothing of their rights, but a great deal of their duties to God and to their neighbour ; that duty was interpreted in easily intelligible ethical terms of regard for the welfare of others, and of a sense of the Christian significance of ordinary things. There was a tendency to equate the Old Testament with the New, manifest for example in the Puritan interpretation of the Christian Sunday in terms of the Jewish Sabbath. Too strong an emphasis on duty rather than charity as the basis of Christian action tends to an anxious legalism. Legalism always issues in Pharisaism, a complacent self righteousness and contempt for those who fail to attain to a visible and measurable standard of conformity to rule and regulation. Yet an age in which moral standards have become so grievously relaxed may perhaps look back not without regret to a time when sin, responsibility and judgment were realities of which the layman, no less than the priest, took account in the ordering of his daily life.

Among the influences that determined the shape of Protestant society, perhaps the first place of all should be ascribed to the Christian home. The Council of Trent had reaffirmed the medieval doctrine that virginity is in itself a higher state and one more pleasing to God than marriage. The churches of the Reformation, returning to an earlier Christian tradition, affirmed that marriage and celibacy are different vocations, but that, in the matter of sanctity, neither is to be preferred to the other. The Christian home became again what it had been in the days of the New Testament, "the church that is in thy house," the small society in which the faith and its duties were most readily learned, the microcosm on the holiness and Christian efficacy of which the well-being of the macrocosm depended. In the early Seventeenth Century, almost every great house in England had its resident chaplain, whose duty it was to read the Morning and Evening Prayer of the Church of England to the assembled household.[1] In simpler homes, especially in the Presbyterian countries, the father of the family exercised his office as priest in his own house, and no day passed without the reading of the Scriptures and family prayer. To this day, it is the custom in most Christian families in Holland that, when the family is assembled for the principal meal of the day, the meal does not start without the reading of some verses from the Scriptures and the offering of prayer.

The strength and glory of Protestant piety is, however, best apprehended by a study of its hymnody. Martin Luther himself was the first and greatest of Protestant hymn-writers. The Reformation sang its way into the hearts of thousands who would never have been able to give an account of its theological implications. The fire passed from country to country and language to language. Clément

---

[1] A touching example is to be found in the sermon preached in 1627 by John Donne in commemoration of Lady Danvers (Nonesuch ed. London, 1932, p. 574). See also G. M. Trevelyan: *Social History of England* (London, 1944), pp. 234–5 ; and, for a later period, C. H. Smyth : *Simeon and Church Order* (Cambridge, 1940), pp. 16–31.

Marot's (1496–1544) metrical version of the Psalms in French supported the Huguenots in the days of persecution. In England, the Independents Isaac Watts (1674-1748) and Dr. Philip Doddridge (1702–51) improved both metrical form and choice of language. Each outburst of revival brought with it a fresh harvest of great hymns. In Germany, Zinzendorf (1700–60) and Tersteegen (1697–1769) expressed in simple language an intense, at times almost sentimental, devotion to the person of the crucified Redeemer. And then came the most remarkable contribution of all, the vast collection of the hymns of the Wesleys, a body of Christian verse unrivalled in depth, range, expression, and solid theological content.

Bernard Manning has remarked that, for the Independent, it is the hymns that really constitute the Liturgy ; the careful choice of hymns makes possible that orderly progression of thought in worship which for the Anglican is provided by the fixed forms of the Prayer Book. More of the theology of the ordinary man is probably provided by the memory of hymns learned in early years than by the Bible itself.[1] And it is in the hymn-book that the essential unity of Protestant devotion is most clearly seen. A study of the collection of hymns used by any of the non-Roman churches of the west shows that in the realm of pure worship the divisions of denominational and theological affiliation break down. In the section of Eucharistic hymns, Thomas Aquinas stands side by side with the Methodist Charles Wesley, with the Presbyterian Horatio Bonar and the Anglicans Reginald Heber and William Bright. Christ is greater than the fragments into which His followers have broken His body ; when men stretch out their hands directly to Him, they find themselves still mysteriously one.

[1] This point is correctly noted by Mgr. R. A. Knox in *A Spiritual Aeneid* (London, 1918), p. 12. It is a curious fact that the only distinguished Roman Catholic writers of hymns in English, J. H. Newman and F. W. Faber, were both Anglicans who had gone over to the Roman obedience.

In the four centuries that have passed since the Reformation the churches of the West have moved further from one another, and have become hardened in their divisions. The non-Roman churches have borne the main burden of Biblical scholarship and of theological speculation. The Roman Catholics have maintained a stronger sense of continuity with the past and with the traditions of the undivided Church. The Protestants have stood for the liberty of the Christian man. The Romans have stood for the corporate unity of the body, as that in which alone the individual can find the fulfilment of his being as a Christian. Each part of the Body has become impoverished by its separation from the other members; none has manifested the fulness of the purpose of God in Christ. Most serious of all, most Christians, born and brought up in a denominational allegiance, have come to accept division as the natural state of the Church of Christ, and have hardly any consciousness of schism as sin. It is not for a later generation to determine the degree of responsibility of individuals for the divisions which it has inherited. The recognition of division as contrary to the very nature of the Christian society is a first and necessary step towards the recovery of that unity without which the Church cannot fully bear its witness to the redemption of the whole of humanity, and of every part and aspect of man's life, through the death and resurrection of Jesus Christ.

CHAPTER VII

THE EXPANSION OF THE WESTERN WORLD

IN 1492, Christopher Columbus, setting out to seek a new route to India, discovered America. In 1498, Vasco da Gama, having rounded the Cape of Good Hope, cast anchor off Calicut. The horizons of a new world opened up before the eyes of the nations of western Europe.

The consequences of these discoveries for the Christian Church did not become immediately apparent. Until the end of the medieval period, the Church had lived almost entirely within the inheritance of the ancient Greco-Roman world. Those parts of the Christian society which lay outside the limits of the Roman Empire, and in which the prevailing language was Syriac, developed traditions of their own, independent of, and in some ways markedly different from, those of the great churches within the Empire. Yet those churches too were found in lands which had been profoundly affected by the Hellenic expansion in and after the age of Alexander, and to a large extent drew on Greek sources for the inspiration of their theological thought. The Church had had contacts, sometimes friendly, more often hostile, with the great Muslim civilisation that spread out from its centres in Baghdad, Mecca, Damascus and Cairo. But Islam drew on both the Old and New Testaments, and can be classed not unfairly under some aspects as a Christian heresy. At the turn of the Sixteenth Century, men saw open before them the way into great lands in which the Church had never existed at any time, and in which great civilisations had grown up without any tincture whatever of Christian influence. Could the Church of Christ break free from the bonds of its geographical and intellectual limits, and grow into the stature of a world-wide Christian society?

The problem was not completely new. Except for the Fifteenth Century, in which the inner weakness of the Church called a halt to Christian progress, there had never been a century in which the Church was not reaching out in new directions.[1] Every spiritual revival had resulted in a fresh beginning of missionary activity. Francis of Assisi felt himself called to a universal mission to all mankind. He set out himself to preach to the Muslims in Palestine and Egypt. His children went much further afield. A small stream of Franciscan missionaries in the Thirteenth Century penetrated India. In 1294, John of Monte Corvino reached Cambaluc, the modern Peking, and remained there for more than fifty years.[2] These Franciscan missions were marked by extreme adventurousness and heroism. But they were small in scale, and during the disturbances which marked the end of the medieval period most of them disappeared. With the opening of the new age of discovery a new beginning had to be made.

From the first, the Roman Catholic explorers and the rulers who supported them were conscious of a mission to spread the faith in the lands newly discovered. Christopher Columbus himself, at the conclusion of his first great voyage, reported that " the Indians have no religion and would readily become Christians, as they have a good

---

[1] There is some evidence that even in the Fifteenth Century the Russian Church was still expanding, and bringing into its fold some of the pagan tribes in the far north and east of Russia.

[2] John was a great missionary, and an intelligent and accurate observer. On his way to China, he spent thirteen months in India; his letters are among our most important authorities for the state of Christianity in India in the Middle Ages. The Pope wished to consecrate him as Archbishop for China ; as the only possible means to accomplish his purpose, he consecrated seven Franciscan friars as bishops, and launched them into Central Asia. One never started ; three died on the way ; the remaining three duly arrived, and consecrated John as their own Metropolitan.

understanding."[1] Some of the Indians brought back by Columbus in his ships were instructed and baptised.

The expansion of the Christian society was formally recognised, when Pope Nicholas V in a Bull of the year 1454 divided the newly-discovered lands between the kings of Spain and Portugal. The line of division ran through the Atlantic Ocean, roughly following the west coast of Africa. The whole of the West was given to Spain, the whole of the East to Portugal. The kings were given responsibility for the evangelisation of all the lands that should be discovered and conquered by their peoples. They were to send out and maintain missionaries. At the same time, they were given the right to create bishoprics and to name bishops for them from among their own subjects, and were given exclusive control over all missionaries going to work in those regions, including the right to exclude all whom they did not wish to admit, and to censor the correspondence of missionaries even with the Holy See. The underlying concept of this new missionary venture was an extension of the idea that the Christian prince is responsible for the spiritual welfare of his subjects, that he must see to it that heresy is extirpated, and that idolatry, which is abomination, is not allowed to exist in any territory under his rule.

The first missionaries were Franciscans. Many other orders, and also secular priests, took part. But it was not long before the Jesuits came to the fore as the great missionaries in every part of the newly-discovered world.

The Society of Jesus came into existence as a militia of the Church, primarily for the re-establishment of the faith where it had been threatened by the spread of Protestantism. At first its organisation was severely criticised, as not falling

[1] Columbus, *Journal of First Voyage to America* (New York, 1924), p. 36. Columbus was wrong in thinking that the Indians had no religion; this is a mistake constantly repeated by discoverers, and, unfortunately, popularised by them.

within any of the categories familiar from the past.[1] Its members were bound by a discipline as strict as that of any of the religious orders. But they were to have an independence and mobility greater even than of the Friars, and yet were not to have the local responsibilities of the secular clergy. Before long, however, it was recognised that the genius of Ignatius Loyola had created precisely the instrument for which the times called. With their emphasis on scholarship, on education, on apologetic preaching and on suitably diplomatic approaches to those who could influence the currents of both thought and action, the Jesuits soon secured for themselves the position of protagonists of the cause of the Counter-Reformation. Laynez at the Council of Trent, St. Peter Canisius in Germany, stood in the breach to maintain what otherwise might have seemed a losing cause.

Just those qualities of devotion, iron discipline and reckless self-giving, which fitted the Jesuits for such forlorn hopes as the reconversion of England, prepared them also to be the most distinguished missionaries of the Roman Catholic Church in the non-Christian world. By the end of the Sixteenth Century, there was hardly a country from Canada to Siam which had not its tale of Jesuit martyrs for the faith.[2]

Although the primary task of the Jesuits was to strengthen or rebuild the crumbling walls of Zion in Europe, Ignatius, like Francis, had from the first understood his task in terms of a world-wide vision. He willingly surrendered Francis Xavier, one of the first group of six companions, and the

---

[1] After considerable delays, the organisation of the Jesuits as a religious order was finally sanctioned by Pope Paul III in the Bull *Regimini Militantis Ecclesiae* of 27 September, 1540.

[2] The records of the early Jesuits, even as seen through the eyes of so sympathetic an interpreter as Fr. Brodrick (*The Origin of the Jesuits, The Progress of the Jesuits*, London, 1940 and 1946), suggest a certain pathological element of over-intensity and strain. If this is so, it means no more than that the Jesuits were children of their age; the Sixteenth Century was a strained and hysterical age. If such a pathological factor was present, it was directed by discipline to the noblest ends.

ablest of them all, to India. From 1541 onwards, each year saw the departure of companies of Jesuit Fathers for the most distant regions of both East and West.

Medieval missions of the Church outside Europe, though marked by conspicuous heroism and devotion, had not led anywhere to the founding of strong and enduring churches. The Sixteenth Century saw the beginning of an enterprise, which was to be carried on continuously, though with fluctuations of zeal, until the present day, and has resulted in the formation of great Christian communities in non-Christian lands and within the framework of non-Christian civilisations. It marked, therefore, a turning point in the history of the Christian Church, and the beginning of a new stage of development in the Christian society.

In the spread of the Gospel in Northern Europe, the conversion of kings and rulers had played a predominant part. In the recovery of areas lost to Protestantism, the Jesuits had found that one of their strongest weapons lay in the appeal to the ruling classes and their establishment in the faith ; in a society still organised hierarchically, influence spreads downwards from above, and there is a strong tendency for the poorer and less educated classes to follow in religion the lead of those upon whom they are dependent in other spheres of life. It was natural that in their missions the Jesuits should attempt to follow a method which had yielded such great successes elsewhere.

In India, the way seemed to lie open with the accession of Akbar the Great (1542–1602) to the Mogul throne. This great man proved to be one of the most remarkable rulers of whom history anywhere has record. Himself illiterate, he was shrewd in statecraft and in his estimate of men, patient and persevering in the pursuit of his aims, and, judged by the standards of his day, humane. He succeeded in uniting under his sway a larger part of India than had ever been ruled by one man since the days of Asoka in the Third Century B.C. A Muslim by tradition and upbringing, he was liberal and open-minded in matters of religion.

Like many of his successors, Akbar was deeply troubled by the power of religion to divide men and to provoke them to hatred ; he was convinced that there could be no stability in his dominions unless the inveterate animosity between Hindus and Muslims could in some way be assuaged. His own solution for the problem was to work out a "religion of all good men," a vague theism without definite dogma, in which he believed that the best of both religions was incorporated, and which men of good sense of all persuasions should be able to accept. Like others before and after him, he had failed to realise that synthetic religions rarely have power to win the allegiance of men in those deep regions of the mind where motives are disciplined and actions determined, that intellectual clarity achieves little unless it is backed by emotional appeal, and that it is not the general but the particular that is the driving force in matters of religion. The new Creed of Akbar, in spite of all the backing of royal authority, never took root in the minds of his people, and failed to survive the death of its author. But this eclectic tendency made Akbar's mind more open than those of other eastern rulers to a consideration of the claims of Christianity. He may even have thought that a religion which was neither Hindu nor Muslim would have the power to unite the striving sects within his dominions. Whatever exactly his motives may have been, in 1579 he sent an embassy to the Jesuits at Goa, asking that a mission might be sent to his court.[1]

Hope beat high. Direct access had been secured to the greatest prince in the east. His conversion could not but be followed by immense success in the establishment of the Church in India under royal patronage. In old Mogul paintings, Jesuit fathers in their black robes are to be seen

[1] The whole history of this episode is set out in Maclagan, *The Jesuits and the Great Mogul* (London, 1932), a most thorough and reliable piece of research.

among the crowd of courtiers surrounding the emperor. In one form or another the mission was maintained until the dissolution of the Jesuit order in 1773. But the results were disappointing. Akbar, with his unquenchable intellectual curiosity, took pleasure in listening to the missionaries, and in hearing their disputes with the learned men of other religions. But his temperament was that of a dilettante, and it is most unlikely that he ever seriously contemplated the step of accepting for himself the faith of the missionaries. Although Akbar, in 1601, gave permission for those of his subjects who wished to do so to become Christians, the Jesuits found themselves reduced to little more than the position of chaplains to foreigners, including Armenians, at the court. There was another flare-up of hope under Akbar's successor Jehangir, when three of the emperor's nephews were instructed in the faith and publicly baptised. But revulsion followed under later emperors who were stricter Muslims, and who, though they continued Akbar's policy of giving financial aid to the missionaries, gradually withdrew the favours by which their esteem in the eyes of the public had been enhanced. The number of converts from Hinduism and Islam remained extremely small. In the end, it became clear that the conversion of India was not to be achieved along the lines of royal favour and mass conversion in the governing class.

At almost exactly the same period, one of the greatest missionaries of all times was making a similar experiment in China. Matteo Ricci[1] (1552–1610) joined the Jesuit mission in China at a moment when it seemed almost impossible that the inveterate prejudice of the Chinese against foreigners could be overcome, even to the extent of making possible the establishment of permanent missions among them. It is reported that Valignani, the Visitor of the Jesuits in the Indies, looking out of his window at Macao,

---

[1] A good short account of this period is to be found in K. S. Latourette : *A History of Christian Missions in China* (London, 1929), c. VI, pp. 78–102.

the tiny Portuguese settlement on the coast, and at that time the one safe *pied-à-terre* of the Christian faith in the Far East, cried out " with a loud voice and the most intimate affection of his heart ' Oh, Rock, Rock, when wilt thou open, Rock ? ' " Ricci achieved a measure of success denied to his predecessors.

It happened that he had studied mathematics, astronomy and cosmology in Rome. The Chinese, with their traditional respect for the scholar, allowed themselves to be interested in the new learning brought from Europe by a man who wore their dress and spoke their language, and was able to open to them new fields of learning. Ricci made a map of the world. He introduced to the Chinese the new science of the calendar. Clocks had been brought into China by the Portuguese, but outside Macao no one knew how to repair them ; in this art also Ricci showed his proficiency, and so made himself useful to a number of leading Chinese, who were much more interested in his technical skill than in the religion which he professed. Such contacts were useful, as securing toleration for the mission. But Ricci, like his brethren in India, was convinced that China could never be won from headquarters in the southern and outlying province of Kwangtung, and that the strategic move was to establish a mission at the very heart of the empire and in its capital Peking.

The difficulties in his way were immense. The old Franciscan mission of John of Monte Corvino had disappeared, leaving scarcely a trace even in memory. Prejudice against foreigners was naturally stronger in the capital than elsewhere. No western sovereign had any kind of diplomatic relations with the Emperor of China, and there was therefore no possibility of political support for the mission.[1] Ricci was left to his own resources, and to the chance of securing favour by his own efforts. Where others had failed, he

---

[1] Here a difference is to be noted between China and India. England was represented at the court of the Great Mogul, from 1614 onwards, by the famous embassy of Sir Thomas Roe.

succeeded. In 1601, the Jesuit mission was established in
Peking. The number of converts was not large. But
among them were sufficient members of the intellectual
élite, and even of the imperial family, to set Christianity
free from being regarded as merely a foreign superstition.

The mission passed through many vicissitudes, but once
established, it never entirely died out. The successor of
Ricci, Johann Adam Schall von Bell, carried his mathematical
prowess to an even higher level. In 1623, he secured the
admiration of the scholar class by accurately predicting the
time of an eclipse of the moon. When civil war broke out,
and in 1644 the Manchus drove out the rulers of the Ming
dynasty, Schall remained in Peking, again secured high
favour by his skill in predicting eclipses, was put officially
in charge of the imperial bureau of astronomy, and secured
from the emperor a declaration in favour of the Christian
faith. It was reckoned that by 1663, there were already
one hundred and nine thousand Christians in the Chinese
Empire. The Christian faith was beginning to take root ;
the Christian society in China was beginning to emerge as
a reality.[1]

So far we have considered the efforts of Roman Catholic
missionaries to penetrate areas where European groups were
small or non-existent, and where the Christian society, if it
came into existence at all, had to face the uncertainties of
the favour or displeasure of autocratic non-Christian rulers.
But the Europeans of the great age of expansion did not
go out only as explorers and traders. They went also as
conquerors. Great areas, some of them homes of ancient
civilisations that the conquerors were quick to destroy,
others populated by very simple peoples, were brought
under Christian rule. Slaves from Africa were introduced

---

[1] Great caution must be exercised in using early missionary statistics.
The sources are rarely consistent with one another, and there is a strong
tendency to exaggeration. The problem of "accommodation," that caused
so much trouble in both India and China, is left over to be dealt with in
another chapter.

into the Spanish Main. Here the task of the Church was very different. It was taken for granted by all that the Christian faith was to be introduced. The question was as to method. Could force be rightly used, or should the Church rely on persuasion alone ?

There is much in the record of the contacts between European races and the weaker peoples of the world, even up to the present time, that is horrifying and shocking to the conscience. In no other area of history is the corruption wrought by power more completely exemplified. There are too many tales of massacre, oppression and extermination. And for the most part, in the early days of European expansion, it was taken for granted that the powers of the state, the army and the Inquisition, could be brought into play, in order to bring the conquered people within the fold of salvation.

In the early history of Christianity in the western world, the most famous name is that of Bartolomé de Las Casas, Bishop of Chiapa, the great champion of the oppressed peoples, and the protagonist of the view that cruelty and coercion can never bring about true conversion to the faith. Throughout the greater part of his long career (he died in 1566, at the age of ninety-two), Las Casas was regarded by colonists and by missionaries as a visionary and a menace. The colonists were convinced that, by his opposition to forced labour, at that time hardly to be distinguished from slavery, he would bring about the economic ruin of the colonies, an argument to be used in the Nineteenth Century against Wilberforce and the advocates of the abolition of slavery in the West Indies. Many of the missionaries were convinced that wild and barbarous peoples could not be won to the faith without such coercion as would help them to see the error of their ways. Las Casas persisted. To him in large part was due the drafting of *The Laws of the Indies*, 1542, that great charter of justice for the indigenous peoples, which, though often infringed, at least set a limit to oppression and cruelty.

It is typical of the spirit of the age that the Laws start with
a long section on the spiritual welfare of the Indians, the
slaves, the Negroes and the peoples of mixed origin. Their
conversion to Christianity is the first object of the solicitude
of the government in Spain ; their social and economic
welfare comes after.[1]

In Asia, the situation was rather different, since there
were no great areas to be so easily conquered by a handful
of European soldiers. But where the Portuguese were in
power, they took the view that a Christian king was directly
responsible for the spiritual welfare of his subjects. The
centre of their eastern empire was Goa on the west coast
of India, a city of great baroque churches, surrounded by
a not very extensive territory that had also come under
Portuguese rule. Before long the city won an unenviable
reputation for debauchery, and for the evil-living of
Europeans set free from the restraints of life in an at least
nominally Christian country. But here, as elsewhere, the
policy of the authorities was to permit no idolatry to defile
the territory of a Christian king. If the inhabitants would
not submit to persuasion, other measures could be taken to
ensure conformity. In a letter written in 1559,[2] we read
that "the fathers, having heard through the neophytes that
the heathen were intending to celebrate a festival of
Ganessa Vinacociti and Vinaico, these being the names of
their gods, came suddenly, and found an idol in the house
of a Brahman. All those present were punished, the
Brahman being condemned to lifelong hard labour, and his
property, by order of his highness, being confiscated. The
same night we went to a Brahman house, and found people
there engaged in the worship of their idol. This we
prevented and took three idols, named Salagramma. The
Brahmans escaped and could not be dealt with ; but orders

---

[1] A good account of Las Casas is to be found in David Jenks, *Six Great Missionaries* (London, 1930), pp. 10–40.

[2] Published in Nuovi Avvisi, parte terza (Venice, 1562), p. 97 ff., and cited in P. Dahmen, *Robert de Nobili*, S.J. (Münster in Westfalen, Aschendorf 1924), pp. 8–9.

were issued that they should be arrested wherever found."
By such means Hinduism was largely driven underground,
and the adherents of the Christian way increased with great
rapidity.

Not content with making their subjects into Christians,
the Portuguese in Goa did their utmost to turn them into
Portuguese. The use of Portuguese names became and
remains common in that part of India. On the testimony
of P. Vico in 1615, we learn that they went so far as to
attempt to introduce the eating of meat, "though the
Indian Magi strove hard against it." Even the use of
Indian clothing was treated as a great concession. To the
early Portuguese nothing could have seemed more obvious
than this policy ; nothing in the end could have proved
more harmful to the development of a genuine and deeply-
rooted Christian society in India. A wise observer, Archi-
bishop Roz of Cranganore, wrote in 1613 that "this is the
reason why none of the higher castes have been baptised,
but only those who have lost their caste or accept baptism
for some worldly reason." The Portuguese boast of the
baptism at Goa of the unimportant Raja of Tanor. "But
as he has given up the usages of his caste and taken on the
appearance of a Portuguese, his people no longer recognise
him as their ruler."

In 1542, Francis Xavier came to Goa, stayed a few
months, and wrought something of a moral revolution.
But before long he was to find in the extreme south of India
a far more fruitful field, in which to bring into existence
a Christian society recognisably Indian. In 1534 all the
fisher-folk of the south-east coast had sought the protection
of the king of Portugal against the land and sea robbers,
who had made their life a misery. They were accepted on
condition of receiving baptism. But for eight years nothing
had been done to teach them anything of the faith which
they nominally professed.

The next three years form an idyll of Christian evangelism.

" The little dark man " went everywhere, over the burning
sandhills where the fisher villages were strewn. His bright
smile and affectionate manner drew the people and especially
the children to him, until he had scarcely time to read his
breviary. He arranged for them to be instructed ; although
he himself knew no Tamil, he arranged for the first rough
translations of Creed and Lord's Prayer and catechism to
be made. He guarded the people, as best he could, both
against their native enemies, and against the wild and lawless
Portuguese of the coast. At the end of three years, he had
an organised church to hand on to his successors.

The Paravars, as these fisher-folk were called, numbered
perhaps thirty thousand. Their situation was peculiar. The
Christian movement was limited to one caste, which formed
an enclave within the surrounding Hinduism. Living by
their boats and by the sea, the Paravars had little contact,
except by way of trade, with those among whom they lived,
and their Christianity exercised scarcely any influence at all
on the way of life of their neighbours. The Jesuit missionaries found the people scattered in small hamlets all
along the sea-coast ; for safety they gathered them into
sixteen large villages. In course of time a Jesuit was
stationed in each village. A large church was built. Something of the atmosphere of an exclusively Christian country
was created.

The fisher-folk were, and are, rude and hardy people, not
easily amenable to discipline ; at frequent intervals, they were
at war with their spiritual overlords, and on occasion even
drove them out. But the Jesuits always came back. With
infinite patience they fashioned the lives of their people.
Strict discipline was enforced. No boat might set out to fish
on Sunday ; a part of each Friday's catch must be given to the
Church. With the support of the Portuguese authorities, it
was possible for the Jesuits to make their discipline effective.
Gradually all memory of a time when the Paravars were
not Christian died away; they might on occasion be sinful

and disorderly, like their fellow-Christians in Europe, but all their thoughts and ideas had been fashioned by the Church and its teaching ; the centre of their life was the church, the one stone building round which their huts of palm-leaf and thatch were clustered. The work of Xavier was in a sense completed, when in 1923 the diocese of Tuticorin was created by the Pope for the coastal area inhabited by the Paravars, and a descendant of one of Xavier's converts, Fr. Tiburtius Roche, was appointed to the see, as the first Indian diocesan bishop of the Latin rite.

Roman Catholics and Protestants alike have united in extolling Xavier's apostolic zeal and the charm of his character. Nevertheless he was a man of his own time, and there are features of his work which, in the light of the Gospel, can hardly be commended. In a letter of 16 May, 1546,[1] he wrote to the king of Portugal that " the second need in India, in order that there may be good Christians here, is that your highness should send the Holy Inquisition. For there are many who live by the Mosaic religion and the Moorish sect, without any fear of God or shame of the world." The request was granted, and the Inquisition continued in its operations in Goa until the beginning of the Nineteenth Century. Eighteen months later, Xavier, still unsatisfied with the co-operation of the civil power in his efforts, wrote to the king : " Let your Hignness inform the Governor who is here, or any other that you send from home, that you entrust to him, more than to any religious persons here, responsibility for the increase of our holy religion in India. . . . If he do not greatly increase our holy faith, assure him that you are determined to punish him, and say with solemn oath that you will hold all his estates as forfeit for the works of the Santa Misericordia, when he returns to Portugal, and further that you will keep him many years in irons. . . . As long as the governors

[1] A reliable English translation of the letters of Xavier is a great desideratum. A critical edition of the originals has been published by the Spanish Jesuits in *Monumenta Xaveriana* (Madrid, 1899), Vol. I, pp. 201–810.

have not this fear before them of being dishonoured and punished, your Majesty should not reckon on any increase of our holy faith." The use of force and governmental authority for the propagation of the faith is attractive to a certain type of mind, and may lead to rapid and sensational successes. But the nemesis of time is hard on such superficial success. Christian communities which had been built up in too close reliance on the Portuguese power tended to decline with the decline of the Portuguese empire. In many parts of the world, these early enterprises did not provide a sure foundation on which the Christian society could be built, and later ages had to begin the work all over again.

The most remarkable of all the Jesuit attempts to create a Christian community among a simple non-Christian people was that carried on for more than a hundred and fifty years in the Reductions of Paraguay. The vast area known as the Chaco is one of the most inaccessible regions of the world even in the Twentieth Century. It suffers from an inhospitable climate. Until very recent times even governments have had very little control over its sparse and primitive inhabitants. From the beginning of the Seventeenth Century, the Jesuits were given complete control over the whole area ; Spanish colonists were excluded, and the utmost watchfulness was maintained to ensure that the rule was not infringed. Under the distant control of the Spanish crown, Church and state were completely identified.[1]

The methods followed were similar to those employed in South India. The nomadic Indians were brought together in thirty-eight villages, widely separated by tracts of untamed jungle, in each of which at the time of greatest development there must have been several thousand inhabitants. The

[1] The nature of the country is vividly portrayed in Julian Duguid's *Green Hell* (London, 1931), a narrative of a journey through the Bolivian Chaco. His novel, *Father Coldstream* (London, 1937), based on careful study of original documents, depicts life as lived in an Indian village towards the end of the Jesuit domination. A full bibliography is given by Latourette in his *History of the Expansion of Christianity*, Vol. III, (London, 1940), p. 154.

land was divided into two parts; one belonged to the Church, and was cultivated by the Indians on a regular system of obligation; the other was left to the Indians to cultivate for themselves, and it was noted that this part was usually less well-tended and less productive than that worked on the principles of a collective farm. The missions were maintained by trade, the disposal of the products of the Indians' labour being entirely in the hands of the Jesuits and those directly in their employ. The trade was extensive, but, although it was the object of continual criticism on the part of the colonists, there is no reason to think that the profits were unfairly used, or that what could just be called exploitation of the people was carried on. The priests were allowed to arm their people, and to organise them for defence against the Indians who had not been "reduced," against aggression by the colonists, or political penetration from without.

The centre of everything was the Church. Noble churches were erected in all the villages. The services were carried out with great elaboration, and the minds of the people were kept occupied by the solemn observance of the feasts of the Church. In particular it was noted that the standard of singing attained by the Indians was very high, though it is not clear to what extent they were taught to understand the words that they were singing. By means of the confessional, and by unremitting vigilance, careful control was exercised upon the morals and habits of the people ; discipline, adapted perhaps from the methods followed in the Jesuit seminaries in Europe, was patriarchal and severe, but not usually so rigorous as to be cruel.

The test of the work carried out by the Jesuits in cultivating this strange garden of Eden came when the Jesuit order was suppressed in 1773. Great as had been their achievement, it was found wanting in the power of survival under adversity. After the departure of the Jesuits, an attempt was made to staff the missions with Franciscan priests, but they had neither the ability nor the knowledge of the people built up by the Jesuits over generations. Immediately the prosperity of the missions began to decline. The principal error of the missionaries had been the attempt to keep their flocks in a state of primitive innocence, and the failure to lead them in the way to the development of independent Christian manhood. No indigenous leadership had been developed. There were, of course, headmen and overseers among the people, but no attempt had been made to educate them beyond a very elementary stage, or to develop in them the capacity for responsibility. No Indian had been allowed to share in the management of the missions, or to have any intimate knowledge of the way in which they were carried on. Above all, no Indian had ever been admitted to the priesthood. In consequence, the great missions remained exotic, a garden enclosed in a world which showed only too plainly the consequences of the Fall. The trim fields and gardens reverted to primitive jungle. The Indians returned to their old barbaric ways. Today, there is little left, in evidence of a great Christian enterprise, but the enduring fabric of the churches, built so solidly as to resist the savage forces of nature and of man.

No Christian society can long survive, unless it has powers of leadership and of renewal within itself. It would be wrong to conclude from one example that the Jesuits and other early Roman Catholic missionaries had failed to realise this, or that their work had no enduring quality, except where the continuing support of governments was available. The most remarkable example, in the whole story of the Church, of a Christian society surviving under conditions of complete isolation is afforded by the history of Christianity in Japan. After a period of great success and prosperity the Church fell upon days of hardship and persecution. From 1614 on, the leaders of Japanese society decided on that policy of complete isolation from the outside world, which lasted until the middle of the Nineteenth Century. In part at least this policy seems to have been dictated by the desire to safeguard Japanese life and culture against the disruptive forces already discerned to be latent in the Christian Gospel. The last missionary was put to death about the year 1715. There was no Japanese priesthood. For a hundred and fifty years, no contact with the outside world was possible. Nevertheless the Church, after a fashion, managed to survive.

When missionary work again became possible, the vestiges of the earlier Christianity were discovered. In March, 1865 a number of Japanese presented themselves to the French missionaries and claimed that they were Christians. Their knowledge of the faith was imperfect and had become mixed with superstition, but no doubt could be entertained as to the reality of their claim to be the descendants of the converts of the Sixteenth and Seventeenth Centuries. In each Christian village, two leaders had been set apart to maintain the Christian tradition, to conduct prayers on Sundays, and in particular to perform the ceremony of baptism. From the point of view of the developed Roman Catholicism of the Nineteenth Century, there was very much in the condition of these survivors from a lost world that was unsatisfactory, and they had almost everything of the faith to learn again. Not all of them were prepared to submit themselves to the new discipline. It is reckoned that about ten thousand put themselves under the care of the French missionaries, but that a larger number, perhaps a very large number, remained aloof. But under all the disadvantages of persecution, of secrecy, of ignorance, of isolation from all the centres of life in the Christian world, the faith had at least in a measure been retained.

Here as elsewhere we are compelled to note the immense importance of the outward forms in which the Christian society expresses the reality of its inner being. Faith, in the Christian sense of the term, is not an abstraction, or an inner emotional experience ; it is a life lived in a community. Unless there is the outward form, by which the society is held in cohesion, there is continual danger that the inward reality may be dissipated and disappear. The continuance of the outward form does not guarantee the continued existence of living faith. Yet over and over again history has shown that wherever the framework of an ordered Church has been preserved, the renewal of life is possible. The secret believers in Japan had lost much ; they had retained enough to serve as the mould into which new life could be poured.

The story of the Christian society is not one of unbroken success and steady progress. There have been many high hopes that have ended in disappointment, many promising enterprises that have led to nothing. Disaster has impeded growth. In not a few places inner decay has destroyed the Church. Mistakes have been made. Reliance has been placed on the power of man, and not on the patience of God. But where, under adverse circumstance, contrary to hope and expectation, the society has survived, it may be taken as certain beyond all doubt that it was founded in living faith, and that it survived because of a continuing relationship to the life of Jesus Christ.

CHAPTER VIII

A LATE BEGINNING

CONTROVERSIES between Christians have little place in the theme of this book. They have been many and bitter, but the record of them belongs elsewhere. On one subject, however, the controversy between Roman Catholics and Protestants was so deep and lasting that mention of it cannot be avoided. Cardinal Bellarmine (1542–1621), enumerating the marks of the true Church, included among them missionary work among the heathen, and pointed to the success of Roman Catholic missions as one of the evidences that that alone was the true Church. Where were the missions of Protestants ?[1] The taunt was repeated by many Roman controversialists. It must be admitted that the Roman Catholics were in the right. At the end of the Middle Ages, the expansion of the known world brought with it an expansion of the horizons of the Roman Church, and imperialism, Spanish and Portuguese, was always at least touched by the sense of Christian responsibility. As early as 1540, Roman missions were beginning to attain grandiose proportions. Three hundred years were to pass before the non-Roman Churches began to put forth efforts for the evangelisation of the world on anything like a comparable scale.

Various explanations of this failure have been given. The predestinarian teaching of Calvin might well seem to cut the nerve of missionary endeavour. In some forms of hyper-Calvinism, the argument has certainly been put in the form

[1] Quoted in C. Mirbt: *Quellen zur Geschichte des Papsttums und des Römisch-Katholizismus* (Tübingen, 1924), p. 362.

184

that, if God has predestined the heathen to salvation, He will Himself see to it that His purpose is attained, and that therefore there is no need for human instruments to concern themselves about what is in no way their responsibility. This is not a legitimate deduction from Christian doctrine as set forth by John Calvin ; it has often been remarked that, though logically Calvinism might seem to point the way to the abandonment of human effort, in fact Calvinists have shewn a zeal and heroism in Christian service that are the envy of those who do not share their theology.[1]

Two reasons are commonly put forward to account for Luther's failure to develop the idea of the world mission of the Church. He was obsessed, it is said, by the eschatological element in the Christian faith and by the expectation of the immediate end of the world ; there would therefore be no time, even if there were the obligation, to preach the Gospel in all the world. Further, he interpreted the words of Romans x. 18, " Their sound went out into all the earth, and their words unto the end of the world" as meaning that even in the time of the apostles the Gospel had been preached to all nations, and that therefore the divine purpose had been fulfilled. Karl Holl has no difficulty in showing that both these interpretations are based on a very narrow survey of Luther's works.[2] The imminence of the Second Coming did not hinder Luther from activity in his own work of evangelising Germany, nor did it preclude, in his view, the work of preaching in countries which, as he

---

[1] It remains none the less true that, in all the volumes of Calvin's works, there is no sign of serious concern for the non-Christian world. The Church is thought of statically and not dynamically, as a closed and not as a growing society. The only argument advanced for missionary work is humanitarian and not theological : " Si nous avons quelque humanité en nous, voyant que les hommes vont à perdition, jusques à tant que Dieu les ait en son obéissance, ne devons-nous point être émus de pitié, pour retirer les pauvres âmes d'enfer et de les amener au chemin de salut." Opera XXIX, 175.

[2] The paper *Luther und die Mission* is printed in Holl, *Gesammelte Aufsätze*, Vol. III (Tübingen, 1928), pp. 234–43, where full references are given. It should be noted that some other scholars consider that Holl is over-generous in his estimate of Luther as a theologian of the missionary cause.

himself says, had lain undiscovered and unevangelised for fifteen hundred years. He makes it one of his reproaches against the Pope, that, if he were a true bishop and shepherd, he had much better set out on foot to convert the Turks, and this time by the mere power of the word of God, and not by that crusading violence which the Popes even in the Sixteenth Century were still trying to stir into a belated renaissance. He shows a special interest in the Turks, to whom he attributes many virtues, and a reverence and devotion in their worship such as is not to be found even among Christians in Germany. Even for the Jews he has a good word to say, and does not regard their conversion as impossible.[1]

The failure of the Protestants to undertake missionary work was due not only to a defect in their theology but also to two very obvious practical hindrances. In the first place, until 1648, Protestants in most countries were fighting for their lives. Even later than that date, such disasters as the revocation of the Edict of Nantes by Louis XIV in 1685 shewed the uncertainty of their position. Secondly, the imperial expansion of the west was at its beginning entirely in the hands of the Roman Catholic powers. It was only by slow degrees and in the face of violent opposition that the British and the Dutch fought their way to a place in the sun.

It cannot be said that Protestants did nothing at all to Christianise the peoples with whom they were brought into contact in the expansion of their empires.

When the Dutch expelled the Portuguese from Ceylon (1658), they attempted to extirpate the Roman form of

---

[1] How little the Reformers had emancipated themselves from medieval ideas is clearly shown by a Church order drawn up by Bucer in 1543 for the Church in Hesse: " The Jews, with their wives and children of the age of 8 years and upwards, must attend all preachings and hearken attentively to the word of God: and the pastors and their assistants must keep careful watch and note all the occasions on which the Jews, their wives and children, are neglectful to attend the worship, and to report to the civil authorities."

Christianity and to replace it by their own. Acceptance of the Protestant faith was recognised as tantamount to a kind of Dutch naturalisation (just as earlier, Indians who became Christians were reckoned to have become a kind of Portuguese), and was accompanied by admission to certain civic privileges. The same policy was followed in the Dutch East Indies. For some years, a seminary was maintained in Leiden for the training of ministers for the East. The whole Bible was translated into Malay. Converts in Ambon, Timor and other islands were numbered in thousands. From the small number of ministers employed, and from the small proportion among them who were able to speak the language of the people, it may be inferred that conversion in most cases was superficial, and political rather than religious in its character. But at least a beginning had been made in the recognition of Christian responsibility for the peoples of the non-Christian world.

The British East India Company (founded in 1600) shewed some care for the spiritual welfare of its own servants in the east, and in its earlier days was prepared for its chaplains to attempt to win the "Gentoos" to the Christian faith.[1] In the Seventeenth Century, only one convert is known to have been made, the young Bengali boy brought to England by the Rev. Patrick Copeland, and baptised in London in the year 1616 under the name Peter, to which later he strangely added the surname Pope.[2]

The noble work of John Eliot (1604–1690) and others in New England had led to the baptism of more than a thousand Indians and the translation of the whole Bible into the Algonquin language.

Yet all this was not very much to set against the triumphs of which the Roman Catholics could legitimately boast.

---

[1] It is interesting to note that nearly a century earlier, the colonising plans of John Rastell, the brother-in-law of Sir Thomas More, included the evangelisation of the heathen in their scope. See R. W. Chambers, *Thomas More* (London, ed. of 1949), p. 141.

[2] See Eyre Chatterton, *The Church of England in India* (London, 1924), p. 16.

The direction of the energies of Protestants to missionary work on a large scale awaited the appearance of a new and remarkable movement within the Protestant churches in Europe, the movement known as Pietism.

Protestantism, especially in Germany, tended soon to lose its first fire, and to harden down into an arid scholasticism on the part of the preacher, and a rather lifeless conformity on the part of the hearer. Luther, out of the depths of his own experience, had proclaimed a grand doctrine of justifying faith. His successors, led away by the intellectualist error, which did not leave their Roman Catholic opponents unaffected, had turned his doctrine into something else. Faith was now no longer that act of utter surrender, in which man in his helplessness cast himself on the mercy of God and found himself accepted through grace, but formal assent to a system of doctrine scholastically set forth. Assurance was associated not so much with the living witness of the Holy Spirit as with rigid orthodoxy of doctrinal belief.

Pietism arose as a reaction against this ossification of religion. In German Church history, Philip Jacob Spener is usually reckoned to have been the first of the Pietists.[1] The aims of the movement were two-fold. The centre of Christian life was shifted from the national church, in which a man was born and brought up, to the intimate fellowship of those united by a common experience and living faith in God. Secondly, a new importance was attached to the Christian individual. It was expected that each individual should make his own endeavour to relate all his experiences and all his actions to the will of God. It is noteworthy that the idea of conversion, as an experience to be undergone by the baptised Christian no less than by the non-Christian enter-

---

[1] Born 13 January, 1635 in Alsace. The first significant expression of the Pietist ideal is to be found in his book, " *Pia Desideria,* or an earnest plea for the improvement of the true evangelical Churches according to the will of God, together with some Christian proposals tending to the same," published in 1675.

ing the Christian faith from without, first comes into pro-
minence in connection with Pietism and the movements
derived from it.

Spener influenced a much greater man than himself,
August Hermann Francke (1663-1727). The ardent piety
of Francke found expression in the great charitable and
educational institutions at Halle, which were to exercise for
more than a century a profound influence on the development
of the Christian society. At Halle, Francke made welcome
the young Count Zinzendorf (1700-60), the founder of the
Church of the Brethren, better known as the Moravian
Church. It was in the chapel of the Moravians in London
that, on 24 May, 1738, John Wesley felt his heart "strangely
warmed by the love of Christ." From the work of the
Wesleys, the new evangelical impulse spread both to orthodox dissenting bodies in England, and to the evangelical
groups in the Church of England. Anglican Evangelicals,
always a minority in the Church, have not merely carried
a wholly disproportionate share of Anglican missionary
enterprise overseas, but, during the short period in which
they were the strongest religious force in England, exercised,
through that passion for social righteousness which resulted
in the abolition of slavery, the great Factory Acts and the
reform of the prisons, a greater Christian influence on the
life of the nation than had ever previously been attained
by any Christian group in so short a period of time. The
movement initiated by Spener had indeed produced astonishing and unexpected results.

The character of Pietism must be clearly understood. It
stood, as it were, half-way between the national type of
Church, into which everyone born in a given area was
admitted by baptism, and the privileges of which he could
exercise provided that he regularly paid the Church taxes ;
and the sect type, in which the only bond of union was a
personal profession of faith in Jesus Christ. The Pietist
leaders were good Lutherans. It was not their intention to

break up, or to separate themselves from, the national Church in which they had been brought up. They desired rather to produce an *ecclesiola in ecclesia,* a society of living Christians within the Church, which would work within the Church and be its true life. We recognise here the same principle as has led to the multiplication of orders within the Roman Catholic Church—the desire for a special type or level of sanctity that would work as leaven within the Church, by accepting heavier burdens of obligation than ordinary Church people could be expected to shoulder. In the early days of Methodism, the plan and purpose of the Wesleys was that their societies should be intimate fellowships within the Church of England. To the end of his life John Wesley bade his followers seek Communion in the national Church, and declared his own unfailing loyalty to the Church in which he had been ordained. It may be that the tendency to separatism was more deeply rooted in the Methodist programme that the Wesleys themselves had realised, and that when the later Methodists withdrew from the Communion of the Church of England, they were following the inner logic of an already developed situation, rather than yielding to the pressure of an unfriendly attitude on the part of the official Church.

It is easy to see the weaknesses of Pietism. At times the emphasis on personal sanctification tended to produce an anxious and introspective individualism. The demand for conscious experience of the grace of God did, in some Pietistic circles, though never in the teaching of the great leaders, obscure the sheer objectivity of the grace of God and of the acts of redemption on which the salvation of men depends. Members of any exclusive society within the Church are always in danger of falling into just that Pharisaism that they themselves would be the first to condemn. Pietists have been inclined to conceive the task of the Church in terms of rescuing a certain number of brands from the burning, rather than as the assertion of the lordship of Christ over every part and aspect of the life of men.[1] Despairing of the present evil world, they have sometimes exaggerated the tendency, present in all the later Lutheranism, so to misinterpret Luther's doctrine of the two realms as to surrender the whole world of the state and of government to the devil, and to deny to the Church any responsibility for the application of the principles of the Gospel to the political, social and economic problems of man in society. In some circles, though never in the strong traditions of Pietism at its best, a sentimental Jesuolatry has taken the place of the robust Trinitarian faith of the New Testament.

But when the worst has been said that can be said, it yet remains the fact that, in the non-Roman western world, the Pietists and they alone took seriously the obligation resting on the Church to preach the Gospel to every creature. Without their contribution, Protestant missionary endeavour would have been a thin and ineffective shadow of what in their hands it has become. This interest of the Pietists in the evangelisation of Jews and heathen peoples was in part a direct consequence of their doctrine of the necessity for every human being of individual conversion. Members of a state Church tend to expect that every man will naturally continue in that form of religion into which he has been born ; the Pietist, accustomed to challenge his Lutheran neighbour with the demand that he should manifest the signs of true conversion, did not find it difficult to extend this thought beyond the Lutheran world, and to believe that the conversion of the heathen was possible, desirable and ought to be attempted. In part, however, the missionary impulse appears to have been connected with eschatological expectations, and with the idea that a great conversion of Jews and non-Christians

---

[1] J. R. Brutsch, discussing, in an unpublished thesis, the missionary plans and methods of Zinzendorf, remarks, " Une critique fondamentale doit être présentée a cette pensée: l'absence complète de la notion d'Eglise. Malgré sa pensée essentiellement christocentrique, Zinzendorf a complètement laissé de coté le réalisme biblique du corps de Christ."

was to be among the signs preceding the coming again of Christ in glory, an event to which every Pietist in every age has looked forward with strained and tender anticipation.

The Moravian Church of the Brethren has always been a small body. Nevertheless, before the death of Zinzendorf, two hundred and twenty-six missionaries had been sent out to different areas of the world. Zinzendorf's attention had been drawn to the missionary problem, when, during a visit to Copenhagen, he had found himself in contact with a negro from West Africa and some Greenlanders. Greenland was one of the first of the mission fields adopted by the Moravians. But their greatest enterprise began with the sending of two brothers to the West Indies in 1732. The latest figures available shew that, in Dutch Guiana, the Moravian Church numbers 140,000 adherents and 34,782 communicants, and that almost the whole population is now Christian.[1] The missionary zeal of this devoted body of Christians has never failed. Many of the early Moravian missionaries were simple artisans, who laboured with their hands and supported themselves, while bearing witness to the Gospel in the simple Christian fellowship of their communities, and in spoken testimony as time and the demands of their work permitted.

Elsewhere among Protestants, the idea of missionary work was beginning to take hold. The great Leibnitz (1646–1716) himself, perhaps the most universal genius that the human race has ever produced, stirred by the accounts of the Roman Catholic mission in China, put forward proposals for the establishment of a Protestant mission in that country.[2]

The most fruitful beginning, however, was to be made at Halle, in connection with the great institutions of the

---

[1] *World Christian Handbook* (London, 1949), p. 298.

[2] The connections between Leibnitz and the Pietist movement have been worked out by Ernst Troeltsch, in a paper *Leibniz und die Anfänge des Pietismus* (Gesammelte Schriften IV (Tübingen 1925), pp. 488–531) in which full recognition is accorded to the importance of Pietism as the home and origin of Protestant missionary work. But Leibnitz was not so much an apostle as a diplomat.

Franckes. The occasion was a curious survival from the
medieval tradition. King Frederick IV of Denmark, though
not himself by any means an admirable Christian, took
seriously his position as head of the Danish Church, and
began to concern himself about the spiritual welfare of
his Indian subjects in the small colonial possession of
Tranquebar on the Coromandel coast. Danish chaplains
were already established in the territory for work among
the Europeans ; but no one was found in Denmark suitable
or willing to undertake work among the Indians. Advised
by his chaplain Lütkens, the king turned to Halle.
Francke was able and willing to produce the needed men.
When, on 5 July, 1706, the two pioneers Bartholomew
Ziegenbalg and Henry Plütschau landed on the beach at
Tranquebar, a new epoch opened in the development and
expansion of the Christian society in the world.

Although Francke undertook to supply the men and the
spiritual resources for the mission, the work was not a
responsibility of either the Danish or the German church.
The missionaries were "royal missionaries," appointed by
the king of Denmark, who set aside certain revenues for
their work, and undertook to maintain it, in so far as it
concerned itself with his subjects within the limits of Danish
territory in India.

The pioneers were faced with endless and at times almost
fantastic difficulties. The chaplains on the spot pursued
them with strange and un-Christian hostility. Ziegenbalg,
who appears to have been more zealous than tactful, fell out
with the governor, and spent some time imprisoned in the
fortress. An urgently needed supply of money was allowed
through carelessness to fall into the sea, and no serious
attempt was made to recover it. The missionaries could
find no one to teach them Tamil, and in the end were reduced
to sitting on the ground with the children in an Indian
school, in order to learn the Tamil letters. Hostile criticism
was rife in Europe. Unreasonable control from authorities

in Denmark, who knew nothing of the problems of missionary work in a non-Christian country, paralysed and threatened to break up the well-considered efforts of the pioneers. Through it all they held on in faith. By slow degrees the mission began to take root and to produce its effects.

Within the first fifty years, certain principles came to be accepted, which have formed the basis of almost all subsequent non-Roman missionary work.

The missionaries found their best opening among the oppressed and the despised. They did not neglect the educated and the influential. Many conversations and disputes between the missionaries and the Brahmans are on record in the periodical letters, through which the missionaries kept friends in Europe informed of their proceedings. But it was at first only among the slaves of the European merchants, and others on a similar social level, that a Christian community was formed. This had its disadvantages. The under-privileged, even when genuinely converted to the faith, bring with them their long-established habits and points of view. They have not been trained to take responsibility for their own affairs. There is always a tendency for them to alternate between tame acquiescence in directions issued to them from above, and peevish irritation at control. The early missionaries accepted their converts as they were, with their good and bad qualities. They remembered the word of the apostle that God hath chosen the weak things of the world to confound the mighty, and believed that, as in the early days of the Church, the Gospel would work upwards from below, from the ignorant and outcast to those whose higher position in the world tended to make them less sensible of their need for the message of the Gospel.

On the whole, their faith has been justified. In the medieval period, the conversion of kings and rulers gave the signal for the acceptance of the new faith by their subjects. We have seen the Jesuits attempting to follow this method of approach in the countries of the east. But, in the main, in modern missions, the conversion of a small number of the élite has not been followed by any rapid development of the Christian community, whereas the calling and education of the poor has brought into being a living Christian community, the witness of which has spread far beyond itself into the life of the nations.

Secondly, the missionaries, although technically the servants of the Danish king, were resolved that no force or governmental pressure should be brought to bear on anyone to change his religion. If they had been under any temptation to follow the example of the Dutch or Portuguese, the hostility of the local officials would in any case have saved them from yielding to it. But it was deeply-held principle rather than circumstances that determined the policy of the missionaries in their evangelistic work. Christ had sent them to preach the Gospel ; it was by the power of the word of God alone that the Church was to be formed. If they had no church to preach in, they would preach in the open air. If they were driven out from one village, they would go to another, confident that in one place or another the good seed would fall on good ground, and that in due course the harvest would appear.

The Lutheran, and specially pietistic,[1] emphasis on the word of God naturally turned the thoughts of the missionaries at a very early date in the direction of the translation of the Scriptures. This third Protestant principle was in sharp contrast to the methods of the Roman Catholics. The Roman missions had been at work in the Tamil country for a hundred and seventy-two years before the arrival of the Protestants. In all that time, they had not, as far as is known, translated into Tamil a single chapter of the Scriptures. Ziegenbalg, as soon as he had acquired a moderate

[1] One of the merits of the Pietists of Halle was a return from the hard and dogmatically-conditioned Scriptural interpretation of the Lutheran State-Churches, to a freer exegesis, based on the text of Scripture only, and nearer, in fact, to the methods and traditions of Luther himself,

knowledge of the language, set himself to the work of translation. In 1714, the whole New Testament appeared in Tamil. The Old Testament was completed in 1729. It has to be admitted that much of the work of the pioneers was hasty and unscholarly. The great Jesuit scholar Joseph Constantius Beschi (*d.* 1742), himself the author of a Tamil epic on the life of St. Joseph, in which biblical, legendary and Indian elements are strangely mingled, wrote unkindly but not altogether untruly that, on looking at a page of the printed work of the Lutheran missionaries, " one rubs one's eyes in amazement ; involuntarily one bursts into loud laughter." No one who has had experience of the difficulty of the task will think lightly of these first stumbling efforts. Rough beginnings can be polished and improved. Here, as in other spheres, it is the first step that counts.

These first attempts of the Lutherans were to point the way to the grandiose achievements of William Carey (1761–1834) and his associates at Serampore. Carey himself translated the whole Bible into Bengali and Sanskrit, and directed or supervised versions in almost all the main languages of India. His colleague Joshua Marshman succeeded in producing the New Testament even in Chinese.[1] All the great languages of India had an extensive poetical literature ; in none of them had prose literature developed beyond elementary beginnings. In many languages of the East, the Bible has played the same part in the formation of modern prose style as Tyndale's English New Testament or Luther's German Bible in Europe ; with this one great difference, that the European versions grew out of a civilisation that had already been profoundly Christianised, whereas the translators in the East were wrestling all the time with the problems of unfamiliar thought-forms and with

---

[1] This was a remarkable achievement. The Serampore Chinese New Testament is a masterpiece of beautiful printing. It is impossible, however, not to regret the time spent on this *tour de force*: a satisfactory Chinese New Testament could not be produced anywhere but in China ; the great Robert Morrison was already at work in Canton, and completed his own version of the whole Bible in 1819.

the recalcitrance of languages that had never undergone
any preliminary domestication to the expression of Christian
truth.[1]

An even more distinguished contribution was made by the
Anglican chaplain, Henry Martyn (1781–1812), who, dying
worn out at the age of thirty-one, left behind him complete
translations of the New Testament in Urdu and in Persian.
Whereas most of the early translators were self-taught men,
doing their best in face of grievous limitations, Martyn
brought to the work not merely brilliant linguistic gifts,
but also the best philological training that the age could
supply. The defects of most of the pioneer translations
have been found to be so great that they have had to be
completely abandoned and the whole work done afresh.
Through all subsequent revisions, Martyn's work has
remained the basis of the Urdu New Testament.[2]

Fourthly, the Protestant missionaries worked with the
intention that as soon as possible members of their new
fellowships should be admitted to the full ministry of the
Church, as they themselves understood it. The ordination
of the first Indian " country priest " after the Lutheran rite
took place in 1726. The number of men so admitted to
the ministry was never large. Candidates were carefully

[1] Much interesting and topical material in S. Pearce Carey's *William
Carey* (London, 3rd edition, 1924). But no later book can really take the
place of *The Life and Times of Carey, Marshman and Ward*, (London, 1864).
by John Clark Marshman. The younger Marshman had lived through
many of the scenes that he described, and wrote the story from within.
Carey did not limit himself to the Bible; historians of Bengali literature
ascribe to his Bengali *Colloquies* an even greater importance in the development of a simple and idiomatic prose style in Bengali.

[2] The limits of this book make it impossible to follow this story further.
It is well known that the number of languages in which some portion of the
Scriptures exists now considerably exceeds one thousand. The vast
majority of these translations has been made in connection with the
missionary work of the non-Roman Churches of the west. There is
agreement among all the missionary agencies of the varying confessions
that the production of the Scriptures in the language of the people at the
earliest possible date is one of the indispensable foundations of the Christian
society. This is one of the clearest differences between Roman and non-
Roman missionary work. Very early examples of Roman versions of the
Scriptures in Chinese exist; but these are exceptions to an otherwise almost
unvarying practice, that the Scriptures are not put into the hands of the
ordinary members of that Church.

selected and trained, and only a few were found able to rise to the standard regarded as necessary. But those entrusted with the ministry did valiant service, especially as towards the end of the century the fires of Pietism began to burn low, and the number of European missionaries to decline. Then some of the country priests alone maintained the continuity of the Church between the small efforts of Tranquebar, and the immense tide of Protestant missionary endeavour that began to come in with the beginning of the Nineteenth Century.[1]

The political associations of the Tranquebar mission before long led the missionaries into difficulties. The Danish territory was very small, and not many years were required for its thorough evangelisation. Naturally the missionaries looked beyond it, and began to spread out into areas where British or French influence was dominant. The king of Denmark was firm in his policy ; the money assigned by him to the mission could be used for one purpose only, and could not be diverted to the support of missionaries living outside the Danish area. The difficulty was overcome through the interest aroused in England by the work at Tranquebar. Alongside the Danish mission, the English mission came into being.

The name is somewhat misleading. As in Lutheran Denmark, so in Anglican England, no one was found desirous of adventuring himself in a distant mission field.[2] All that happened was that those of the Tranquebar mission who worked in other than Danish territory were taken over and supported from the funds of the Society for the Promotion of

---

[1] The impression must not be given that at this point the difference between Roman and Protestant methods was greater than it actually was. As we have seen, the Jesuits were very slow and cautious in admitting any of their converts to a rank in the mission higher than that of catechist. Other missions were less strict. Many Goanese were ordained to the priesthood. In certain areas, results may have suggested to the Jesuits that theirs was the better policy.

[2] This is not quite fair to Denmark. Though the first missionaries were all Germans, there were later a few Danes in the Danish mission. There were no English in the English mission.

Christian Knowledge in London. This led to some unusual situations. German Lutheran missionaries not merely drew their support from the Church of England. On many occasions they served as chaplains to British soldiers and civilians, and not merely evangelised the heathen, but baptised, married, buried, and celebrated the Holy Communion according to the Prayer Book of the Church of England. Relations between the Church of England and continental Protestantism at the time were such that this arrangement seems to have aroused no unfavourable comment in either country.[1]

Of the missionaries of the English mission, by far the most distinguished was Christian Friedrich Schwartz, a prince among men, who laboured without a break from 1750 till 1798. Schwartz was unique, both in the simplicity of his character and in his capacity to win the confidence of men of every kind. British generals and Indian rulers equally found him irresistible. A new aspect was given to the work of the mission when for a period Schwartz became the Dewan or Prime Minister of the Raja of Tanjore. No change took place in his daily habits ; he passed without the least sense of incongruity from the high affairs of state to catechising children in the Christian school. No suggestion was ever made that he used his political influence unfairly in favour of the mission. But there is no doubt that the influence of Schwartz in the state added prestige to the new religion, and led many to become enquirers who would otherwise have held aloof. By the end of his life, Schwartz

[1] The first Tamil translation of the Prayer Book was made by German Lutheran missionaries. It need hardly be said that the idea of comity did not exist in the Eighteenth Century. A Roman Catholic described the Protestants in the choice phrase, " The Lutherans, bent on their work of the destruction of souls." Protestants took over discontented or neglected Roman Catholics wherever they could. On their own principles, both parties regarded themselves as justified in their attitudes and policies. Even in the Twentieth Century, the spirit of rivalry and of hostility has not been wholly eliminated.

is recorded himself to have baptised not less than 2,000 converts.[1]

The fame of Schwartz spread throughout the world. But it is not to be supposed that his efforts and those of his companions and of the Moravians remained isolated in the world of the non-Roman Churches. As early as 1701, the Anglican Society for the Propagation of the Gospel had been founded, specially with a view to work in British possessions in the western world. The Dutch continued their work in Ceylon and in the East Indian islands. But almost all these enterprises were on a small scale, and were hampered by certain national and racial limitations. The immense importance of the work of William Carey lay in the world-wide sweep of his imagination, and of the challenge that he presented to the churches as a whole.

Anglo-Saxons have tended to exaggerate the part played by Carey, forgetting that he was building on the experience of the pioneers of the Eighteenth Century. But without exaggeration his achievement places him in the front rank of those who have extended the borders of the Christian Society. His first great book was published in Leicester in 1792, under the characteristic and cumbrous title, *An Enquiry into the Obligations of Christians to Use Means for the Conversion of the Heathens. In which the Religious State of the World, the Success of the Former Undertakings, and the Practicability of Further Undertakings are Considered.* The work was based on a comprehensive survey of the history of the Christian Church, of the population of the world, of all existing missionary activities, including those of the Roman Catholics, and ended with practical proposals for the preaching of the Gospel throughout the world. Essentially, Carey's work was inspired by a return to the Bible, and to

---

[1] It is a curious illustration of the ignorance of even eminent men concerning the spread of the Gospel that an Indian civilian, giving evidence before the House of Commons in 1793, stated that he had known Mr. Schwartz, who was a very respectable man; but he believed that he had never made more than one convert.

the simple convictions of the apostolic Church. But even biblical theology is influenced by contemporary factors. The horizons of thousands of British readers had been enlarged by the narrative of the voyages of Captain Cook. A new world consciousness, a new sense of imperial responsibility were coming into being in the nations of northern Europe. The Christian application of the new knowledge would not have been apparent, unless someone with Carey's vision and passion had set it forth in a way that the plain man could understand ; but when it was set forth, the soil was already to some extent prepared to receive the missionary idea. In Carey's work the eschatological element is less present than in much Protestant missionary writing. He takes his stand on the plain principle that the kingdom of Christ is to be established in the world, and that it cannot be established without the preaching of the word of God to every nation ; whether the church has ten years or ten thousand to accomplish this task is not his concern ; he is prepared to leave that to the providence of God, and simply to arouse the churches to do at once what, with the resources at their command and with the help of God, is within their power.

The Pietist strain had been strong in all the earlier Protestant missions. The concern had been with the individual. Men are perishing without the knowledge of Christ in a sinful world that is going headlong to destruction ; some at least must be rescued before the day of judgment from the general condemnation. So to the individual the appeal is addressed. When individuals responded and were baptised, all the problems of organisation and of the formation of a Church had to be faced. But generally speaking there was no thought-out policy in advance. The Protestants had not, like the Roman Catholics, the sense of an already existing world-wide Church, to which any new churches in the formerly non-Christian regions were simply added as extensions. They reproduced faithfully the pattern of church life with which they had been familiar in their home land. Like the pietistic groups in the formal churches of the continent of Europe, the Christian groups overseas were islands in the surrounding sea of non-Christians, fed in the same way by the study of the Bible, by singing the same type of hymns, and with the same individual sense of responsibility to God for personal conduct.

With Carey's thought and in his work, the whole scheme takes on a grander outline. He is already thinking in terms of the evangelisation of whole countries, and of what is to happen when whole populations become Christian. He sees in advance that the foreign missionary can never make more than a small contribution to the accomplishment of the work that has to be done, and that therefore the development of the local ministry on the largest scale is the first and greatest of all missionary considerations. Above all, he sees that Christianity must be firmly rooted in the culture and traditions of the land in which it is planted, even though its first task be to overthrow the old world of non-Christian thought and to re-create it from its own ashes. When Ziegenbalg wrote a pioneer book on *The Genealogy of the Dravidian Gods*, he was sharply criticised by the mission board, on the ground that his task was to preach the word of God in India and not to propagate heathen superstition in Europe ; in consequence the book remained unprinted for a hundred and fifty years. Carey and his companions launched themselves courageously into all the intricacies of Hindu thought. These studies they did not regard as in any way a distraction from their missionary work. On the contrary, they regarded a full understanding of Hindu thought as an essential part of their equipment, not only because the preacher of the Gospel cannot be clearly understood if he speaks merely out of the self-confidence of his own knowledge, but also because they understood that it is not only the souls and bodies of men that need to be redeemed—the thought-world of a non-Christian nation is also one of those realms that are to be taken captive and brought into subjection to Christ. The signal once given, the non-Roman world was quick to respond. The London Missionary Society was founded in 1795, the Church Missionary Society four years later. One missionary organisation after another followed rapidly in every country of the west. By the end of the Nineteenth Century, almost every Christian body, from the Orthodox Church of Russia to the Salvation Army, and almost every country, from the Lutheran Church of Finland and the Waldensian Church of Italy to the newest sects in the United States, had its share in the missionary enterprise overseas. At last the challenge presented by the Roman Catholics was being seriously taken up. In at least one sense, the concept of the Holy Catholic Church, which had been obscured at the time of the Reformation, was being recovered by the Christian churches outside the Roman obedience.

CHAPTER IX

THE FAITH AND THE GREAT RELIGIONS

THE Christian society was born within the womb of Jewry. One of its first tasks was to make itself at home in the world of Greco-Roman civilisation. This was the less difficult, because the Old Testament had already been translated into Greek, and a fruitful interplay between Hellenism and Judaism, which had modified both these somewhat irreconcilable worlds, had prepared the way for the acclimatisation of the new message in the minds of men. The Scriptures of the New Testament were written in Greek, the *lingua franca* of all educated men from Spain to the borders of India. There was at first resistance in the Church to any assimilation of the Gospel to the world of thought by which it was surrounded. But for good and evil the decision was taken in the other sense. Christian scholars learned to re-think their Christian thoughts in terms of the culture of the day, and to express them in thought-forms that would be familiar to educated men among their contemporaries. Both worlds, that of Christian faith and that of classical thought, underwent modifications in the process. Once made, the decision could not be reversed. Through the whole of subsequent Christian history, the ancient classics of Greece and Rome have been accepted as the basis of Christian education, a position from which, even in our own day, they have been only slowly and partially dislodged.

The nations of northern and central Europe had no developed culture of their own, which could successfully resist the onward march of the composite Greco-Roman Christian civilisation. It is true that this civilisation did not remain unchanged. The Celtic, Scandinavian and Teutonic races, as they were brought within the orbit of the Christian culture, impressed upon it something of their own genius and racial experience. Even within the Roman Catholic Church, there is a place for national and linguistic differentiation ; the Church in Germany is not exactly what it is in France or Italy. The Slavonic peoples have diverged further from the original tradition than the races which were more directly subjected to Greco-Roman influence. Yet among them the inheritance of Byzantium is still creative. Even Protestantism, with all its emphasis on freedom, has not broken away completely from the older tradition, but has developed in the main within the framework established by the great Fathers of the Church between the time of Origen and that of Augustine.

It is obvious that, as soon as the Christian society breaks out of the familiar Greco-Roman world, all the initial problems have to be faced again in a new guise. Ideally the Church remains always and unchangeably the same. As history shows, it cannot in fact escape the destiny of constant action and reaction with the world in the midst of which it is set.

The world, as it has come to be known through the researches of recent years, may be divided into a number of great cultural regions, within each of which subsist a number of varieties, and, in certain parts of the world, surviving elements of more ancient cultures now submerged. As the Christian society moved eastwards, it found itself confronted by three great patterns of culture, each with its own system of thought, each linked to great historic religions that have sprung from its cultural background and in the course of history have profoundly modified it.

Islam is the only one among the great religions of the world which is post-Christian, and much in its intellectual development has been conditioned by the Christian sources from

which in part it has been derived. Yet, with all its similarities, the Muslim way of life and its outlook on the world
are so different from those of the west that this vast area,
stretching from the Atlantic ocean almost to Australia, can
be conveniently regarded as one distinct cultural region. The
dominance of one religion, Islam, and one language, Arabic,
give it a unity even more intricately integrated than that
of the Latin west in medieval Europe. Common action
unites men even more effectively than common thought.
The five daily hours of prayer, and the repetition of the
same prayers in exactly the same way throughout the Muslim
world, are more than an external conformity ; they are the
outward expression of a spiritual trend towards unity that
is of immeasurable strength.

The world of Indian culture is not so firmly unified, but
also presents itself as a distinctive area of human life and
thought. The history of India has been broken by innumerable invasions and by the domination of one alien
power after another. In contrast with this, the history of
Indian thought presents an unbroken continuity of more than
three thousand years, with countless variations within itself,
yet always returning again to the expression of certain
central ideas. This is the territory of the great world-
denying religions. The spiritual quest of India has been
for the true unity underlying all the changing phenomena
of the material world. Once the spiritual has been identified
with the non-material, as it has been in Hindu thought,
the material world is condemned as the place of frustration
and alienation. History can have no inner principle of
meaning as the unfolding of a divine purpose. Redemption
is not so much moral, through deliverance from sin, as
metaphysical, through the enlightenment that leads to
escape from the *Samsāra*[1] of unending change. The last

---

[1] The wheel of being, to which, according to Hindu thought, the soul,
Ātman, is bound through ignorance and through the commission of acts
which demand expiation. There are various ways of release: that offered
by Hindu philosophy is the *Jnāna-mārga*, the way of wisdom, which

thing that is desired of eternity is the survival of the
individual personality ; salvation is the end of differentiation,
and the absorption into the undifferentiated One of that
which through birth in time had become separate.

Hinduism has been the matrix of two other great religions,
Buddhism and Jainism. It is this that makes it difficult
to define exactly the limits of its area. It is convenient
to treat Burma and Ceylon, where Buddhism survived
after its disappearance from India, as part of the world
of Hindu culture. But, in one of the former extensions
of the Indian sphere, Indonesia, Hinduism has been overlaid,
except in the island of Bali, by Islam, and in Cambodia by
Buddhism. And the immense extensions of Buddhism in
Tibet, China and Japan, which were never under the Hindu
influence, must be treated as one determining factor in a
widely different cultural pattern.

This third area, that of the Sino-Japanese culture, manifests, like the Indian, the characteristic of immense stability
underneath constant political and superficial change. Here,
however, the emphasis is less spiritual and more consciously
ethical. Chinese thought has concentrated itself on the
pattern of human society, and on the duties of the virtuous
man in society. Confucianism is the focal point, from
which the other religious developments of China must be
considered. There have been specifically religious and even
mystical strains, through which the craving of man for
warmth in religion has been satisfied. But this mystical
element has been always in the background of Chinese
experience ; the foreground has been occupied by the
picture of the Confucian wise man, on whose devoted
attention to the details of correct conduct the stability of
Chinese society has for centuries depended. This reverence
for the existing order, as it has come to be crystallised in

consists essentially in the recognition that the $\bar{A}tman$ in man is the same
as the universal Self of the Universe, the *Brahman*, and that the appearance
of separate self-hood is mere illusion.

the experience of the past, is set forth in the characteristic Chinese practice of ancestor-worship.

The Japanese are in almost every way different from the Chinese. Just as Christianity was modified by the racial experience of the groups to which it came, so Buddhism, and all else that has come from China, has been transformed into a Japanese pattern. But culturally the Japanese have not shewn any great creative gift, and therefore it is usual to include Japan with China in the one great cultural area, the more naturally since the extension of Buddhism has made so strong a link between the two countries.

The early missionaries were hardly aware of the cultural conflict that the introduction of the Gospel into such contexts was bound sooner or later to produce. To most of them, Christianity in its western form was Christianity ; western civilisation was Christian civilisation, besides which there could be no other. Therefore to make an Indian or a Malay a Christian was *ipso facto* in greater or less measure to turn him into a Dutchman or a Portuguese. It is easy to condemn too readily this point of view. Every Christian society, and every individual Christian, combines with the faith much that is not intrinsic to it ; it is almost impossible to detach oneself from presuppositions and ways of living that in fact derive not from the New Testament but from the traditions of men. This problem has pursued all missionary work from the beginning. None the less, the consequences of such an alien presentation can be disastrous to the progress of the Gospel. If Christianity appears in association with western habits that are shocking to the mind of another people, such as the eating of meat, or a greater familiarity between the sexes than is permitted in most eastern societies, the prejudice called into being by the unnecessary accretion is such as to make it almost impossible for the Gospel to be seen as it really is. The faith is condemned before it is even examined.

If it were possible to present the essential Gospel, free

from any human alloy, to do so would undoubtedly be the duty of the Christian messenger. Since this is, in practice, impossible, there seem to be only two alternatives—that the missionary should present the Gospel frankly as he has known it, in the form it has assumed in his own Church and country, or that he should endeavour as best he may to assimilate it to the culture and the thought-forms of the people to whom he goes. Which of the two courses is the more perilous has long been a matter of debate among the advocates of missionary enterprise.

One of the greatest attempts ever made to grapple with this problem was that of the noble Italian Jesuit, Robert de Nobili, who reached Madura, the cultural capital of the Tamil country in South India, in 1606. De Nobili observed at once that the customs of the Portuguese and of their converts in the area were such as to arouse an ineradicable hostility to the Gospel in the minds of the members of the more cultured classes. Helped by his Italian nationality, which at once made possible a distinction between him and the Portuguese, as well as by a singularly versatile intellect, he decided to abandon European ways and associations, and to make himself an Indian among the Indians in order that the Gospel might have free course among them. After a period during which he was observing very closely the habits of life of the Brahmans and acquiring the language, he adopted the dress of a Brahman ascetic, and followed in every particular the rules of life by which every detail of the Brahman's day is governed, except that at certain points Christian ceremonies were substituted for those which were distinctly idolatrous. He even went so far as to wear the sacred thread, by which the " twice-born " castes are distinguished from the lower orders, though his thread was of different material from that worn by an Indian Brahman.[1]

[1] Unlike most of his predecessors, de Nobili realised that it was essential for a missionary to master the language of the country in which he worked. Max Müller has described him as the first European Sanskrit scholar. He acquired sufficient fluency in Tamil to debate readily in that language

Almost immediately the new policy began to take effect. Instead of shunning the foreigner, Hindus of good quality began to come about the man who lived among them so simply and familiarly, and in whose house they were sure not to meet anything that could shock their susceptibilities or infringe the purity of their caste. The moment was in some ways favourable. India has always been familiar with the appearance of new ascetic teachers, and of reforming sects differing in the details of their practice from their predecessors, and directed to the recovery of the initial purity of the Hindu faith. At the end of the Sixteenth Century, the Tamil race seemed for the moment to have exhausted the springs of the great creative period in literature, architecture and religion, which had lasted for nearly eight centuries ; intellectual curiosity was still alert, but there was little that was new to satisfy it, and therefore the keen dialectic of de Nobili, against the background of a rigid asceticism with certain new forms of austerity, was well calculated to attract attention and an initial degree of favour. On 1 Dec., 1607, de Nobili was able to write, with pardonable self-satisfaction : "Whereas previously in twelve years it had proved impossible to make a single Christian, in six months I have baptised no less than ten."

The number of high-caste converts was never large. Later legend has swelled the figure to fantastic proportions. Sober study of the figures supplied in the Annual Letters of the Jesuits reveals that in 1643, after thirty-seven years of work, not more than 600 "pagans of noble caste" had been baptised. Two years later, the Letter records frankly that a great many from the higher ranks had apostatised.[1] It

with Hindu scholars, and to leave behind a number of written works in Tamil. The best account of de Nobili known to me is that by Fr. P. Dahmen, *Robert de Nobili* (Münster in Westfalen, 1924). The chapter in *Six Great Missionaries* by Fr. D. Jenks (London, 1930) is more readily accessible to English readers.

[1] The same uncertainty attaches to all early missionary statistics as to the numbers in the Old Testament. In general, actual figures in tens and hundreds are to be taken seriously; thousands have to be viewed with suspicion; hundreds of thousands may be discounted.

remains true that de Nobili, by his policy of accommodation, had found a new way into the heart of an alien and hitherto almost unapproachable civilisation.

His policy was not without its enemies and critics. The upholders of the older policies regarded the work of de Nobili with a mixture of rage, jealousy and incomprehension ; some of them even went so far as to declare that he had abandoned the faith and become a Hindu. The attacks were concentrated on three points—the use by Christians of a spot of sandal-wood paste on the forehead, the wearing of a sacred thread, and growing the hair in a tuft at the back of the head, all usages permitted by de Nobili as having only a social significance, and condemned by his opponents as being integral parts of Hindu usage and inseparable from the Hindu religion. It is unnecessary to follow the details of the long contest, pursued with relentless vigour over more than a century. Suffice it to say that, though de Nobili's practices were modified in certain particulars, in the main his cause was declared to be the good one, and the authorities of the Roman Church accepted in principle the idea that without derogation from the holy doctrines of the faith there might be a measure of adaptation to the customs and even to the prejudices of a non-Christian country.

A precisely similar storm blew up in China. Roman Catholics pray for the faithful departed, and invoke the prayers of the saints. To what extent do these practices justify the retention by Christians of the Chinese custom of ancestor worship and veneration of the memory of great teachers like Confucius ? Were these local customs of the kind that Gregory the Great had told Augustine not to be too hasty in suppressing among the Anglo-Saxons ? Or were they departures from the faith that would in time involve heresy? Could masses for the dead be said on behalf of non-Christian Chinese ancestors ? Above all, since the Chinese language contains no word which can without question be used as the correct translation of the word GOD, which of the available

terms can be used without prejudice to the distinctiveness
of Christian truth ?[1] Again, must Chinese priests be
required to learn Latin ? Is it not better that they should
master classical Chinese, a difficult enough task, to put them
on the level of the Chinese *litterati* without whose respect
the witness of the Church in China is likely to remain
ineffective.[2]

On all these matters controversy raged back and forth
for nearly a hundred and fify years. The Jesuits, on the
whole, followed Ricci in giving wide scope to the continuance
of traditional Chinese usages, believing that the Chinese
Christians themselves, as they grew in understanding
of the faith, would be able to discriminate between those
which were purely social in character, and those which
in any way conflicted with the purity of the Christian
faith. The other orders and the secular clergy were ranged
almost unanimously in the hostile camp. The situation
was complicated by the participation of the emperor
Kang-Hsi, who in 1700 issued a declaration upholding the
policy of his friends the Jesuits. Rome decided otherwise. By the Bull *Ex illa die*, promulgated by Clement XI
in March 1715, reiterated by Benedict XIV in the Bull

[1] This dispute has left its mark on English literature, in the Pope's speech
in Browning's *The Ring and the Book*, 11, 1591-1604:

   " Five years since, in the Province of To-kien
   Which is in China, as some people know,
   Maigrot, my Vicar Apostolic there,
   Having a great qualm, issues a decree.
   Alack, the converts use as God's name, not
   Tien-chu but plain *Tien* or else mere *Shang-ti*,
   As Jesuits please to fancy politic,
   While, say Dominicans, it calls down fire—
   For *Tien* means heaven, and *Shang-ti* supreme prince,
   While *Tien-chu* means the lord of heaven; all cry,
   ' There is no business urgent for despatch
   As that thou send a legate, specially
   Cardinal Tournon, straight to Pekin, there
   To settle and compose the difference.' "

[2] "In 1659, 1669 and 1673, the privilege was given to the vicars apostolic
to ordain to the priesthood natives who did not know Latin well. They
were required, however, to know enough Latin to understand the sense
of the mass, and the sacramental formulas." K. S. Latourette, *A History
of Christian Missions in China* (London, S.P.C.K. 1929), p. 133, n. 1.

Ex quo singulari of 11 July, 1742, almost all concessions to Chinese customs were forbidden, and the missionaries were ordered to set forth the Catholic faith in form and custom, as it had been consecrated by centuries of experience in Europe. Latin was to be, and still is, the sole ecclesiastical language of the Roman Church in China.

The slowness and the hesitations manifested by Rome will be criticised only by those who have failed to realise the novelty and the depth of the problems involved. For the first time since the age of the Fathers, the Church was faced with all the problems involved in integrating the faith with great systems of culture, determined by non-Christian religions and venerable by their antiquity.[1] As has been realised with increasing clearness in modern times, systems of thought and of religious practice are held by those who profess them, in their totality. A custom, even one which seems in itself to be morally neutral, when detached from its original context and introduced into another, either remains as an undigested bloc of alien material in the new system, or is transformed by it. A new idea introduced from without into a homogeneous system of thought ends by changing the whole character of the system. The missionaries were right in desiring that Indians and Chinese should not be unnecessarily shocked by western additions to the original Christian deposit. Rome was right in seeing that the Gospel is always an explosive and revolutionary force, and that any attempt to disguise this fact is likely in the end to change the Gospel into something else.[2]

[1] The Franciscan missions of the Thirteenth Century had been too sporadic to raise the problems in full intensity. The heroic attempt of Ramon Lull (c. 1231–1315) to rethink the Gospel in terms of Islamic dialectic and thus to meet the challenge of the Muslim World was never adequately followed up. See Allison Peers, *Ramon Lull—a Biography* (London, 1929).

[2] Social custom in India, where uninfluenced by western habits, demands that a married woman should not in any circumstances be touched by any man other than her own husband. I know, from personal experience, the extreme reluctance of women converts of good standing to accept the necessity of the laying on of hands in Confirmation. But the Church of India rightly refuses to compromise on what it holds to be the essential element in this sacramental rite.

The problem may be summed up as follows : How is it possible for the Christian faith ever to penetrate a non-Christian society, if it presents itself from the start as so alien as to be immediately repudiated by the society it seeks to penetrate ? How can it retain its distinctiveness, as a Christian society, if it identifies itself with a society the basic presuppositions of which are wholly different ?

There is a distinctiveness of the Christian society which derives from the distinctiveness of the Christian message. Probably the apostasy of so many of de Nobili's converts is to be accounted for by their failure to realise this from the start. They accepted the Gospel as preached by de Nobili and his colleagues as a new system of philosophy, accompanied by certain new disciplines, which could be practised within the Hindu framework. They had not taken account of the fact that the Gospel involves a total view of God, of man and of the world, and that this must work itself out in a complete reconstruction of life in every aspect and in all its details. When this was borne in upon them, the majority were unprepared to go the whole way in accepting the consequences of their profession of faith, and so withdrew.

As the non-Christian religions themselves became better aware of the significance of the Christian message, they closed their ranks in uncompromising hostility. The problem of integration or segregation was solved, not by thought-out policy, but by the hard facts of the situation.

Missionaries have been severely criticised for separating their converts from their normal surroundings, and for gathering them in Christian settlements of which the foreign missionary was the natural head and leader. It may be that this line of least resistance has at times been too easily followed, and justified by the pietistic concept of separation from the world. But in many situations it is hard to see what other line could have been followed.

In Islamic countries, as we have seen, a considerable

measure of toleration has been afforded to existing Christian communities. But the Muslim attitude to the Muslim who desires to forsake the faith of his fathers and become an "idolater" is very different. The law demands the death of the apostate. Even in countries where western influence makes it impossible for this law to be put into effect in its full severity, the situation of the convert may be one of grave peril, in which life itself is endangered. In many instances, the only course open to the missionaries has been to take the convert under their personal protection, or to send him to some place far from his home, in which his identity would be unknown, and he could find safety in the shelter of an established community.[1]

In Hindu India, the virtue of tolerance of new ideas is carried almost to an extreme. Hinduism is so flexible and versatile that it finds room within itself for both the most spiritual and the most materialistic philosophies.[2] But this tolerance breaks down if a seeker goes beyond the entertainment of new ideas to the point of deserting the community in which he has been born and of seeking entrance into another. Baptism is the rock of offence. To this day, if a Brahman accepts Christian baptism, the funeral ceremonies will be performed for him, and from that moment he will be regarded as dead by all the members of his family. In a slightly lower level of society, a similar result is reached by refusing to the convert the right to draw water from the village well, to buy in the village shop, to inherit his share of the property of the joint-family of which he is a member, and to participate in any of the communal functions of the village. In

---

[1] It is still so commonly believed and asserted that there have never been any Christian converts from Islam that it is worth placing on record the fact that, in every Muslim country, there has been a small but steady stream of converts. One of the most distinguished was the Rev. Imad-ud-din, who was awarded in 1884 the Lambeth degree of Doctor in Divinity for his services in the work of Bible translation and Christian literature, the first Indian ever to receive this distinction.

[2] The philosophic system of the Lokayatas is strictly materialistic. See Dasgupta, *History of Indian Philosophy* (Cambridge, 1922), Vol. I, p. 78; and Vol. III, pp. 512 *et seq.*

the extreme case, he has no choice but either to renounce
his faith or to join the Christian family in a segregated
mission society.

The number of converts from the higher and educated
classes has never been large in any eastern country. It
is easy to see that the development of a true Christian
society among them presents innumerable problems, for
which no easy solution can be found. Societies grow only
from deep roots. An eastern society cannot grow from
western roots. But if the members of the group have been
cut off from their natural eastern roots, how can they ever
grow into a society at all ? The tendency has been for the
small Christian groups to withdraw into themselves, to build
themselves up on biblical foundations, in a Christian thought-
world mediated largely through western minds, to develop
a society rather self-consciously alien from that by which
it is surrounded, and lacking those natural points of social
contact with members of other societies through which the
spontaneous expansion of the Christian society is possible.

The extreme example of this tendency is shewn in the
history of the great church of the " Thomas Christians " on
the Malabar coast of south-west India. The Christians
seem to have been originally merchants from Mesopotamia ;
they retained their connections with the Nestorian Patriarch
of Babylon, and received their bishops from him. In course
of time they settled down, and, like that other community
of merchants the Parsis of Bombay, became an integral part
of the Indian community. They had in their hands almost a
monopoly of the immensely profitable traffic in pepper and
spices. Local rulers accorded to them privileges, recorded
on copper-plate tablets which have been preserved, by which
their status in society was determined. In effect, the
Christians were integrated into the Indian caste-system,
being given a position roughly equivalent to that of the
Nairs, the great Hindu land-holding class, and second only
to that of the Brahmans. Whatever may have been the

intention of the rulers, the result was that Christianity as a religious force was insulated and rendered innocuous. The Christians, finding themselves unable to make fresh converts among the higher castes, and not wishing to share their privilege with those socially inferior to themselves, gave up the attempt to evangelise, and remained for a thousand years a separated Christian community, remarkably free from contamination by the influences of the surrounding non-Christian religions, but also exercising remarkably little Christian influence on its neighbours. This was a genuinely Christian society ; but a Christian society which fails to expand and to convert is in danger of losing one of those characteristic marks without which it cannot be more than nominally the Body of Christ.

The growth of oriental scholarship and of national feeling in the east combined, towards the end of the Nineteenth Century, to produce a new outlook in the small educated Christian communities. The supercilious attitude towards eastern religion and learning, represented at its most complacent by Macaulay, gave way to almost superstitious veneration for the treasures of a culture now known to be considerably older than that of Europe. Christians, and others, in the east learned from western scholars to look back to their own great traditions, to respect them, and to regard them as a part of God's providential dealing with humanity.

One of the first questions provoked by this new attitude of reverence for the past was exactly that raised by Marcion in the Second Century as to the place of the Old Testament in the Christian Church. The Old Testament is a Jewish book, the record of the providential dealing of God with the Jewish people. Is the Gospel for ever bound to that Jewish background, or is it so emancipated from it as to stand in its own right ? Is Christ the fulfilment of the aspirations only of the Jewish race ? Or is he also the crown and fruition of the long search of the eastern peoples after truth ? May not the ancient scriptures of the ethnic religions be regarded as playing, in the history of the eastern nations, the same providential part as was played in the history of Israel by the revelation given in the Old Testament ? Should not Christianity be presented to these peoples as the crown and fulfilment of the best that their fathers had known, and not as the destructive force that alienates a man from his own national and cultural heritage and sends him out alone and unprotected into a world for which nothing in his previous training has prepared him ?[1]

Instances are on record in China, in which selections from the writings of Confucius have been read in Christian worship. Indian Christians have proposed that selections from the ancient Hindu Scriptures should take the place of Old Testament readings, as being more intelligible and more closely related to the life and thought-world of the Indian to whom Christ has come as Saviour.

Those who advance such proposals have failed to give weight to the truth emphasised above, that every religious system is a whole, and that a piece taken out of one system and transferred to another cannot be other than an old patch on a new garment. They fail also to recognise the unique place of the Old Testament as witness to a unique work of God, incommensurable with any other, in the preparation of the world for the coming of Christ, and as containing the groundwork of thought, on which alone the teaching of the Church can be surely based.[2]

And yet those who are seeking new ways for the integration of the Christian society in a non-Christian world are raising a real problem, and one to which the Church has never found a finally satisfactory answer. Christ stated that He came to fulfil the Law and the Prophets and not to destroy them. How was this fulfilment accomplished ? And if he

[1] This attitude is perfectly expressed in the title of a book of Christian apologetic, *The Crown of Hinduism*, by the well-known scholar J. N. Farquhar (Oxford, 1913). The book itself is much freer from syncretistic tendencies than its title might suggest.
[2] This problem has been fully dealt with by Godfrey Phillips in *The Old Testament in the World Church* (London, 1942).

came to fulfil one system, the imperfections of which were to be shewn up by the perfection of that which God wrought in Him, is it not possible that He came also as the fulfilment of other systems which have never till recent times known His name ?

This view has been put forward, not only by the heirs of ancient cultures who have entered into the riches of Christ, but also by Christian scholars of the west, who believe that the providential operations of God are not confined to one line of revelation, but include all nations in their majestic scope. One has written, " Christianity is related to other Faiths as their complement, their fulfilment, their realisation. And when that which is perfect is come, then that which is in part shall be done away."[1] Some would go so far as to say that the Christian should regard himself as a co-worker with the forces within each religious system which make for righteousness.[2]

In strong reaction from this point of view, others have stressed the complete discontinuity of the Christian revelation from every other system of thought. Though acceptable men of faith may have lived, or may live today, under non-Christian systems of thought, those systems themselves are manifestations of rebellion against or disobedience to God. " There are, to be sure, longings and apperceptions in the religious life of mankind outside the special sphere of the Christian revelation, of which Christ, what He is and has brought, may be termed *in a certain sense* the fulfilment. Yet, it is mistaken and misleading to describe the religious pilgimage of mankind as a preparation or a leading up to a so-called consummation or fulfilment in Christ. . . . Even when we recognise that Christ may *in a certain sense* be called the fulfilment of some deep and persistent longings and apprehensions that everywhere in history manifest

[1] W. St. Clair Tisdall in *Christianity and Other Faiths* (London, 1912), p. 212.
[2] *Rethinking Missions* (New York, 1932), the report of a commission of American Laymen on the missionary work of the Church, p. 327.

themselves in the race, this fulfilment, when we subject the facts to a close scrutiny, never represents the perfecting of what has been before."[1]

The controversy, with its far-reaching consequences for the idea of a Christian society in a non-Christian world, continues. The aim of the champions on both sides is in essence the same, both to safeguard the uniqueness of Christ in His capacity as Saviour and as Judge of all that men have achieved outside the Church and within it, and also to do justice to God's providential ordering of the whole of human history, of which Christ is seen to be both the centre and the consummation.

In the meantime, the Christian in the non-Christian world has to live his life, and without waiting for the end of controversy has to plan such an ordering of the Christian society as will make it in truth the Body of Christ, the effective witness in a surrounding society that has not yet acknowledged Him. The present century has been a time of varied experiment in the acclimatisation of the Christian society in soils as yet largely alien to it.

Some of these experiments are concerned with things that in themselves are external, such as the ordering of worship and its relation to national and cultural traditions. But worship, though in one sense external, is the most characteristic of all the outward expressions of the life of the Christian society, and we have seen at point after point how deep an influence forms of worship have had on fashioning the Christian thinking of communities, and maintaining the continuity of Christian life under circumstances that might otherwise have dissolved it. In the ancient world, the eastern and western churches developed different and characteristic forms of liturgical expression. It would be

---

[1] H. Kraemer, in *The Authority of the Faith* (Tambaram Series, Vol. I, O.U.P. 1939), pp. 2–3. Dr. Kraemer is the protagonist on one side of this controversy. Many conflicting points of view are to be found expressed in the volume just referred to. A useful summary of the whole issue is to be found in E. C. Dewick, *The Gospel and Other Faiths* (London, 1948), pp. 92–116.

strange if these two traditions had exhausted all the liturgical possibilities, and if the younger churches did not in time arrive at new forms, in which something of their individual apprehension of the truth of Christ could find its natural expression.[1]

Acclimatisation of thought is even more difficult than acclimatisation of worship. But in this field also a beginning has been made. Christian thinkers in Asia, dissatisfied with the western impress on all the theological thinking to which they have been introduced, have naturally been driven to ask whether the Gospel, without detriment to its essential content, cannot be re-thought and re-expressed in the categories of thought by which the mind of the eastern nations has been formed. Unless we are content merely to repeat without alteration the biblical phrases in which Christian truth was first expressed, we are bound to make use of thought-forms current in the world outside the biblical sphere. Unless we make this adventure, we cannot find answers to the questions which are raised by contemporary men, and to which no answer can be given directly in the words of Scripture.

It must be admitted that so far the contributions made by eastern Christian thinkers have not been impressive. In some of their writings, little more has been done than to substitute words from ancient languages for those current in ordinary Christian usage. This can be illuminating ; but unless the substitution is accompanied by deep labour of thought, there is the danger that the ancient word may carry with it from its earlier history connotations that are irreconcilable with Christian truth, and that so the expression of that truth may be obscured rather than illuminated.[2] In

[1] One of the first acts of the Church of South India, after its inauguration on 27 September, 1947, was the appointment of a liturgical committee. A form for the service of Holy Communion has been issued by this Committee, but experiment seems not to have gone further than new combinations of elements already existing in eastern and western service-books.

[2] This is the weakness of an interesting book, *Re-Thinking Christianity in India* (Madras, 1938), produced by a group of Indian Christians about the time of the Tambaram Missionary Conference.

other cases, the writers have not gone beyond the juxtaposition of Christian and non-Christian ideas and phrases, without clear definition of the identities and differences between them, and manifest therefore a tendency towards a syncretism, in which the distinctiveness of the Christian message is in danger of being lost.

Such weaknesses are inevitable in a period of pioneer experiment. Most of the churches that live daily in contact with the great religions of the east are themselves young. Their scholars have been burdened with the labour of assimilating what they have needed from the resources of the west, and have hardly yet had time to spread their wings in the realms of original Christian thinking. There are signs that the day of experiment is passing, and that that of solid achievement is in sight. Both in India and in China individuals and groups of theologians are beginning to speak with a new confidence, and to make original contributions to the world of Christian thought.[1]

This laborious process of the rebirth of thought is indispensable, if the younger churches in the east are ever to be more than " colonies of western imperialism," located but not rooted in the countries in which they are situated. But it is possible that the direct assault of preaching and the inner labour of theological thought are not the only effective means by which the Christian society can make itself at home in an alien situation. A society which is in any degree Christian has a power which radiates far beyond its

[1] I may refer by way of illustration to the work of Dr. T. C. Chao in China, and to the group of younger Indian theologians, who under the leadership of D. T. Niles, are preparing a complete survey of the expression of Christian truth in relation to the religions prevailing in India, Burma and Ceylon. Many scholars of the younger churches have defended the opinion that the task of bringing independent eastern theology to its maturity would be achieved more quickly if eastern students were not required to spend so much time in mastering contemporary western theology, and were brought more directly into contact with the masterpieces of Christian thought in the patristic age, when conditions more closely resembled those obtaining in churches still perplexed by an overwhelmingly non-Christian atmosphere, and in which questions are posed more sharply and uncompromisingly than they are in the dialectic of modern western thought.

own limits, and produces effects which it is impossible exactly to assess. The churches tend to think in terms of direct witness and measurable achievements; they "have hardly any conception of the little ways which act with capillary influence and leaven the whole body."[1] The number of those who, having heard the Gospel, accept it outright has always been small. The number of those who feel its attractive power may be very much larger.

Even at an early period in the Nineteenth Century, highly educated Hindus began to find in the teachings of Christ something for which they had looked in vain in the Hindu Scriptures. The most famous names are those of Raja Ram Mohan Roy (1772-1833), the founder of the Brahmo Samaj, and Keshub Chunder Sen, both Bengalis of high caste, and both friends of the early missionaries in Bengal.[2] Neither of these ever felt it necessary to break completely with Hinduism or to join the Christian Church. Each believed that salvation must come to India through the renewal of Hinduism by the fresh light that they had found in the Christian Scriptures. Yet they and their followers, and especially Keshub, were able to speak of Christ in terms of passionate devotion hardly excelled in the highest flights of the mystics of the west. The Brahmo Samaj has never had a large membership; the type of ethical theism without strong emotional content which it represents has never had power to attract more than a small number of the élite. But it has had wide influence in introducing Christ to India not as an importation from the west, but as One to whom the allegiance of India is naturally due.

A far more remarkable instance of the influence of the

[1] This striking phrase was used by an Egyptian Christian, quoted by S. A. Morrison in an article on " The Indigenous Churches and Muslim Evangelism " in *The International Review of Missions* (July, 1936), p. 319.

[2] The classic account of these and other reforming movements in Hinduism and Islam is J. N. Farquhar, *Modern Religious Movements in India* (London, 1929). In this work, the extent to which the reform movements were directly or indirectly indebted to Christian teaching is carefully worked out.

Christian society outside its own borders is afforded by the career of M. K. Gandhi (1869–1948). The time has not yet come when a critical biography of this enigmatic man can be written, but the main facts of his career are already well-known from his own writings and speeches. Mr. Gandhi first came deeply under the influence of the Christian Scriptures while he was practising as a lawyer in South Africa. From his own account, it is clear that he at one time seriously considered becoming a Christian ; but in the end, like Ram Mohan Roy and Keshub Chunder Sen, he decided that he could find his deepest inspiration in the Hindu Scriptures, adding to their teaching the insights which he had gained from the New Testament. From this position he never afterwards departed. Profound as was his reverence for the person and teaching of Jesus, he never committed himself to such exclusive loyalty as is involved in baptism. His most characteristic doctrine, that of non-violence, seems to have been derived rather from Tolstoy than directly from the Gospel. His noble championship of the poor and the depressed classes was the expression in act of what he had learned from the example of Christ Himself.

Mr. Gandhi's influence on the development of the Christian society in India was ambivalent. By his character he challenged that society to live more faithfully to its own ideals. By his constant references to the Gospels, he opened the way to the study of the Christian Scriptures for thousands of educated Indians, who might otherwise have disdained them. On the other side of the account, by his strenuous opposition to what he called " proselytism," he helped to convince many of his fellow-countrymen that, in order to express in word and act the warmest devotion to Jesus Christ, it was not necessary for them to separate themselves from the society in which they had been born. If Mr. Gandhi had had his way, there could have been no further growth in the Christian society in India.

An even more striking illustration of the radiation of the

Christian society comes from what is recognised as being from the Christian point of view the most unapproachable of other religions, Islam. For centuries Islam and Christianity had little real knowledge of one another. To the Christian, Muhammad was simply the false prophet, and there an end. The Muslim, believing that the Christians had hopelessly corrupted their Scriptures, felt under no obligation to study them. Since the Eighteenth Century all that has changed. Carlyle's well-known study of Muhammad as hero represents a first and uncritical stage in the discovery of the real Muhammad by the west. As research has proceeded, the stark grand outlines of the Prophet's character have more and more clearly been revealed. And at the same time, Muslims have been reading the Gospels with alert and critical eyes. A confrontation of Jesus and Muhammad was inevitable.

The place of Muhammad in Islam is different from that of Jesus in Christianity. Though sometimes spoken of as mediator, he is neither God nor Saviour. Yet as the unique and final mouthpiece, according to Muslim doctrine, of the revelation of God, his importance is far more than that of any mere man. Tradition has woven a mixture of truth and legend about him ; to the Muslim, it is axiomatic that he was the best and most perfect man who ever lived. But the character of Muhammad, grand as it is, is, as is to be expected, that of an Arab leader of the Seventh Century. There is much in it that is unacceptable by the standards of the Twentieth Century, and much of which Muslims cannot but be rather uncomfortably conscious in their contacts with Christians.[1]

In recent times, many biographies of Muhammad have been written by Muslims. An acute student, who has read

[1] Professor D. S. Margoliouth, after an exhaustive study of the original Arabic records, goes so far as to write, "The character attributed to Muhammad in the biography of Ibn Ishaq is . . . exceedingly unfavourable. . . . This is a disagreeable picture for the founder of a religion, and it cannot be pleaded that it is a picture drawn by an enemy." Hastings, E.R.E., Vol. VIII, pp. 877-8.

them all, notes that there is a constant tendency to redraw the portrait so as to make it more acceptable by modern, and in particular by Christian, standards. Characteristics which are regarded as less desirable are not stressed. Awkward episodes are explained away, or presented in a light quite different from that in which they appear in the original sources. "The influence of western ideals of life and conduct based on the life of Jesus is very noticeable, and the life of Muhammad must be pictured so as to compare favourably with that ideal. . . . In spite of many unfavourable features, the picture (given in the original sources) gives us the presentation of a figure which claims our sympathy and frequently stirs our admiration, but it is no ideal figure. These modern writers are equally conscious that it is no ideal figure, but the Prophet must have been an ideal man, therefore an ideal figure must be constructed, and the principle behind the reconstruction is the gospel figure of Jesus."[1]

This is an admirable example of the capillary action of Christian witness. Every such example is to be welcomed as evidence of the life-giving power of Christ. Such penetration of non-Christian society by Christian ideals may in the end prepare the way for the final triumph of Christianity. But its significance must not be mistaken ; at best it can be no more than a by-product, since the aim of Christian witness can never be anything less than faith in Christ, and incorporation by baptism into the Christian society. That society, if it is alive, will produce effects far beyond its own limits, and may even in time effect a revolution in the standards of judgment applied in the non-Christian world. But interest in the teachings of Christ and a general acceptance of them can never take the place of personal commitment to Him. It is only as a society, and only through those members of it who have been renewed by the grace of

[1] Arthur Jeffery, "The Real Muhammad and the Ideal," *International Review of Missions*, July, 1929, pp. 390–400.

God revealed in Christ, that the Church can fulfil its work of witness, and bridge the gap in time between the first coming of Christ in the Incarnation, and His second coming to set the seal on all the purposes of God in history.

CHAPTER X

THE GOSPEL AND PRIMITIVE PEOPLES

FROM time to time, explorers have reported the discovery of a people which has no religion, no worship, and no sense of God. In every case that has come under skilled investigation the initial assertion has been disproved. Among many simple peoples, religious rites are secret and not readily revealed to the first foreigner who comes along. Closer and more sympathetic contact has revealed that some of the supposedly non-religious peoples are among those which have the most elaborate rituals and the most complex religious ideas.

Primitive man does not think logically, as do some among his more civilised brethren. But this does not mean that he is wholly irrational. He thinks always pictorially, symbolically, by association. Living as he does in the closest proximity to nature and its forces, and often on the bare edge of subsistence, he is more aware of the mystery and terror of nature than are those protected by the surroundings of civilisation. This primitive sense of mystery may he below the level of what can specifically be called religion ; but no strict dividing line can be drawn between mere irrational awe and the beginnings of worship. " To the primitive hunter, for example, the beasts are not merely a source of food supply, and an occasional danger, they are mysterious beings which are in a sense superior to man and nearer to the divine world. The strength of the bull, the swiftness of the deer, the flight of the eagle, the cunning of the serpent are revelations of ,he super-human, and consequently divine, power and glory. And the same is true of the attitude of the primitive farmer to the earth and the fruits of the earth. However low is the level of his culture, man cannot but recognise the existence of laws and rhythms and cycles of change in the life of nature, in which his own life is involved. . . . Behind these appearances there are divine powers—gods or spirits or undifferentiated magical forces, which must be propitiated and served, if man is to live."[1]

Propitiation of natural powers, control of them, co-operation with them—these are the three pillars of primitive religion. And since a right relation to the unseen powers is all-important for the welfare and survival of the race, at certain times of the year the whole energy of the people is directed to the carrying out of an almost liturgical series of observances. Few peoples in the world are so backward in most of the ways of civilisation as the aborigines of Australia. But when their life came under the scientific observation of Spencer and Gillen,[2] it was found that in certain tribes the whole community might be occupied for three or four months at a time in what, at a slightly higher level of development, would certainly be described as religious practices.

In a very different part of the world, New Mexico, the studies of Miss Ruth Benedict have revealed a similar pattern of living. Of the Zuni culture, she writes, " No field of activity competes with ritual for foremost place in their attention. Probably men among the Western Pueblos give to it the greater part of their working life. It requires the memorising of an amount of word-perfect ritual which our less trained minds find staggering, and the performance of neatly dovetailed ceremonies that are charted by the calendar and completely interlock all the different cults and the governing body in endless formal procedure."[3]

[1] Christopher Dawson, *Religion and Culture* (London, 1948), p. 41.
[2] The first book published by these outstanding anthropologists, *Native Tribes of Central Australia*, was published in 1899.
[3] R. Benedict, *Patterns of Culture* (New York, 1935), pp. 59–60.

In some areas, though it is recognised that man is dependent on the powers of nature, it is also believed that the powers of nature are dependent for their stability and order on man and on the due performance of his ritual task. The free Dyak of Borneo has the proud consciousness that, if the order of nature should in any way fall into disarray, it is his responsibility and privilege to set things right again by the mystery of head-hunting—to the Dyak a religious and not merely a savage business—and all the rituals associated with it. The Dutch occupation of Borneo was objected to for many reasons, but above all because, by the prohibition of head-hunting, it had introduced an irreparable breach into the divinely appointed order of the world.[1]

Man can survive in almost any climate, however inhospitable and unkindly. The Eskimo has adapted himself to life in the Arctic. The Australian aborigine successfully holds on in a desert where the white man would very quickly perish. But the bleaker the aspect of nature and the more constant the struggle to survive, the more precise must be the adaptation of man to his environment, and, generally, the more elaborate the rituals by which that adaptation is consecrated and maintained from generation to generation. By all these factors the life of primitive man is held together in one indivisible whole.

What is plainest in extreme cases is true of the life of primitive man everywhere. His beliefs and customs may appear to an outsider to be a strange patchwork collection of irrational superstitions, illogically held together. It may well be that primitive man himself has no recollection of the origin of the rites that he performs and can give no rational account of them to the enquirer. But for him they are all linked together in one system, unquestioningly held in its entirety. The whole of life is woven in a single web. To

[1] A curious parallel to this viewpoint is to be found in the Brahmanical idea that the gods are dependent for their welfare on the offering of sacrifice, and therefore the Brahman, without whom the sacrifice cannot be properly offered, is in his own way greater than the gods.

change one part is to affect the whole. To make any great modification may be to tear the whole fabric irreparably.

The success of missionary work among primitive peoples has been so much greater and more spectacular than among the adherents of the great ethnic religions that there is a natural tendency to suppose that it is beset by fewer problems in that area than in the world of more developed civilisations. The resistance of primitive peoples to a new religion, backed by the prestige of a stronger culture, is certainly less. The problems of contact and conflict, however, though different, are none the less formidable. The Gospel is a new factor of immense potency. Once admitted into the life of a primitive people, it cannot but tear the seamless robe of the established order. The missionary, whether he knows it or not, comes inevitably as a destroyer. To those who idealise primitive life, this must always seem an evil thing. Even the Christian, who believes that the Gospel must be preached to every creature and that every system of life must be subjected to the redeeming power of Christ, may regard the destruction of ancient ways of living as dangerous. Unless the missionary is successful in helping his people to weave a new web of life, he may find that in the end he has left them defenceless, dead to the old world, and with no power to be born again into the new.

Missionaries have often been blamed for things which cannot rightly be laid to their charge. To them, for instance, have been attributed the degeneracy and even the disappearance of simple races in the South Seas and elsewhere. Undoubtedly the policy of early missionaries was in some respects unwise. Shocked by the universal and almost complete nakedness of the South Sea islanders, the pioneers laid so much stress on the wearing of clothes, that the acceptance of the Gospel and the acceptance of a gift of wholly unsuitable European clothing came to be regarded as almost identical. This undoubtedly had bad effects on the health of people wholly unprepared for such a radical change in a basic human habit. In many cases, harmless activities and pastimes were forbidden by the missionaries as savouring of idolatry. But the missionary was never more than one of a large number of disturbing factors. Usually he was running a losing race with the explorer, the trader and the government official.

The record of the white man among the simple peoples of the earth is not one on which a European can look back with any pleasure. In the Eighteenth Century, British, French, and Dutch in America vied with one another in the sale of " firewater " to the Red Indians, long after experience had clearly shewn the disastrous effects of this traffic on the race. In 1860, when John Paton was living on the New Hebrides island of Tanna, white traders deliberately landed four young men suffering from measles. Their answer to the missionary's remonstrances was " Our watchword is— Sweep these creatures away, and let white men occupy the soil."[1] In 1876, the last indigenous Tasmanian died. The whole race had been systematically exterminated.[2]

The arrival of responsible representatives of civilised governments put an end in the course of time to the worst features of the exploitation of the simple by the more powerful races. It is often assumed, by the critics of white imperialism, that the alternatives before the African and Oceanic peoples were either freedom in the ways of their ancestors, or subjugation to alien and colonising powers. The issue is much less simple than this. The course of early Nineteenth Century history suggests that the real choice was between ruthless exploitation by men who had no other purpose than gain, and control by governments which, however deeply influenced by commercial and imperialistic considerations, had retained at least a minimum of regard for the human rights of their subjects. On the

---

[1] John G. Paton, *An Autobiography* (London, undated), p. 150.
[2] R. Allier : *La Psychologie de la Conversion chez les Peuples Non-civilisés* (Paris, 1925), Vol. I, p. 32, and see the whole section, pp. 28–37.

whole, the record of western governments in this field, though very far from perfect, is one in which the good may be held to outweigh the evil.

None the less, governments also come in as grave disturbers of primitive ways, as renders of the fabric of societies which by long usage have become ill-prepared for change. In parts of Africa, the two great pastimes of the people were fighting and hunting. Fighting was, for obvious reasons, suppressed. Because of the rapid decrease in game and the danger of its complete disappearance, severe restrictions had to be placed on hunting. What was the tribesman to do ? He could recognise that life had become safer and more prosperous, but it had also become very dull. And when simple peoples lose the zest for living, they are likely to deteriorate, to dwindle and to disappear.

It is hard to establish controls, in the light of which the effects of the Gospel on the survival of simple races can be accurately calculated. Too many factors operate, and it is difficult to isolate those which are specifically Christian. In certain instances, however, the Christian factors have been so strongly marked that some conclusions may, with due caution, be reached.

The island of Kusaie in Micronesia, when discovered in 1806, had a population of about two thousand. In the course of eighty years of rape, ravage and disease, this had been reduced to about two hundred. Missionaries of the American Board took up work in 1861. It was reported in 1945 that the whole population was now Christian, and that the numbers had risen to twelve hundred.[1]

One of the smallest and most ancient peoples in India is the tribe of the Todas, living patriarchally in the Nilgiri Hills. When discovered, they numbered between eight hundred and a thousand. But the proximity of European civilisation,

[1] I cite without comment the report of an American journalist that "Kusaie is now an unbelievable island of twelve hundred angels." Quoted in H. P. Van Dusen, *They Found the Church There* (New York, Scribners, 1945), p. 75.

after Ootacamund had been opened up as the summer seat of the government, brought about its usual consequences, and the number began steadily to decline. Government measures to check drinking and to deal with the ravages of syphilis were so far successful that among the non-Christian Todas actual decline was checked, but between 1921 and 1941, no increase in numbers was recorded. In the meantime, a number of the Todas had become Christians. Some married Toda women, others had to marry outside. Of twenty-six Christian Toda marriages, all but five had proved fertile, no distinction being observable between those marriages in which both parties were Todas and those in which one party came from another community. The average number of children to each fertile marriage was, at the time of recording, 3.766. Apart from the difference in religion, conditions of life were much the same for Christian and for non-Christian Todas. This is at least presumptive evidence that the Gospel, by giving new hope in life, and by introducing a different moral standard, had supplied to a people threatened with extinction fresh powers of resistance to the disintegrating effects of western civilisation, and an unexpected capacity for recovery and survival.[1]

Just because of the closely integrated organisation of primitive society, it is difficult for any individual to act on his own initiative, or to make such a decision as that demanded by the appeal for Christian conversion. Kings and priests are allowed by tradition to be individuals, but this is because they are endued with special mysterious powers ; and even these are circumscribed by the duty of interpreting the customs of the people as enshrined in the wisdom handed on from the fathers. Lesser folk, though marked by individual characteristics, are regarded as expressions of the common life of the tribe, and a means by which that life

---

[1] The facts have kindly been supplied by my friend and former pupil, Mr. M. Mangaladass, a catechist of the Church of South India in Ootacamund.

is carried forward. Any inclination to be different is severely judged and opposed ; the tribe depends on its homogeneity, and anyone who tries to be different is threatening the existence of the tribe by making a rent in the seamless web of its life. Cases are on record, from the Congo area in Africa, in which attempts made by women to follow missionary teaching in so small a matter as keeping their houses and gardens tidier than those of others called down severe disapproval and retaliation.

In face of this problem, many missions, while aiming consciously at conversion, have postponed the appeal, and have planned so to penetrate the whole consciousness of a tribe or people that eventually a group decision favourable to Christianity can be reached. What is impossible in dealing with masses of people in a large country may be achieved in a community numbering not more than a few thousands, and well organised under a small number of recognised chiefs. Dutch and German missionaries in East Indonesia and in New Guinea have gone further than most others in the attempt to meet in this way the problem of the foundation of the Christian society.

Group decisions are in no way alien to the mentality of a primitive people. Just as marriage, directed as it is towards the continuance of the race, is regarded much more as the concern of the whole community than as the private affair of two individuals who may happen to think of getting married, so religion may naturally be regarded as a matter on which the whole people should decide together. Enough decisions of this kind are on record in missionary history to make possible an analysis of their probable consequences.

In the first place, it must be recognised that such a decision is in most cases negative. There shall be no more idolatry, no more human sacrifice or eating of human flesh, no more strangling of twins at childbirth, or whatever the contested customs may be. These practical renunciations are the expression of a change of allegiance ; henceforth the old gods are not to be worshipped, but the God of the strangers is to take their place. The idols are broken. In some cases, as seems often to have happened in ancient England, the idol sanctuary is turned into a Christian Church.

The day of the breaking of the idols is always a memorable day, no less in the Twentieth Century than when Boniface cut down the oak of Donar at Geismar in Hesse.[1] To the primitive worshipper, the idol is never a mere representation; it is itself endowed with mysterious life and power, perilous to the man who approaches it without due authorisation, still more to the man who lays violent hands upon it.[2] The wise missionary never performs the work of destruction himself. The act must not be regarded as a trial of strength between the newcomer and the local gods, but as the decisive repudiation by the people of their old allegiance. When the deed is done, there are usually mixed feelings of terror and relief; but in either case a new day has begun.

Yet such enthusiastic beginnings often lead on to disappointment on both sides. The primitive people have acted without any full understanding of the weight of the yoke that they have taken on themselves. So much has been done. Idolatry has been abandoned, and with it many of the worst excesses by which it is often accompanied. What more can the missionaries want ? The missionaries on the other hand, seeing their converts go on in ways that startlingly belie their Christian profession, wonder whether there was any deep sincerity in the original decision to accept the Gospel. The disappointment on both sides is natural, but it is easy for the underlying cause of it to be overlooked. If simple people accept a new god, on the ground that he

[1] Levison, *op. cit.*, p. 76.
[2] In India an *image* does not become an *idol* until a special ceremony has been performed to call down into it the presence of the deity. The heathen do not, in reality, "bow down to wood and stone." I have referred elsewhere to the perplexity of the Christian judge who was called on to decide in his court whether a certain figure of a Hindu deity was technically an idol or not.

is stronger and wiser than the old, they will inevitably accept him as a god of the same type as that to which they have been accustomed, wiser, perhaps, kinder, less capricious, but still a god fashioned by man in his own image, and that the image determined by the ancestral traditions. In view of the almost unlimited capacity of traditionally Christian man to do the same, this is not surprising. But a change in names signifies little, unless there has been a corresponding revolution in ideas, and unless the original concept of God has been transformed after the likeness of Jesus Christ through the working of the Holy Spirit in the inner consciousness of simple man.

Where outward progress is too fast, it may happen that time is not allowed for this slow and difficult transformation to be achieved, and the life of the now professedly Christian people may harden down into a pattern which makes the realisation of a fully Christian society well-nigh impossible.

The commonest substitute for the genuine transformation is a strict Christian legalism, not that discipline of the law which is necessary in the training even of a Christian people, but the choice of certain aspects of outward Christian behaviour as those by which the character of the new society is to be determined. But this again is often a manifestation of an unchanged mentality ; the chosen observances often bear too close a resemblance to the taboos of pre-Christian days, and are maintained in force by much the same sanctions of menace and fear. It is no unusual thing for Christians drawn from a primitive background to be fanatical Sabbatarians. In part this may be derived from the views and habits of puritanically-minded missionaries, but in part it is a spontaneous development. The Christian rest on one day in seven is one of the differences which first strikes the neighbouring non-Christian, accustomed to work every day except on the somewhat irregularly recurring and protracted festivals of his own religion. The strict observance of the day makes heavy demands, especially in an agricultural community, where one day may make much difference in getting in the crops.   But the costliness of the observance is part of its value ; if so much has been given up for God's sake, what more can He reasonably demand ?[1]

Such Christian aquiescence is harmful because, by substituting the law for the Gospel, it makes much more difficult the apprehension of what the Gospel really is. In such cases, it is more than probable that under the respectability of conformity, a very dark inheritance from the unchristian past will linger on.   There is much in the life of primitive peoples about which they do not speak readily to a foreigner, and to which they refer only in guarded language even among themselves.   It is very difficult for a foreigner to penetrate fully into the thought-world in which the non-Christian lives.[2]   In almost every primitive community in the world, beneath the daylight world of familiar things, there is the dark or twilight world of magic and witchcraft, in which everyone believes, and of the reality of which all have what to them is incontrovertible evidence.   The African or Papuan is aware that the European does not believe in the same way in this dark world and may be inclined to ridicule his beliefs.[3]   There is a tendency therefore for it to be quietly assumed that this, like other more open manifestations of the old way, has been put away with the acceptance of the Gospel.   But unless the dark world has been brought out into the light of day, fully faced and deliberately abandoned in reliance

[1] See a magnificent exposition of this problem in R. Allier, *op. cit.*, Vol. II., pp. 54–68, under the title *La Moralité Formaliste.*

[2] An interesting example is the Tamil Christian catechist referred to by W. H. R. Rivers in his book on the Todas (London, 1906), pp. 8–9, who after working among the Todas for a number of years helped Rivers in his anthropological investigations.   Realising how little he had come to know of the real habits and ways of thought of the people among whom he had lived, this man became so much discouraged that in the end he gave up his work and went elsewhere.

[3] On the question whether there is any reality, other than that of suggestion, in this world of black magic, those who have lived closest to primitive peoples are the least likely to be dogmatic.   See Godfrey Callaway, S.S.J.E., *Witchcraft* in I.R.M., 1936, pp. 216–226.

on the power of Christ to overcome all the powers of darkness, it is much more likely that it will continue to exercise its power as an unspoken, and perhaps almost unconscious, influence in the life of the people.

This is something deeper than the mere persistence of superstition among only half-Christianised people. It is no uncommon thing in an Indian Christian village for a woman whose child is ill to make a special offering in the Christian church, and also to go by night to sacrifice a cock at the demon shrine, in case the illness may have been caused by the malevolence of an evil spirit. Such practices can be dealt with by fuller education. But if something undesirable has been driven underground and repressed, the consequences are so similar to those of the repressions observed in the individual by the student of abnormal psychology as to suggest that there is a racial personality akin to the personality of the individual and susceptible to the same influences. As is well known, if something has been driven out of the conscious mind of the individual and suppressed, it continues a life of its own in the unconscious realm, and acquires compulsive and autonomous force, so that the actions of the person affected seem to pass on occasion out of his own control.

Nothing in the life of young churches is more perplexing than the persistence and emergence of magical practices among those who have been Christians for generations. If questioned, such people will almost certainly answer that these things are wrong and that Christians ought to have nothing to do with them. But if asked why they continue to permit them, they may find it hard to answer ; they feel themselves in the grip of something that they cannot understand, and yet which on occasion seems to act with irresistible force. When such a lesion has taken place in the early stages in the growth of a Christian community, it is very hard indeed for healing to be brought about. The evil, dwelling now on a sub-conscious level, cannot be cast out by exhortation or discipline, but only by the penetration of light and grace into ordinarily inaccessible levels of the human personality.

Such are some of the problems of the new Christian society, as it emerges from a pagan background. Most of them are familiar from the perplexities and struggles of the early Church.[1] As the builder of the Church tries to face and overcome them, he finds himself driven back to a recognition of the supreme importance of the individual. While it is perfectly true that " a primitive tribe lives wholly in a communal and collective apprehension of life, and that it is therefore unnatural to them and detrimental to sound Christianisation to proceed along the line of separating iso-lated individuals from the tribe and making them Christians in isolation from their given and inescapable basis of com-munal life,"[2] it is nevertheless true that the most primitive man, though less individualised and individualistic than the member of a more advanced community, is never completely submerged within the community. He remains an individual, with his own loves and hates, his own incommunicable experience of life.[3] The primitive artist, shaping his club, works within the established pattern of his people ; yet he always manages to add that which is his own and not merely derivative. He can on occasion assert himself against the popular opinion. Even where the life of the community is most fully integrated, there are degrees of influence and authority even among those who are technically equal. So it comes about that in every religious movement or revival, we almost always find the individual, or it may be the group of two or three, who take a stand against the custom of the tribe or against what has become the custom of the half-Christian community.

[1] On this see the two very able books of Campbell N. Moody, *The Heathen Heart* (Edinburgh, 1907) and *The Mind of the Early Converts* (London, 1920).
[2] H. Kraemer: *The Christian Message in a non-Christian World* (London, Edinburgh House Press 1938), pp. 349–50, commending the work of A. C. Kruyt and N. Adriani among the Toraja people in central Celebes.
[3] See J. Kruyt : *Community and Individual in Central Celebes* in I.R.M., 1940, pp. 231–239.

Whenever such a stand is made, it is certain to be followed by a measure of persecution. From the side of the community, action against the innovator is the natural consequence of conservatism, the instinct of self-preservation on the part of an organism which feels itself threatened by change. But to the innovator, it feels like religious persecution for the sake of his new found faith; much of his own future and of the Christian cause depends on his ability to stand firm, provided that his ground is well chosen, even when the issue is clouded by the confusion between social and religious attitudes.[1]

There is a tendency in contemporary writing to draw a distinction between the *individual* and the *person*. It may be that the capacity to stand alone and to endure hardness for the sake of conviction is that which transforms an individual into a person. Certainly the Christian society can never prosper unless it has within it a sufficient number of such persons. Of all the factors that contribute to bring about the change, none can compare in importance with the direct response to what is felt to be the call of God. If the Christian society cannot reach its true nature except in so far as it is, and in each generation is renewed as, a community of free persons who have chosen Jesus Christ as the way, the truth and the life, the first in any community who make that choice and stand by it are at the crucial turning-point which makes possible development from a group of individuals, conditioned by their environment and by mere acceptance of it, into a genuinely Christian society.[2]

---

[1] A perpetual cause of difficulty in the Indian village is the question of contributions to village festivals; to most of the villagers this seems a mere matter of social duty; to the convinced Christian it may appear as participation in idolatry. In another area, the problem may be that of taking part in communal manufacture of native beer.

[2] The difference, in a primitive Christian community between those who have merely accepted Christianity with the group and those who have gone forward into personal experience of Christian life is so marked as to suggest the working out of a theology of the Holy Spirit as the true centre of personality in man.

But even when the fellowship of convinced Christians has been formed, the problems which face the guide and friend of the community are not all solved.   If he is wise, his desire is that the break with the past shall be marked by as little violence as possible, and that the Christians shall not make the mistake of taking over with their Christianity what are merely western accessories of it.   Here the difficulty may arise from the attitude of the Christians themselves. Missionaries have, no doubt, sometimes in the past been unnecessarily iconoclastic, and have believed in the virtues of civilised traditions which have nothing essentially to do with the Gospel.   But sometimes the convert is more radical than the missionary in his determination to make a complete break with the past.   He is aware, as no outsider can be, of all the implications of that past.   He understands its totality, the way in which every part of it is woven in with every other part, so that it is not possible to make a discrimination between the sacred and the secular, and to say that one part is rooted in the heathen past and other parts are innocent.   To him it is all one, the web woven without seam, of which we have spoken.   His desire is that his Christian future shall be as different from the past as possible.

One of the points at which this problem presents itself most sharply is the use in Christian worship of traditional melodies. Nothing could seem more natural and suitable, and the missionary is often anxious that experiments in adaptation shall be made.   He sometimes encounters unexpected opposition.   For example, in the island of Bali, where the old life shows a marvellous integration of diverse elements into an artistic whole, when some of the younger Christians began to write Christian songs in the traditional rhythms to the familiar tunes, the synod of the Church discussed the matter, and reached the surprising decision that, while such songs might be sung in informal gatherings, they must not be used in the regular worship of the Church.   The decision was defended on the ground that, in the old days, the meaning of the songs had been little understood and that the whole significance of them lay in the tunes ; these were so closely associated with non-Christian worship that the association of ideas could not be broken. It was the view of the elders that a time might come when that association would no longer exist in the minds of the new generations of Christians and that then such tunes could be safely used ; but that, in a young Church, where the pull of the old ways was still so strong, nothing must be done in official worship to bring back to Christians memories of things better forgotten.

The same applies to the dramatic dances, which play so large a part in the life of all primitive peoples. Such dances are very highly stylised ; every movement, every gesture has its significance. And since every tribal dance is not only a recreation but a ritual, and, at a level where the distinction between sacred and secular is not recognised, plays its part in the expression of the religious life of the people, the adaptation of these beautiful and complex forms of art to Christian purposes presents far greater difficulties than is usually suspected by those who have no intimate knowledge of the life of the people concerned.

The beginnings of a new attitude can be noted when the first Christian generation has passed away, and a new race is growing up, which has never known anything but the Christian tradition. This is especially true where the whole tribe has become Christian, and the heathen ways have passed out of existence. Unfortunately, it is possible in fifty years for much to be irrecoverably lost, and for the reaction in favour of the old traditions to come too late. To secure the continuity of artistic tradition without endangering the purity of Christian life is a task that requires most delicate judgment and understanding.

Some recent experiments in Africa give ground for hope

that it may be possible to begin construction, before destruction has gone too far.[1]

One of the features common to almost all primitive cultures is the initiation rites and ceremonies by which boys and girls at the age of puberty pass from the status of children to that of full members of the tribe. These include initiation by the elders into the secret lore of the tribe, the *arcana* which are guarded from all except those who have by birth and initiation a right to know them. In the case of boys, the period of initiation includes segregation from the life of the family and the tribe, and severe physical disciplines, intended to test the fitness of the boy to be reckoned a man. Though in many instances there is much that is gross and revolting in the rites themselves, the underlying principles of responsibility, trustworthiness and courage seemed to offer a foundation on which a Christian building could be set up. The early Christians thought of initiation into the Christian family in the same way. There was the severe preparatory discipline of fasting, and then the *traditio arcani*, the revelation of the carefully guarded secret of the faith ; and so at last the convert was accepted into the new manhood in Christ. To associate the period of preparation for confirmation with just such segregation for special instruction and for testing in the reality of resolutions made to follow Christ, to build on the sense of solidarity of the tribe the sense of solidarity with the great family of Christ on earth, seemed the natural way to bring Christian experience into association with what to the African is one of the most deeply rooted traditions of his race.

All such experiment has its dangers. Wrong associations persist long after it might have been thought that they had been exterminated. Simple people find it hard to distinguish between the sacramental and the magical. Superstition

---

[1] One of the pioneers in such experiments was William Vincent Lucas, Anglican Bishop of Masasi from 1926 to 1945. See the brief memoir of him by W. G. de Lara Wilson (London, n.d.) which includes a selection from the Bishop's writings on this theme.

tends to creep back, as it does in much older Christian societies. But the permanent survival of the Christian society must depend on its capacity to take firm root in different soils, to draw into itself all that is assimilable in the elements contained in those soils, and so, to produce diversity of flowers and fruits in different ages and climes. Already the young churches which have come into being among simple peoples have shewn a capacity for spontaneous joy which often puts the older churches to shame, and a power of missionary expansion beyond their own borders, which is evidence that they are rooted in the living Christ, and not merely in the traditions that have come to them from the older parts of the Christian society.

CHAPTER XI

THE GROWTH OF INDIGENOUS CHURCHES

IN all the affairs of men, theory tends to follow upon practice, even when the presupposition is that practice will be determined by theory. An enterprise is taken in hand, because it seems to be right and necessary; but those who take the first steps rarely see where the enterprise will carry them; events belie anticipation, and progress is made only by continual adaptation to the unforeseen. The expansion of the Christian society has followed upon the general Christian conviction that the Gospel is the message of salvation for all men; the course of events has been erratic rather than straightforward, haphazard rather than systematically planned.

This has been true even in the history of the expansion of the Roman Catholic Church, the most fully centralised and most efficiently organised of all the Christian bodies.

When the Pope assigned to the kings of Spain and Portugal the eastern and western worlds, with the duty of providing missionaries and bishops for all the new territories, he laid it down in so many words in the Bull that no subsequent Pope might alter or annul these privileges. At the time it seemed certain that the empires of Spain and Portugal would be and would remain, as long as time lasted, the greatest in the world. With the decline of the power of these nations, and their increasing incapacity to fulfil the task laid upon them, the Church was compelled to change its policy, and to work out new adaptations of means to ends. The change was attended by serious difficulties. In the east, the Portuguese held firmly to their rights, treated as interlopers and enemies the Vicars Apostolic whom the Popes sent into their domains, and did their utmost to hinder their work. The great quarrel over the "Padroado" was not settled until well on in the Twentieth Century, and still survives in the form of minor quarrels and maladjustments in the work of the Roman Catholic Church in India.

If such complications occur in the work of the greatest and most prudent of all the churches, still more must they be expected in the history of other Christian bodies in the process of their expansion. Only rarely have missionaries had a clear idea of the kind of Christian society that they desired to create, or of the kind of local organisation that would fit it to be a living and permanent society.

In the process of expansion, the problem has been to discover outward forms sufficiently flexible to enable the new society to adapt itself to its environment, sufficiently stable to hold it together in times of spiritual dryness or persecution, sufficiently firm to make possible a genuine unity of the Christian society throughout the whole earth.

For good and ill, Christian expansion in the last four centuries has been associated with the political and commercial expansion of Europe. Where European governments have taken complete control of an area outside Europe, it has generally been assumed that the admission of Christian missionaries should follow as a matter of course. As long as India was a preserve of the East India Company, permission for missionaries to reside was steadfastly resisted ; when the British people began to feel their imperial responsibility, the opposition of the Company was gradually worn down, and the renewed charter of 1813 included a clause by which the ban on missionary effort was withdrawn. In India and Africa, governments have co-operated warmly with missions in educational and medical enterprises. In countries not under direct European control, treaties imposed by the force of European arms, such as that which in 1844 began to open China to the west, have included provisions for the admission of missionaries to territories from which they had formerly been excluded. Sometimes the missionary has been far ahead of governments ; but almost always in the end his status and protection have become the concern of his government at home. In countries such as Tibet, which has remained firmly sealed off from the western world, or Afghanistan, where resistance to the admission of missionaries has been successfully maintained, the Christian society has not been able to take root. Elsewhere, the missionary of modern times has come in on the wave of western power and prestige.

It proved impossible for the enterprises of the Church to remain unaffected by the attitude of the political powers. It would be difficult to prove a direct connection between the colonialism of the period of western political expansion and the policies of missionaries in relation to their own work, and it is probable that the connection, if it existed, was never more than sub-conscious ; but it is just by such action and interaction of different forces that the form of the Christian society is affected and modified.

The imperial powers started out with a policy of the strictest control of all colonial possessions from the metropolis. The affairs of the Spanish colonies were kept under rigorous supervision by the king himself, acting through the Council for the Indies ; no kind of independence was contemplated or thought of. Parkman has shewn how the development of French Canada was thwarted by constant interference from France, and by a colonial policy directed not towards the interests of the colonists but consistently to those of the home country. The British system was always more liberal ; but it was long before even the British contemplated the granting of real independence or self-government to colonies overseas.

The churches were not much in advance of the state. Most missionaries seem to have accepted the view that the foreign missionary was a permanent factor in the life of the new Christian society, and that the dependence of colonial possessions on the home government would be reflected in the complete dependence of colonial churches on the churches at home. This view was carried to such a point in Britain that the Church of England never provided a bishop for America, and anyone in the colonies desiring to be ordained had to make the long voyage to England to seek ordination from the Bishop of London.

The organisation of most missionary societies has been very different from that of the Christian society. The missionary society has been the group of directors and members in the home Church. The missionary has been the agent or employee of the society, in many cases excluded by specific regulation from becoming a member of it. The direction of the work has been concentrated in the home country, and has generally included minute and vexatious control over all the operations overseas. The work of Ziegenbalg and his colleagues in south India was almost brought to a standstill by the unsympathetic directorate in Copenhagen, which issued a set of regulations based on a theory of what missionary work ought to be, bearing no relation whatever to the conditions at that time existing in India, and impossible of execution. Of all the great western missionary societies, the China Inland Mission alone has, from the beginning, had its central direction in China. This benefit it owes to the genius of its founder and first General Director, Hudson Taylor (1832–1905). He laid it down as the principle of the work that all planning and direction must be in the field of operations, and that councils and committees in the sending countries must be regarded not as the directors, but as supporters and auxiliaries of the responsible authorities in the field.[1]

The missionary was thus a man under authority. But

[1] It should be noted that it was comparatively easy to make this system practicable, since all the work of the China Inland Mission is in one country. It would be much more difficult for a society maintaining work in a number of countries to adopt it.

he was also a man in authority; it was all too easy for him in his own sphere to make that authority absolute and to believe that it would be permanent. In many cases he came to simple peoples as a guide endowed with all the prestige of the west. At the beginning of the new society, he was the sole fount of Christian knowledge. In some areas, he was the sole repository of almost every kind of useful knowledge, being architect and builder, farmer and digger of wells,[1] doctor and nurse as well as preacher of the Gospel. He determined what should be done, and how it should be done. The function of the convert was to listen and to obey. Even the missionaries of the London Missionary Society, which laid it down as a principle that it existed not to promote any particular denomination but to make the pure Gospel available to the heathen, were in fact successful in reproducing accurately the main features of the form of Christianity to which they themselves were accustomed.

For the most part the converts were well-pleased to have it so. The authority of the missionary was usually exercised as the authority of love. The Christian community grew up as a family of obedient children under the care of wise and loving parents. Occasionally the desire for political protection and influence played a part in the growth of the community. Even in China, where political independence was always maintained, there were those who saw advantage in connection with the foreigner, and in the measure of protection that he might be able to give in unsettled and dangerous days.[2] But even where no subsidiary interests were concerned, there was a strong tendency for the young

---

[1] The successful digging of a well by John G. Paton was a potent factor in the conversion of the people of Aniwa in the New Hebrides. *Autobiography* (London, 1919), p. 345.

[2] There was a tendency for the French Roman Catholic missions in China to attempt to play the same sort of role as they had played in Palestine, as the protectors of the Christians under the rule of the Turks. This may explain why, in the violent reaction of the Boxer movement at the end of the Nineteenth Century, the Roman Catholic missions were the object of even more intense hostility than the Protestant missions. See Latourette, *History of Christian Missions in China*, pp. 508–13.

Christian community to be content with the attitude of passive acceptance of the good things given and not to aim at an independence which was neither granted nor desired.

The charge that missionaries deliberately lent their services as agents of the imperialistic policy of the colonising peoples cannot, in general, be supported by adequate evidence. Yet, with the progress of colonial expansion, there was a hardening of the attitude of the white to the coloured races. The intrinsic superiority of the white man came to be assumed without question. It was taken for granted that the coloured races were incapable of managing their own affairs, and that, though ultimately a time must come when relationships would change, the period of tutelage would be very long, so that no immediate steps need be taken to consider what should be done in the event of the docile children beginning to grow up, and to claim their right to the control of their own affairs both in church and state. There is evidence that the early missionaries were more prepared to treat their converts as equals than their successors in the middle of the Nineteenth Century.

But one movement in human affairs tends to be balanced by its contrary. Even before the end of the Eighteenth Century, there had been a violent reaction against the accepted view of colonialism. The American Revolution had broken the connection between Britain and most of the British colonies in North America, and had brought into existence a new democratic nation conceived in liberty. At the beginning of the Nineteenth Century, the same process took place in South America. By 1830, the dominion of Spain and Portugal west of the Atlantic had been brought to an end, and its place taken by a collection of turbulent, ill-organised but virile republics, all resolved that never again would they be brought under domination from across the seas. These were risings of white colonists against their own home governments. To men of wide vision it was even then clear that the same process must sooner or later follow in Asia and Africa, and that European domination must be regarded only as an episode and not as a permanent feature of the human situation. If this was true in political affairs, it must sooner or later be true also in the affairs of the Church.

When does a Church cease to be a colony of another Church, and become a genuine Christian society existing in its own right, drawing its spiritual vitality directly from Christ the head of the society ?[1] It is clear that as long as a Christian group is dependent on foreign personnel, foreign leadership and foreign support, its situation is precarious. An alteration in the political balance of the world may cut it off from its sources of supply ; then, if its own resources are inadequate, it will wither away and possibly, as has happened more than once in history, disappear. If its continuance is to be assured, it must have within itself everything that is needed for the maintenance of its life, its ministry and its witness. Slowly and hesitantly this new conception of the nature of the younger churches entered the consciousness and the policies of the Church as a whole.

The first step was the development of Christian leaders in the younger churches, who could stand on an equal footing with the foreigner, and in the end take his place.

The extreme centralisation of the Roman Catholic Church has made difficult the development of any kind of independence in its more distant dependencies. A good start was made when two Indians and one Chinese were raised to the episcopate in the Seventeenth Century. Then there was a period of regression. The early experiments may have been in some ways unsatisfactory. The extreme disorders of the Eighteenth Century made necessary a period of strict control, while reorganisation was in progress. It was not till the present century that a decisive step forward was taken.

---

[1] In the true sense of the word there can be only one Christian society. The problem of the relation of geographically separate and partial societies to the whole is held over for consideration in the last chapter.

The initiative was taken personally by Pope Pius XI. He saw clearly that in the increasingly uncertain political conditions that followed on the first world war, the dependence of young churches on a foreign episcopate constituted a danger, and that the work of the church was not completed until each country and area was fully provided with an indigenous episcopate, able to give individual leadership and to maintain unimpaired the full system of the Church, even though for a long period communications with the centre of direction in Rome might be interrupted. On October 28th, 1926, therefore the Pope himself consecrated in Rome twelve bishops drawn from many races.

From that time, the creation of new sees and the elevation of priests of many races to the episcopate has gone forward with remarkable rapidity. At the beginning of this century, there was not in India a single Indian diocesan bishop of the Latin rite ; at the time of writing there are twelve, not including Indian bishops of the Oriental rites in South-west India.[1] A further step was taken when, in 1947, for the first time a Chinese was chosen as a Cardinal of the Roman Church. To some extent the independence of the new hierarchies is limited by the system of appointing apostolic delegates. The apostolic delegate is the personal representative of the Pope, and, as such, takes precedence over all archbishops and bishops. His task is to watch over the order of the Church, and to prevent any departure which has not the approval of the Roman authorities. A Roman Catholic might argue that, without some such check, the rapid creation of new and inexperienced hierarchies would be too dangerous, and that the granting of new independence must always be balanced by the strengthening of the links with the centre, without which the one society is in danger

[1] The new policy was very clearly set forth in the sermon preached by the first Indian diocesan bishop of the Latin rite, Mgr. Roche, at the consecration of Mgr. P. Thomas, one of the most distinguished of Indian Roman Catholic scholars, as Bishop of Guntur, on 29 June, 1940. Mgr. Thomas was later transferred to Bangalore.

of dissolution into a number of unconnected islands.

The early non-Roman missionaries did not set themselves to produce leaders. They aimed at training men of God, in the expectation that some among them would be found fit to carry great responsibilities in the Church. It may be said that on the whole the older churches have been much too slow in entrusting authority to the members of the younger churches. The apostles had to make use of such materials as they had ; they put their churches into the hands of the leaders on the spot, and, in spite of many mistakes, those churches took root and flourished. The parallel is not exact in all respects ; many of those leaders in the early church had been prepared by the discipline of Judaism for the reception of the Gospel ; they worked under the supervision and direction of the apostles. Yet in the main the criticism is just. The only way to train men in the bearing of responsibility is to give them responsibility, and not to be too much disturbed by the failures of those who do not rise to the height that is expected of them. This principle, always admitted in theory, now holds the field in the development of all missionary strategy.

Progress may be illustrated from the history of the Anglican episcopate overseas. The first non-European ever to be raised to the position of bishop in the Church of England was Samuel Adjai Crowther, rescued as a boy from slavery, and consecrated in 1864 for work in Nigeria among his own people. There was never any doubt of Crowther's goodness and devotion. But at his death the diocese was found in considerable disorder ; the experiment of an African diocesan bishop has not yet been repeated, though Crowther has been followed by a number of distinguished African assistants to European bishops. The first Indian bishop was not appointed till 1912, when V. S. Azariah, a Tamil, was consecrated to the then tiny see of Dornakal. Even at that date, there was much opposition to the appointment both from missionaries and from Indian

Christians. Azariah proved to be one of the greatest leaders in the history not only of the Indian Church but of the Church of Christ. Under his guidance, the number of Christians in his area was quadrupled in his episcopate of thirty-two years ; his wisdom, his power as a teacher and his humility at once made him a distinguished figure in any company in which he was called to move.[1] The first Chinese assistant bishop was appointed in 1911. Until 1948, more than half the bishops of the Chung Hua Sheng Kung Hui (The Anglican Church in China) were foreigners ; in that year the balance was reversed, and for the first time the Chinese were in a majority. In Japan, all the ten diocesan bishops are Japanese ; bnt the Japanese Church has recently shewn its superiority to racial prejudice by electing two foreigners as assistant bishops.

A similar account of progress might be drawn from almost any country, and from the work of almost any of the larger missionary bodies.

Whereas the Roman Catholics, until recent times, have concentrated on the education of their priesthood, a work done far more thoroughly by them than by any non-Roman body, the Protestant missions at an early date launched out on an immense enterprise of general Christian education, of which they are now reaping the fruit. Unless a very narrow view is taken of the function of the Christian society, it is called to make its voice heard not only within the walls of the church, but wherever men gather together, and wherever the destinies of men are determined. The Christian layman should everywhere be the spearhead of the Christian advance, since he alone has access to so many fields of service from which the ordained minister is debarred. It is remarkable that, at a time when not more than one person in fifty in Asia is a Christian, China and Japan have already had Christian Prime Ministers, and India has

---

[1] See the short life by Deaconess Carol Graham (London, 1946). Azariah died on 1 January, 1945. A full history of the life and times of Bishop Azariah is a great desideratum of the Christian Church.

seen a Christian governor, Christian members of cabinets, and Christian presidents of assemblies. A hundred years ago, the most sanguine prophet of the Christian society would not have dreamed that these things could come to pass within a century.

A second field in which a remarkable transformation has taken place is that of the giving and receiving of money.

One of the chief perplexities of the missionary's position has been that he has been the paymaster as well as the father of the Church. For a long time this was not felt as a perplexity. Many of the missionaries came from churches in Europe, in which the whole financial responsibility for the Church was undertaken by the state, or was covered by the inheritance from medieval times. Many of them received their own salaries of royal bounty, and with them sufficient income to cover the needs of their missionary work. It did not seem necessary to ask that the converts should share in the burden of what was being done for them. Many of them were so very poor that it may have seemed almost unjust to ask anything of them, when they had scarcely enough to maintain themselves in life at all.[1]

It must not be supposed that Christians in the new churches were left without any outlet for their generosity. At an early stage of growth, they took over responsibility for minor local expenses, such as the lighting of churches. At intervals they contributed generously to the needs of Christians elsewhere ; for example, at the time of the great persecution of Christians in Uganda in 1886, Christians in South India raised a considerable sum for the relief of those who were in distress. But almost all those in the service of the mission were paid by the missionaries from funds

---

[1] The regular collection in church has become so familiar a part of Sunday services in England that most people have forgotten how very recent its introduction is. There should always be a collection at the Holy Communion, but this was very rarely celebrated. Special collections were taken at intervals by order of the government. It appears that the regular Sunday collection was first instituted by the poet Hawker of Morwenstow (1803–1875) in the middle of the Nineteenth Century.

which were exclusively under their control. As has been pointed out by Chinese Christians, the introduction into village communities, resting on a minutely balanced economic system of production and exchange, of a class of persons living by money payments from without was in itself a serious disturbance of the existing order of things. But much more serious was the situation in which the Church took no responsibility for the support of those who ministered in it, and in which to the spiritual authority of the missionary was added the undefined but immense power of economic control.

The old ways worked well over a long period of time. It was only gradually that the new principle of self-support, as an essential condition of healthy church life, made its way, often in the face of opposition from those who had long enjoyed the benefits of " free salvation," and did not readily see why they should now be required to pay for what, as they had been so often assured, had been given by God without money and without price.

It may be questioned whether the term self-support is one which should ever have been used in a Christian connection. It at once introduces a self-regarding motive which is contrary to the spirit of the Gospel. And self-support can be interpreted variously and attained by various means. In some missions, self-support was limited in interpretation to the payment by the local congregation of the salary of its own minister, and a distinction was made on this basis between self-supporting and missionary congregations. The result might well be that a Christian group, avid of independence, would concentrate all its efforts on raising enough to pay its minister, to the neglect of other Christian obligations, and might reject a well-qualified man in favour of another, to whom a smaller salary could be offered. A still worse situation resulted when self-support was limited to the internal affairs of the Christian society, its expansive work in evangelisation being left to foreign money and foreign personnel, a dichotomy of the static and dynamic in the life of the community indefensible on any reading of the New Testament. In any case, there is something artificial in the use of the term. Almost all missions have looked forward to the ultimate conversion of large numbers of people, and have therefore built up a structure of educational, medical and social work heavier than can be carried by the new churches, until their numbers and economic strength have grown far beyond the present level. Even in highly developed churches, the complete withdrawal of foreign aid would cause widespread disruption.

Nevertheless, the principle, though imperfectly stated, was sound and necessary. Economic dependence implies a state of adolescent tutelage ; it is incompatible with full manhood in Christ. The emphasis should, however, have been laid from the beginning primarily on the claim of God to a share in the gifts He has given to His children, represented by the Jewish law of tithing, and on the Christian obligation to share with others who are in need. The Gentiles who contributed to the relief of the necessities of the poor saints in Jerusalem did not claim any spiritual domination over them ; they recognised that the ministry of Christian giving is one of the sacramental means by which the unity of the whole Christian society has been expressed. It has been noticed that missionary expansion is most rapid in those bodies, such as the Church of the Seventh Day Adventists, in which all members are required, as a condition of Church fellowship, to give to the service of God the tithe of all that they acquire.

In almost every mission field, it has been found desirable to set up some form of organisation through which the mind of the local Christian community can be expressed, and in which the layman can take his share in the government of the Church. In practice from the very beginning converts were consulted on the affairs of the Church. Western customs and times of service could not be im-

posed in strange climes without any modification. The
use of the marriage token (tali) in South India, instead of,
or in addition to, the ring required by western custom, is
an early example of local modification, introduced in
recognition of the feelings of the Indian Christian. In such
matters as the admission of new members, local elders were
consulted and attention paid to their views. But in the
end the decision rested with the missionary. A great step
forward was taken, when formal councils were set up, and
it was made clear that the decisions of these councils would
not be overridden in their own fields of competence.[1] At
first, it was found that the members regarded themselves
as having been called together merely to register assent to
decisions already taken for them, since timidity for a time
outweighed the desire for independence. That stage was
quickly passed through, and now almost every Christian
community, however young, has its graded system of
councils and synods, in which responsible decisions are
taken, and in which any infringement of local independence
from without would be quickly resented and opposed.

It might be supposed that a change in name could not
in itself have a profound significance in the development
of the self-consciousness of a Church ; but recorded facts
bear witness to the contrary. In 1930, the Anglican Church
in India ceased to be a part of the Church of England, and
became the Church of India, Burma and Ceylon.[2] The
immediate practical changes were simply that the Church
obtained the right to elect its own bishops instead of
receiving them by appointment from England, a reversion
to early and genuinely Christian practice, and that no
appeals in ecclesiastical affairs could thenceforth lie from
India to England. But the effect on the minds of Indian

---

[1] Such a system of Church Councils was set up in 1890 in the area of the
Church Missionary Society in Tinnevelly in South India.
[2] The steps by which this change was brought about have been fully set
forth by Archdeacon C. J. Grimes in *Towards an Indian Church* (London,
1946).

Christians was immediately apparent and far greater than could have been brought about by any mere change in organisation ; they felt in a new way that this was their Church, for the maintenance and growth of which they must now more fully take responsibility.

Effectiveness in the transmission of the faith is the only unmistakable sign of manhood in Christ. No individual Christian has given certain proof of his full possession of the faith, unless he can say of some other man, as Paul said of Onesimus, " My child, whom I have begotten in my bonds."[1] No part of the Christian society can establish beyond doubt the reality of its participation in the life of the society, unless it has proved its capacity to bring into being new communities in Christ, where none existed before. Of the churches in the western world, scarcely any has has failed in the last century to give this evidence. It is not possible to say that God has conspicuously blessed the missions of one Christian confession more than those of another. Roman Catholics, Orthodox, Anglicans, Free Churchmen have gone out in the name of Christ, and where they have worked, Christian communities have come into being. A further stage is reached when those new communities themselves give proof of their vitality by going beyond their frontiers to win others and to pass on the life that they have themselves received. The present century has shewn in many parts of the world that that stage in the life of the younger churches has now been reached. The Indian Missionary Society (Anglican) of Tinnevelly, founded in 1903, the work of the Methodist Church of South India in the Nizam's Dominions, the mission of the Church of Christ in China among the aboriginal peoples of the western Chinese frontier, and many others that might be named, are all enterprises carried out by the younger churches themselves, without western aid or direction. They could not have attained such success as has been granted them, if the crea-

[1] Philem : v. 10.

tive power of Christ Himself had not been at work within their fellowships. The stage of colonial dependence has really been exchanged for that spiritual independence, which is so much more important than the mere outward forms of self-government.

The progress of the churches may well be regarded as parallel to that which takes place in any normal family. The period during which the children are dependent on the parents is followed by a time of conflict and criticism, when new adjustments of relationship have to be made. With patience and goodwill on both sides, this passes into the third stage of fellowship and co-operation between parents and their grown-up children. In many younger churches, the period of growth has been marked by tension, and even by sharp conflict. Submission to the missionaries has been followed by revolt, criticism and fault-finding. In the natural desire for self-assertion, leaders of the younger churches have sometimes been inclined to believe that from the beginning missionaries have done nothing but make mistakes and lay false foundations. But in many areas, that time of contention is passing away, and a new era of happy co-operation is beginning. In some places it is possible to see all three stages contemporaneously in existence. The older generation is content to remain in the attitude of quiet veneration for those by whom the faith was originally brought. Those of middle age are self-assertive and suspicious, always inclined to believe that the foreigner is actuated by impulses of domination and a desire to thwart the independence of the younger church. The new generation accepts the westerner as a colleague, and finds no difficulty in co-operation with him on a basis of natural and unquestioned equality.

As the younger churches enter on their new life of independent self-expression within the world-wide family, they are faced with the task of re-thinking their relationships to the past, and to the older churches. How much of the tradition of the church must they keep as sacred, and how much can they reject as not belonging essentially to the faith ?

In this process, there cannot but be peril. New heresies may spring up as a result of liberty, just as they did in the early days of the Church. So far this tendency has hardly manifested itself ; the younger churches tend towards strict conservatism and orthodoxy in matters of doctrine and biblical interpretation. In other questions of practical concern, however, they are faced with decisions for which western precedents may be found inadequate. For instance, how far are they to be bound by the marriage law of the Church as they have inherited it ? There is no one marriage law of the Church. There are wide differences between the Roman Church and the Orthodox, and modifications have come in in Protestant areas, partly through the relaxation of old requirements, and partly through the action of the state. But all these traditions, whatever their differences, stand within one stream, deriving on the one hand from the Old Testament, and on the other from the inheritance of Roman law. At many points this tradition differs from those of lands which have never come under Jewish or Roman influence. Some marriages which are permitted by Christian codes are forbidden by ethnic tradition. In parts of Africa, all marriages between cousins, permitted though not encouraged by the custom of the west, are regarded as incestuous. In South India, all the children of a group of brothers are regarded and referred to as brothers and sisters, and any possibility of marriage between them is rigorously excluded.[1] On the other hand, marriage of a man to his mother's brother's daughter is so common as to be almost obligatory. In some groups, marriage of a man to his elder sister's daughter, forbidden by Christian law, is regarded as natural and right. In yet other communities,

---

[1] This is rendered necessary by the joint-family system, in which a number of families may live together in one large house, built round a single courtyard. Naturally conversion to Christianity does not immediately modify this social custom.

a man is almost compelled by custom to marry the widow of his deceased elder brother.[1] How far are the older churches justified in insisting that the younger must be bound by traditional solutions ? At what point would they be justified in breaking off communion, if younger churches, in their own very different setting, decided to go their own way, and to try new experiments ? The Roman Catholic Church solves the problem by maintaining a strict law, but giving dispensations so widely and easily as almost to make the law of no effect. If this solution does not commend itself, at what point does legitimate experiment pass over into unjustified rebellion against what the wisdom of the Church in past ages has decided ?

This is but one illustration of a problem that will come up in many forms, and from many angles. Many of the problems are wholly new, since the Christian society is now world-wide, and living again through that period of tension, represented in earlier Church history by the epoch of the Fathers and of the great Councils, in which the relations between the Christian civilisation and that to which it had fallen heir were being regulated.

Another peril which will certainly lie in the path of the younger churches is nationalism. Nationalism in any extreme form can grievously disrupt the God-given unity of the universal family of Christ. The English reformers may have believed that, in setting up a Church of England in separation from Rome, they were doing no more than to make possible the English expression of the Catholic faith within the undivided family of Christendom. But if, as actually happened, the Church of England becomes isolated from the general life of Christendom and self-contented in its isolation, where is the common life of the family ? The consequences of the Reformation were less disastrous than they might have been, because of the

[1] All these problems are set forth in the Lambeth Report on *Kindred and Affinity as Impediments to Marriage*, a thorough and balanced study of the whole subject.

common heritage by which all the churches of Europe have
been to some extent held together in mutual understanding.
The perils will be greater in the vast non-Christian world,
where the disruptive forces are greater, and where the
centripetal force of tradition has had so much less time to
grow. To believe in an Indian expression of the Catholic
faith of Christendom is one thing. To speak of the Indian
Church, as though it were something possessing a separate
existence, and in which equal stress is to be given to the
epithet and to the noun, involves a denial of something
essential to the life of the Christian society.

The attitude of the Church in the great struggles for
political independence which have perturbed the East in
recent years has tended to be ambiguous. Almost all older
Christians stood aloof, or regarded nationalist movements
as a peril to the Church, partly through the sense of being
a minority dependent for safety and protection on foreign
friends, partly through genuine affection for missionaries
and respect for western traditions. This gave justification,
in the mind of the ardent nationalist, for regarding the
Christian as the enemy of his country, and as a running-dog
of western imperialism. When the younger generation of
Christians began to be affected by the national movement,
with its emphasis on national self-respect and its passion
for political equality, there was a tendency for those involved
to go to extremes, and to compromise their loyalty to the
Christian faith, since nationalism presented itself almost in
the form of a second religion, incompatible in its local
emphasis with the international element which is inseparable
from the first. A small number of Christians felt this
incompatibility so strongly as to abandon Christianity and
to return to the religion of their fathers.[1] Happily, the

---

[1] A new problem is posed by the attempt now being made in some
countries to give to nationalism a continuing emotional content by
identifying the traditional religion of the country with it. In Ceylon,
Buddhism has undergone a marked revival since the beginning of this century ; it is frequently stated that Buddhism is the basis of Ceylonese culture,

political détente that has followed on the achievement of independence by so many eastern nations has resulted in an easing of the tension within the Church, and in a changed attitude on the part of many non-Christians towards it. Christians have in many countries played a notable part in the national movements and in the reconstruction that has followed on the attainment of independence. The strain between loyalty to the Church and loyalty to country is no longer so acutely felt.

National isolationism has not as yet become a serious danger to any younger church. For a time, national leaders newly installed in positions of authority in the Church tended, while thanking the missionaries for all that they had done in the past, to say that the period of foreign co-operation was now over, and that the Church itself would undertake full responsibility for all that needed to be done in the country in which God had set it as a light and a witness. But the task proved unexpectedly heavy In India, only two per cent. of the population is Christian, in China barely one per cent., in Japan less than one per cent. The Christians are in the main drawn from the poorer and more ignorant classes. The miracle of the existence of the younger churches cannot conceal the many weaknesses from which they still suffer. In consequence the younger churches themselves have begun to ask again for the help of colleagues from the west. They have made it abundantly clear that only those will be welcome who are prepared to come as servants of the Church, and to identify themselves wholly with it in its sufferings and in its aspirations. There is to be no return to the old days of domination. But equally there is to be no national or racial exclusiveness. In matters of importance, the younger churches have shewn marked

and that only a Buddhist can be in the fullest sense a patriotic Ceylonese. A similar process can be seen at work in Burma, where the severe restrictions at present imposed on missionary work can be interpreted as the result in part of a continuing suspicion of western influence, in part of a desire to give to Burmese nationalism a religious sanction.

capacity to transcend all feelings of national or racial difference. In the (Anglican) Church of India, the inclination still to elect European and not Indian bishops is so strong as to cause some dismay to those who believe firmly in the principle of indigenous leadership.

The independence of the younger churches has been fully recognised and accepted. But the very word independence raises many problems. Independence of what ? If the answer is independence of foreign control, no difficulty arises. But is there any sense in which any part of the Christian society can be regarded as independent of all the rest ? The small Christian groups of New Testament times enjoyed much independence. But they were firmly held together by apostolic teaching and supervision, and by an intense sense of interdependence in the one fellowship of Christ. If divisions had never arisen among Christians, this mutual interdependence would never have been threatened.

In the present state of the Christian society, with its marked divisions, expressed in mutual excommunication and refusal of fellowship at the table of the Lord, the problem becomes increasingly acute with every expansion of the society, and with the reproduction of western divisions in non-Christian countries. When a younger church is a member of one world-wide Christian family or denomination, independence is balanced by a sense of wider loyalties and of mutual responsibility within the family. Where, however, as has happened widely in recent years, small Christian communities have come into existence through the preaching of ardent evangelists, whose aim has been to preach the Gospel, but who have had little concern about the form or organisation of the Church, the standing of such communities within the wider family and their relationships to it remain undefined. A vague sense of spiritual fellowship with other Christians is much less than the New Testament sense of community in Christ.

It seems that here we are driven back on one of the

fundamental problems involved in the nature of the Christian society. Almost all Christians would agree that, when a man is baptised, he is baptised into the body of Christ, that is into the whole company of the redeemed, who in every country and in every age have found their unity in Christ. But in practice, Christians are divided in the way in which they view this fellowship. For some, the immediate reality is the local community ; that is, the fellowship into which a man is admitted by faith, and of which formally he is a member. Behind that local community, the larger fellowship of which the local community is only a part is sometimes no more than vaguely apprehended. To others, the great community is the first reality, loyalty to the whole of which no less than loyalty to Christ is accepted in the profession of faith in baptism. Membership in a denomination, in a local community, is only as it were an accident, a necessity of our present condition, since, as long as we are in the body, the Christian family must have its local expressions, and its incorporation in countries and cities and villages. This is more than a difference of emphasis ; a difference of theological outlook is involved. It is clear that, if the sense of the part carries the day against the sense of the whole, inter-dependence is something that has to be learned, and is not accepted implicitly as belonging to the very nature of the Christian society.

Yet another problem is raised by every recognition of national distinctiveness in the field of religion. How are we to understand God's providence in the ordering of the history of the nations ? To the Christian, Christ is the centre, the interpreter and the judge of history. The main line of revelation is through the history of the Jewish people and through the prophetic word of the Old Testament. But it is possible firmly to hold this truth, and yet at the same time to believe that God has watched over all the nations of the earth, and has given them a share in the good gifts of His love, even in their isolation from the truth of Christ. If this is true, then racial characteristics and insights, the profound psychological differences that arise from difference of language and tradition, are treasures to be guarded and not to be abandoned ; and the fulness of the Christian society cannot be realised, until all these in their integrity, purified and transformed by Christ, are brought into the city of God. The saying of Bishop Westcott is well known, that the Church will not fully understand the meaning of the Gospel of St. John until it is interpreted in a commentary brought forth from depths of wisdom hidden in the Indian mind. The simple joyousness of the African, the austere simplicity of the Muslim world, the ethical sobriety of the Chinese, the passionate self-devotion of the Japanese to a cause may be equally indispensable to the perfection of the Church, if the manifold wisdom of God in Christ is to be fully revealed and understood.

It is only in the light of such a concept that the use of the word *Churches*, to designate separate and local parts of the Christian society, can in any way be justified. If, in the calling into being and the liberation of the younger churches, the conscious aim is to set the nations of the world free to find themselves in Christ, and to express in their own way what they have found in Him, but always within the fellowship of the one society, then, however many the risks, and however many the mistakes made by the way, the enterprise is seen as justifiable and necessary, as a part of God's purpose to bring the nations, as nations, to walk in the light of the city of God. But, if Christian communities carry the assertion of independence to the point at which interdependence is no longer seen to be equally necessary, their misconception of the nature of the Christian society may be so serious as to cause grave hindrance to the fulfilment of the purpose of God to sum up all things in Christ.

* The " Padroado " was finally brought to an end on 20 July, 1950, except for the diocese of Goa, which is in Portuguese territory.

CHAPTER XII

THE DISINTEGRATION OF THE WEST

AT the end of the Nineteenth Century, the situation of the Christian society was such that, whether attention was directed to its vast geographical expansion within the space of a hundred years, or to the apparently impregnable stability of the supposedly Christian west, an observer might well have concluded that it was destined within a measureable span of time to carry all before it, and to establish itself as the universal home of all mankind. Even those who saw most clearly the defects of western civilisation tended to identify that civilisation with the cause of Christianity, and to believe both that any extension of the influence of the west would be favourable to the spread of the Gospel through the world, and that the Gospel itself was one of the strongest influences making for common understanding and the development of a universal humanity.

This optimistic estimate was reinforced by a misapplication of the Darwinian hypothesis of evolution. The earlier applications of the theory to human affairs had been on the whole pessimistic ; the world seemed to present itself under the aspect of ruthless and merciless struggle, in which the gentler emotions vainly attempted to place a check on the elimination of the weak. But if evolution be interpreted not merely as a principle of change but also as a law of progress, and if the term progress be given a Christian colouring, it is not difficult to reach, as a conclusion, belief in the inevitability of the arrival of the kingdom of God upon earth.[1] This optimistic view survived the disasters of the

[1] I believe that the optimistic view of evolution was first made current in England in Benjamin Kidd's *Social Evolution* (London, 1894), a book which was widely read and influential at the turn of the century.

first world war. It was supposed that this had been the last manifestation of the power of the lower elements in human nature, and that, now that these had been purged away by suffering, humanity would enter on a new course of progress, in which the animal would more and more recede and the spiritual take control. This accorded well with the views of that liberal humanism from which the League of Nations drew its strongest support. It was recognised that the process would take time ; but since God has aeons to work in, and the history of civilised man on this planet has been but a moment of astronomical time, there was no reason to be disturbed by apparent regressions or delays, which could not do more than retard the inevitable momentum of the whole historic process. Since the nature of the process was revealed in Christ, the Christian had the assurance that he was working along the lines on which the cosmic whole was moving to its perfection.

There is a curious parallelism between this Christian inevitabilism and the Marxist doctrine of freedom as the realisation of necessity. The Marxist is equally convinced of the existence of an inevitable trend in history. Man may oppose himself to that trend, but in that case his only destiny is to be swept away by the march of events ; whereas if he aligns himself with the movement of history, he has a triumphant sense of freedom and achievement in the accomplishment of his own historic destiny. To the Christian who believed in the coming of the kingdom of God by evolution, the apocalyptic element in the New Testament was naturally repugnant and unintelligible ; it was explained away as part of the Jewish furniture of the apostolic mind, a superfluous deposit within Christian thinking from the needs of an earlier day.[1]

The history of the world between 1914 and 1949 has

[1] Even so profound a Christian thinker as Baron Friedrich von Hügel admitted that he found the apocalyptic passages in the Gospels an almost unassimilable element. See *Essays and Addresses* (London, ed. of 1924), pp. 119–143.

effectively destroyed the optimism of the pre-war period. Two wars, the Russian revolution, the much greater revolution that has followed it in Asia, the discovery of the weakness of the churches throughout Europe, persecution, destruction and terror have combined to bring about a situation in which the sombre pictures of the Apocalypse no longer seem so irrelevant as once they did. It has become apparent that prosperity and progress may conceal the inward gnawing of decay, and that two conflicting processes may be at work together within a single organism.

Many of those who have tried to understand this ambiguous condition of the Christian society have concluded that the principle of disintegration was introduced at the time of the Renaissance, and that its consequences, though retarded by periodic religious revivals, have been working themselves out slowly ever since.

The Renaissance was a glorious epoch in the history of the human race. The rediscovery of the world of Hellas opened again to the mind of Europe original sources of inspiration that have continued to quicken it until the present day. Men recovered the sense of wonder and of delight in life. From wonder came again the lost faculty of observation, and from this the impulse to discover, to invent and to create. Man found the world to be a delightful kingdom, and became conscious of his own position as its king.

But there is only a short step from delight in life to that wanton "boastfulness of life" condemned by the Apostle.[1] To look through the portraits of Renaissance leaders given as illustrations to Burckhardt's *Civilisation of the Renaissance in Italy*[2] is a disturbing experience. Here are represented ambition, skill, intensity of feeling, finesse, refinement, arrogance. There is not one single face in which the spiritual qualities are dominant. The Renaissance set man in the

[1] 1 John ii. 16.
[2] In the admirable edition published by the Phaidon Press (London, 1937).

centre of the human picture ; it was a movement for the glorification of man, for the development of his gifts and of his power over nature. But it did not encourage that humility and submission before God, without which man loses the balance of his nature, and, falling into idolatry, makes himself his own god.

This man-centred concept of the universe has worked itself out in many ways.

The glory of the medieval artist was his anonymity. He worked in a tradition, a fellowship in the mystery, and was content to let his work pass into the common stream of human life. " In the long run intellectual artistic creation depends on the living power of a tradition, that is, on hearing the response of other men. A wrong turning was taken when at the Renaissance the artist began to put himself and his individual achievement at the centre, to develop a pride in his own accomplishment, and so became increasingly isolated and solitary."[1] This tendency has not affected all the arts equally ; that it has been widely operative can scarcely be denied.

Next to the artist stands the philosopher. Modern research has shown that Descartes (1596–1650), like Luther, was more dependent on the medieval tradition than had sometimes been supposed. Nevertheless, the thought of Descartes does mark a new beginning. Man, as rarely before, is in the centre of the stage. Much post-Renaissance philosophy is marked by a supreme confidence in the power of human reason to stand outside the universe, to comprehend it, to reconcile all contradictions and to impose upon it the order of a rationally coherent system. The absurd conclusion of the Hegelian system in the glorification of the contemporary European state as the final self-expression of self-developing spirit pointed to a defect somewhere in the process of thought. It was not

[1] J. H. Oldham in *Question*, Vol. 2, No. 1 (London, 1949), p. 120. Dr. Oldham refers to *The Dilemma of the Arts* by A. J. Weidle (London, 1949).

generally remembered that man himself is part of the universe that he contemplates, and that he himself is the deepest problem of all.

The Eighteenth Century marked the triumph of reason in human affairs. It was an age of genius and of high achievement. Excluding the irrational elements in human nature, it tried to achieve within the limits of reason a graceful and proportioned ordering of human affairs. It was willing to accept those parts of religion that could commend themselves to reason, and accepted the principle of benevolence as that by which the actions of man should be determined. But deeper elements of religious faith were rejected. External conformity to the traditions of Christian faith could not mask that profound scepticism which finds expression in the writings of Gibbon and of Hume (1711–1766). Such religion could not in fact control the rebellious nature of man ; the lives of some at least of the devotees of reason were not such as to commend their creed to a race desperately in need of the power of redemption.

If one part of human nature is suppressed and disregarded, it will always take its revenge. The Romantic movement gave expression to just those aspects of human nature which the Eighteenth Century had most disapproved—emotion, the sense of mystery and strangeness in the universe. The rediscovery of mystery was undoubtedly one of the factors in the great religious revivals by which the Nineteenth Century was marked. In the profound but often obscure philosophy of Coleridge, and more especially in the novels of Sir Walter Scott, men rediscovered a world that they had forgotten, and were predisposed to reconsider a religion that offered satisfaction to cravings of the human spirit that had been starved. Yet in the Romantic movement also there was the characteristic weakness that it tended to concentrate on the individual in his isolation, to give expression to his emotions and experiences, to encourage the experience of emotion rather than the experience of life, and in religion to make religious experience an end in itself.

The Christian society, so far from adapting itself to meet the new and clamant needs of a secular society which was fast drifting away from it, had been falling into an isolation that, if carried beyond a certain point, could not but make it ineffective as an instrument of redemption.

The process of clericalisation was continuous and increasingly harmful in its effects. There had been from an early period tension between the rich and the poor within the Church, between the ecclesiastical potentates and those over whom they ruled. This was harmful, but much less harmful than the gradual emergence of the clergy as a separate order, with vested interests of their own, and a position in society that inevitably set them in opposition to the needs and demands of Christ's little ones. This process had reached its furthest limit in the Church of pre-revolutionary France. The higher clergy were a privileged order exempt from taxation, and assured of the possession of wealth, privilege and status, without regard to whether the services, for the sake of which those privileges had been originally given, were being performed or no.[1] In England, the clergy of the established Church had become a part of the possessing class, with too great a stake in the maintenance of the *status quo*. The poor country priest might maintain his link and his sympathy with the poor. The higher clergy were almost invariably on the side of reaction. Lecky was scarcely exaggerating, when he passed his famous judgment that for a hundred years the Church of England had been

[1] The early career of Talleyrand is a striking illustration of the extent to which this process could be carried. Since Duff Cooper's beautifully proportioned *Life of Talleyrand* (London, Cape 1932) has passed through nineteen editions, it is not necessary to labour this point for English readers. Those who know their Talleyrand best from *Rewards and Fairies* will be glad of the historian's note that: "Fiction is often an aid to history, and the penetrating eye of genius can discern much that remains elusive to the patient researches of the historian." Page 81.

opposed to every reform. When Sir Samuel Romilly brought forward in Parliament a proposal to abolish capital punishment for theft in shops to the value of five shillings, the Archbishop of Canterbury and six other bishops walked into the opposition lobby to record their disapproval.[1] As long as the poor could be kept suppressed, all might go on with little change. It was certain that, if ever the poor attained to emancipation, the official church would pay dear for its attitude of aloofness to their needs. The French Revolution gave a first indication of what the future might bring. When the storm was over, the official churches settled down again contentedly to their alliance with the forces of reaction. As the new working-class, brought into being by the Industrial Revolution, came to self-consciousness, it was taken for granted in most European countries that the Church would always be on the wrong side.[2]

Changes in the climate of thought are always difficult to trace, and there may be wide disagreement about them. On one subject there can be no difference of opinion. From the middle of the Eighteenth Century, hard demographic facts were breaking up the old order of western society and of the Church. For centuries recurrent epidemics, wars, famines, and an immensely heavy death-rate among children had kept the population almost stable. Now at last birth began to win in the race with death, and European man began to multiply. Vast new aggregations of population came into being. The churches had no means to deal with them. Even if they had been alive to the signs of the times, they were hampered by their own traditions of property, and by

---

[1] L. Radzinowicz: *A History of the English Criminal Law and its Administration from 1700* (London, 1948), p. 353, n. 30, Dr. Radzinowicz refers to "the failure of the Established Church to take a lead in any important movement for reform."

[2] "In 1879, when the first organised strike took place in Sweden, the strikers wished to have morning prayers, and invited a clergyman to take these for them. The clergyman not merely refused, but notified the police, who called out the military to compel the strikers to come back to work." *The Church's Witness to God's Design* (Amsterdam Assembly Series, London, S.C.M. Press 1948), Vol. II, p. 78, n. 1.

their entanglement with the state. The number of ordained clergy remained almost what it had been. In England, until well after the middle of the Nineteenth Century, the city of Manchester remained one single parish, the clergy of its collegiate church being unwilling to accept the loss of income from fees that would have been involved in the legal creation of new parishes. In Norway, the number of parishes and priests remains almost exactly as it was at the time of the Reformation. When a parish in Oslo reached a population of twenty-four thousand under the care of a single minister, the government was still unprepared to take the legal action without which the formation of a new parish was impossible.

In England, the consequences to the Christian movement of this sudden change were mitigated by the spread of Methodism. The Established Church was dangerously wedded to the cause of the possessing classes. The older dissenting bodies were small and had their own aristocratic traditions. Methodism became the religion of the proletariat. Methodist chapels sprang up everywhere. Their proceedings and the extravagances of the Ranters were extremely distasteful to all persons of culture and refinement. But the Methodists brought into the lives of the dispossessed emotional satisfaction, a sense of being loved, the opportunity of responsible action, and, in their class meetings and on the temperance platform, an admirable training ground in public speaking.[1] Where there was no Methodist movement, generations of men grew up who had had no connection at all with the Church, and regarded it with sullen hostility. The common phrase "recovery of the working-class for the Church" is meaningless in some countries of Europe. The working-class in its modern form has never belonged to the Church ; it is almost as much a

---

[1] The importance of this in the development of the Trade Union Movement and the Labour Party in England can be readily discerned by reference to the brief biographies of the leaders given in R. C. K. Ensor, *England*, 1870–1914 (Oxford, 1936).

virgin field for missionary endeavour as the heart of China.[1]

The development of scientific thought and historical criticism challenged the churches to readjustments in their traditional formulations of thought and doctrine. These the churches were ill-equipped to make. In facing Darwin and his followers, the Christian apologist tended to take his stand on a line that could not be defended, and was inevitably overwhelmed. Neither party was aware at the time that the victory and defeat were only tactical, and that the great strategic issues still remained to be decided. There was widespread alienation from a Christianity that seemed to desire, by the imposition of outworn dogmatic tests, to limit the freedom of scientific enquiry and experiment.[2]

The real lines of the conflict have only gradually been clearly drawn. The great scientists of earlier days had stood well within the humanist tradition. Newton[3] and Leibnitz were both men of profound religious conviction, and neither had found any intrinsic disaccord between faith and scientific progress. The development of a new type of scientific thought and education produced new conflicts. Humanism, whether Christian or secular, is more concerned with persons than with things. Modern physical science is occupied with things and the relationships between them. Even where, as in medicine, it is dealing with human beings, it tends to eliminate the personal factor and to treat man only as an animated body. It relies for its spectacular results

[1] Dramatic attention has been called to this state of affairs in a series of publications by French Roman Catholic writers, notably the Abbé Godin's *La France, Pays de Mission?* (Paris, 1943: English translation, under the title *France Pagan?* London, 1948).

[2] There were notable exceptions to the obscurantist attitude of the churches. For instance, F. J. A. Hort at Cambridge took from the start a more constructive view of the new scientific movement. But public attention was directed in the main to the unsuccessful apologetic of the conservatives, and it took time for Christian thought to recover from the discredit in which it had become involved.

[3] In 1687, Newton wrote, as the concluding sentences of his *Principia Mathematica* the following : " The whole diversity of natural things can have risen from nothing but the ideas and will of one necessarily existing being, who is always and everywhere, God Supreme, infinite, omnipotent, omniscient, absolutely perfect."

on the evidence of that which can be measured, numbered and weighed. It is well known that those trained to use only one kind of evidence find it hard to adjust their minds to assess the weight of evidence of a different category. The kind of evidence that the Christian faith can produce is ruled out by many scientists as irrelevant. The kind of proof that science calls for is mostly of the kind that Christian faith ought not to be expected to produce.

As science has become the dominant force in educational process, it has tended to produce a general climate of thought unfavourable to Christian faith. There was a time when most men, if questioned, would have confessed to an inclination to believe in the possibility of human survival after death. In the Twentieth Century, the majority would probably deny the possibility or profess themselves sceptical. Such inclinations lie deeper than rational conclusions ; but they are part of the raw material of thought, by which apparently rational convictions are affected.

Yet one more source of weakness within the Christian society has to be recorded. The later Lutheranism, mis-applying Luther's doctrine of the two realms, had tended to shut the Church up within the ghetto of its own ecclesiastical concerns, and to deny its responsibility to serve as watchman and critic of society and of the state.[1] In any extreme form, this doctrine involves a surrender of the world to the devil, and a denial both of its redeemableness and of its actual redemption in Christ. Statesmen have always been unscrupulous and violent, but in the past they had usually thought it necessary to find some plausible excuses for their worst acts. When Bismarck (1815–1898) with characteristic Prussian efficiency and thoroughness introduced his *Real politik*, the serious thing was not that he was successful, but that scarcely a voice was raised, in criticism

---

[1] On this, as on so many other subjects, what Luther really taught bears little relation to what he is supposed to have taught. His real doctrine of the two realms has been briefly set out by Bishop Anders Nygren in the *Ecumenical Review*, Vol. I, No. 3 (Geneva, 1949), pp. 301–10.

of his actions, in the Church of a great Christian country. The epitaph on Christianity was pronounced, with the pungency of which he was master, by Friedrich Nietzsche (1844–1900), when he wrote " The Christian values and the *noble* values . . . it is we others, free spirits, who have been the first to establish this contrast, the greatest contrast that exists."

The first world war shook the credit of the Christian society throughout the world, and especially in Asia. It was not until the post-war period that it became clear that the society had moved out of the period of stability into that of movement, peril and persecution.

The Babylon of the Apocalypse, the typical representation of human society arrayed in rebellion against God, has clothed itself today in the garments of the totalitarian state.

When Adolf Hitler, on his accession to power, took action to bring the Churches in Germany under his control, it was not immediately evident that a conflict had begun, no less serious than that of the early Christians against the Roman emperors, in which, sooner or later, Christians must stand upon the Christian line, at the cost if need be of martyrdom and death. It is the merit of the leaders of the so-called Confessing Church that at a very early stage in the controversy they detected the significance of totalitarianism, as the claim of the state to complete control over all the thoughts and actions of men, in consequence of which God is either eliminated from the field of action, or becomes a convenient tool to subserve the purposes of the state. In such a situation, any criticism of the state on the grounds of religious loyalty can be regarded by the authorities as political disaffection, as interference in the field which the state claims as legitimately its own, and as punishable on purely political grounds. This is no new situation. There has never yet been a religious persecution which was admitted by the persecutors to be such. And the situation can easily be confused for simple Christians, especially for those well schooled to civil obedience, so that the reality of the spiritual struggle is not immediately apparent.

The Barmen declaration of the German Confessing Church (1934) is a declaration of war between the Christian society and any society which claims to be exempt from the judgment of God. In uncompromising terms it asserts the lordship of Christ over the Church and over the world, and asserts the right of the Church to listen to the voice of Christ alone. Just what adjustment is to be made between a Church and a state each claiming autonomy in its own sphere remains a problem. It is categorically denied that the Church can ever become a department or an instrument of the state.[1] The Roman Catholic authorities made a similar stand. In consequence relationships between Roman Catholic and Protestant forces in Germany became closer than at any time since the Reformation.

Hitler and his companions were under no illusions as to the menace to their schemes represented by this Christian dissidence. Every "pope" in the country was carefully watched and reported on.[2] Many endured the horrors of the concentration camps. A considerable number never returned. It had become evident that two incompatible loyalties had come into conflict, and that the Christian society was faced with a challenge more radical than had for centuries been presented to it.

In Russia the official Church was singularly ill-equipped to face the blizzard that burst upon it, when, in the early stages

[1] The principal facts can be conveniently found in Stewart Herman, *The Rebirth of the German Church* (London, 1946), pp. 64–83, but the Declaration itself is not quoted in full. The key sentences are: "Jesus Christ, as witness is borne to Him in the Holy Scriptures, is the one Word of God, to which we must hearken, and which we must trust and obey. We repudiate the false doctrine which asserts that the Church can and should recognise, beyond and beside this one Word of God, other events and powers, forms and truths, as a source of the message that it must proclaim and as a revelation from God."

[2] I have myself read, in the original files, many reports of the Gestapo on Roman Catholic priests and Protestant pastors. In many cases, minute details of word and attitude are recorded.

of the Russian revolution, the moderate elements were swept away, and power was taken over by the Bolsheviks, the party pledged to put into effect the full rigour of Marxist doctrine as interpreted by Lenin. Since the time of Peter the Great (1632–1725), the Russian Church had surrendered its spiritual independence to the state. The patriarchate had been abolished, and the Church put under the direction of the Holy Synod, the Chief Procurator of which, a layman, exercised supreme governance on behalf of the emperor. The worst features of the old Byzantine system were reproduced. Under the last of the Chief Procurators, the able and rigid Pobedonostsev, (1883–1903), the Church was kept under strict control and made to serve as an instrument of the reactionary policy of the government.[1]

It is rightly pointed out by Russian writers that this is not the whole truth about the Russian Church. Orthodox theology regards the continuance of the hierarchy as indispensable for the formal existence of the Church ; without it the channel of divine grace would dry up. But if the hierarchy should prove unfaithful, the real life of the Church can continue for long periods in almost complete separation from it. The tradition of the stylites and the hermits was not dead. There was an unbroken line of saints and mystics, profoundly venerated by the common people, through whom in the worst days of state domination the inner spiritual tradition of the Russian people was kept alive.[2] Nevertheless, the close association of Church and reaction made it certain that in a revolutionary epoch the Church would be one of the first objects of attack.

Even now, it is not possible to state with any accuracy

---

[1] "In the days of Pobedonostsev and Sabler, the influence of the State and its conservative ideology penetrated the Church to its core, and paralysed all manifestations of a free religious life . . . its supreme organ was composed of those willing to serve the government, and ready to comply with the demands of the Chief Procurator." Miliukov, *Outlines of Russian Culture*, Part I (Philadelphia, Univ. of Pennsylvania Press 1943), p. 152.

[2] This point of view is argued very strongly by, for example, Nicholas Zernov in his book, *The Russians and their Church* (London, 1945).

the numbers of those who suffered death in the first assault of the communists on the Church. It seems probable that about thirty bishops and considerably more than a thousand priests were among the victims. From the point of view of the revolutionaries, these men were political opponents of the new regime, who had to be eliminated because of their opposition. Communism being based on an atheistic and materialistic philosophy cannot but regard every form of religion as being at best an otiose survival from the pre-scientific age, at worst a potentially dangerous enemy of progress. Communist procedure was logical. Churches were closed, priests deprived of their civil rights, and the utmost freedom given for atheistic and anti-Christian propaganda. After the first fury of persecution had died away, it was hoped that, without further recourse to violent methods, religion, being no longer rooted in the process of history, would die away and would present no further problem in the new communist order.

The Christian faith presented unexpected powers of survival. In spite of persecution and propaganda, a number of churches remained open, and were thronged by the faithful. The essential communist purpose did not change, and, as long as communism remains Marxist, cannot change. But prudence suggested a change of tactics. In the new Constitution of the Union of Soviet Socialist Republics, freedom of religious worship was guaranteed, civil rights were restored to priests, and a *modus vivendi* was reached between the communist state and the Church. The enthusiastic support given to the state by the Church in the conflict against Germany cemented the new relationship, and the Church was able to breathe again.

No reliable statistics have become available as to the number of practising Christians left in Russia at the time of the promulgation of the new constitution. Certainly they did not constitute more than a tiny minority of the population. Since then the patriarchate, temporarily restored during the revolution, has been reconstituted, the vacant bishoprics have been filled up, and theological seminaries opened. The Christian society seems to have found means to subsist within a society that is basically anti-Christian and still regards the disappearance of all religion as necessary to the final fulfilment of its aims.

The spread of communism beyond Russia, and the establisment of communist governments in Balkan countries, in Czecho-slovakia and Hungary, raised in new forms the problem of the continued existence of the Church as an independent international society, with loyalties other than those of the citizen to the state and liable at times to conflict with them. The situation of the Christian society in such a context has been dramatically expressed in the following parable :

There are three possible forms of the limitation of freedom, all of which have been experienced by individuals, as by churches, in this century in the new conflicts between Christ and His enemies. First there is house-arrest. In this stage, the Church is free to continue its activities within the walls of the church building. There is freedom to hold religious services. But it is clearly indicated that there is a division of territory : the state claims complete control over everything that concerns the life of man in this world, and is willing to leave to the Church the concerns of the other world, the more readily because to the authorities of the state that other world is mere illusion without reality of any kind. But this freedom does not include liberty to instruct young people in the faith, education being the concern solely of the state and being limited to those subjects which the state regards as true and useful. Nor does it include liberty of communication beyond the limits of the ideological world of communism. Any transgression by the Church of these limits, any attempt to exercise influence in the spheres marked out by the state as its own, is certain to bring about a renewal of hostility.

The second stage is imprisonment, in which every kind of activity is made impossible. It is possible for the Church, through the confiscation of all property and the prohibition of all public assemblies, to be deprived of every traditional form of activity, and to be reduced to a surreptitious and illegal existence. In the past, the Church has from time to time been subjected to such imprisonment and has survived. The third and worst stage is that of the concentration camp, in which the victim is not only deprived of liberty but is compelled to work ceaselessly for the benefit of an order that he knows to be fundamentally hostile to all that he himself believes. Opinion in the Christian world is divided as to whether the Church in communist-controlled countries has already reached this stage or not.

The Christian society has given evidence of remarkable powers of adaptation to the most varied forms of the organisation of human society. It can co-exist with different forms of government, though to some it is by nature more closely allied than to others. The difficulty of adjustment is greater, when the Christian society, the Messianic society, constituted, as it believes, with a view to the redemption of the human race, has to live within another society, which is itself inspired by a quasi-messianic ideal of a different kind. The National Socialist ideal was a kind of perverted messianism, looking forward to the fulfilment of the destiny of humanity through the dominance of a master race. The messianic elements in the communist outlook are so clearly marked that communism has not unjustly been called a form of Christian heresy. Here the eschatological kingdom is the realm of earthly bliss to be realised in the classless society. The chosen people is the proletariat, the sinless victim of cruelty and exploitation in the past, itself regarded as exempt from the vices that have destroyed all earlier and less perfect human societies. The messianic message is that to which the Christian churches have paid lip-service, but which they have failed to proclaim effectively

—deliverance for the poor, the breaking of every yoke, the year of release and the overthrow of the arbitrary and tyrannical powers of the world. The messianism of the master race has for the moment passed away. The messianism of the classless state is on the march.

But there is yet a third messianism, with which the Christian society finds itself confronted in the modern world.

It has always been hard for the pride of man to accept the view that it is not within his own power to control his destiny. The wonderful achievements of science and of technology in the Nineteenth and Twentieth Centuries have given to man a new sense of power and self-direction. Scientific humanism, in all its many forms, is based on the optimistic view that man is able, by the right use of knowledge, to bring in an *order of things that will secure sufficiency, prosperity and full self-development for all. The application of science to agriculture and to the problems of communication, has, in fact, brought within sight the abolition of want and penury in their extremest forms.[1] The necessity of some form of economic planning and state control is accepted almost universally in the west, in view of the increasing complexity of the interdependence of nations and societies.

Those who put their faith in a planned society would, however, go much further than this. The social sciences, they would claim, are only in their infancy, compared with the physical and the biological sciences. We have hardly begun to apply modern knowledge to man as he is in himself, and to the problems of his relationships. Modern psychology has begun to penetrate the mystery of the disharmonies in man that lead to aggression in the individual and so, by the accumulation of individual aggressions, to wars between

[1] This would not be admitted by all. There is a neo-Malthusian school which holds that, with the present rate of increase in the population of the world, the pressure of population on soil is bound steadily to increase, and that the threat to the general standard of living is already serious.

states. Scientific study has begun to uncover the nature
of human relationships in society, and so to make a beginning
in reducing to scientific and therefore controllable order
what had previously been no more than empirical data or
experimental adjustment. So far from human society
having reached a stage of permanent decay, it is only at
the beginning of its long evolution.[1] The phenomena
presented by man in society are so much more complex
than those studied by physical science and the number of
those who have given their attention to the scientific study
of them has been so small, that progress so far has been
slow. But just as the application of science to physical
nature has produced a revolution in man's control over his
outer environment in nature, so the application of science
to the organisation of society will produce a revolution in
man's control over his inner environment, man himself.
What has hitherto gone forward at haphazard, in the dark
or at best the twilight of intuitive understanding, will now
go forward in the full light of reasoned and accessible
knowledge.

All such doctrines are in their essence messianic. According to them, all the evils in human society are due to ignorance,
to wrong education, or to the bad social conditions that
have resulted from them. By knowledge, all these can be
eliminated, and man set free to realise that which he has
it in him to be. If in this messianic scheme there is a
chosen people, it is the scientists, the planners who are the
bearers of the redemptive message. If there is a redeemer,
it is the process of history itself, which carries man along
with it into his predestined kingdom.[2]

Faced with these alternative and powerful messianisms,
the Christian apologist is disturbed to find that what he

[1] E.g. Koestler, *Insight and Outlook* (London, Macmillan 1949), p. 167:
"*Mutatis mutandis*, human society compared to insect society must be
considered to be still at an infautile or even larval stage."
[2] The modern doctrine of history as redemptive has been fully and very
ably analysed by Dr. Reinhold Niebuhr, in his most recent book, *Faith and
History* (New York, 1949).

says appears to most men either irrelevant or unintelligible, and that what he offers is unattractive. If he speaks of eternal life, as the perspective in which the Christian society always moves, he awakens no response in men who for the most part have accepted either dogmatically or instinctively the view that there is no human immortality apart from that of the race, and that this is conditioned by the certain fact that sooner or later life on this planet will become impossible. Redemption by a divine act from without is not readily accepted by those who are committed to the idea of an immanental redemption through a process of which man himself is a part. The idea of service to humanity has been transformed by the development of the welfare state, a much more powerful machine for the provision of loaves and fishes than the Church could ever be. If the Christian speaks of absolute rights and wrongs, he is confronted by the doctrine of the relativity of all things, and especially of ethical concepts as epiphenomena of the changing economic conditions in which men live.

The malaise of the Christian society in the west is very evident. It may be that the cause is deeper than the changing climate of thought among men. To survive at all, the Christian society must be willing to accept some kind of adjustment to the larger society around. But if that adjustment lead to too close an identification of the Christian society with the existing social order, then in a changing world the Church may well fail to see the signs of the times, and to recover that mobility which makes it possible to enter into a new order of things and again to serve as a creative power within it.

The inveterate tendency of the Christian society is to identify itself with the existing order and to resist change. Revolutionary in its own principles, it too easily forgets the startling proclamations of the *Magnificat*, and accepts an easy spiritual interpretation for what, if literally applied, would disrupt most human societies. The Christian revolutionary has often been ostracised by his own kin, and has found himself more at home with the ostensible enemies of the Church than with its friends. It is too easy for those caught up in an unwelcome revolutionary situation to find in the Christian tradition the expression of their own nostalgia for a state of things that can never come again. For this reason, the reports of crowded churches and enthusiastic congregations in countries under communist control do not make entirely reassuring reading. Even if the Church does not lend itself directly to the forces of reaction, as at certain times it has been prone to do, there is yet a danger that it may find itself the home of those who are out of touch with the movement of the times. This may lead to the re-creation of the Christian ghetto, and may make it yet more difficult for the Christian society to move out into creative activity in the new order of society.

The Twentieth Century scene is characterised by an immense revolution—the emergence into power of classes and peoples that have hitherto been powerless and suppressed. The Christian cannot discount the possibility that, whatever the excesses and violence involved in the process, the process itself may yet be part of God's providential ordering of history. Whether that be so or not, it is certain that the process cannot be reversed, and that humanity will not move back into the pre-revolutionary situation. It is certain also that in many countries the revolution has rejected the guidance of the Church and has repudiated Christian principle. Is it right to conclude, as the revolutionary does, that the day of the Christian society is over, and that at best it can hope for no more than survival as a parasite on a society it can no longer effectively influence ?

The events of the revolution make it necessary for the Christian society to reconsider its own nature. Until recently, there has been marked confusion of thought. The very success of Christianity in imposing a pattern on the western nations has blurred certain fundamental distinctions. Christian society has been assumed to be that ordering of human affairs, in which secular thought has been so far penetrated by the ideas of the Gospel that there no longer remains any basic clash between the Gospel and the principles by which the affairs of state are ruled. It was this identification against which Søren Kierkegaard (1813–1855) so passionately protested, the idea that we are all Christians now, and that the truth of Christianity has become self-evident through the nineteen centuries of its progressive advance.[1] If ever the issues were obscured, they have become plain again in a revolutionary world. Augustine is seen to have been right in his analysis ; the kingdoms of this world are founded on *superbia*, man's claim to be his own master and his own god ; the kingdom of Christ is founded on *humilitas*, the submission of man to a power outside himself that both judges and saves. No earthly order ever represents in its pure form either of the contrasting principles, and it is possible for a kingdom of the world to be deeply penetrated by the divine principle. Yet the contrast remains irreconcilable as long as the world shall last. Nothing more than a temporary and uneasy truce is possible. The Church, therefore, must remain till the end, potentially at least, the Church under the Cross. It must be neither surprised nor dismayed if old allies turn out to be new foes, and if its protests on behalf of the sovereignty and judgment of God bring down upon it at times the hatred and hostility even of those who claim to be acting in the name of God.

The enucleation of the Christian society from the world, and the fresh recognition of its distinctiveness and separateness, must in the end be greatly to its advantage.

At the same time, the Christian society is called to recognise

---

[1] Especially in *Judge for Yourselves* and *Training in Christianity* (English translations, Oxford, 1941).

how many of its contemporary difficulties arise from its too close identification with the principles and practices of bourgeois society.[1] Almost all the Christian bodies have come to believe in the virtue of property and security, in the indispensability of a ministry regularly paid and secure in its social and economic position. Proletarian society thinks in very different terms. It is accustomed to insecurity and uncertainty. It lives from hand to mouth. It regards generosity as more important than thrift, comradeship as preferable to the maintenance of individual rights, recklessness as on the whole more desirable than prudence. Having been conditioned through centuries by the hard experience of poverty, it finds it very hard to believe in the virtue of the well-to-do. The proletarian does not find himself readily at home in the churches as they are now organised ; the churches are almost wholly debarred, by their organisation and their identification with the existing order, from entering deeply into the new world that is coming into existence.

The Constantinian situation of alliance between Church and state is successfully maintained in many parts of the Christian Church, but already it is felt to be an anachronism. The cry "Back to the catacombs" has been raised by some responsible Christian leaders. For the Church to hide itself in the catacombs, unless necessity is laid upon it, would seem to be a counsel of despair. But signs are not lacking that the Church may be driven by circumstances out of its Constantinian security, and back into a situation much more like that of the Church in the days of the persecutions. It has been laid down by the communists in China that no minister of religion may draw a salary in that capacity ; for him to do so is taking money from the poor, an offence in a society in which only the productive worker has the

[1] Cf. Wolfgang Trillhaas : *Studien zur Religionssoziologie* (Göttingen, 1949), p. 25 : "Protestantism is not a return to primitive Christianity ; the hour of its birth marks the conscious movement of Christendom into the bourgeois age ; in a measure, it is a twin-brother of the bourgeois world."

right to live.   As in the early Church, the minister will have to earn his living like anyone else, giving only such leisure as is left to him to the service of the Church.   It is not unlikely that all Church property will be confiscated, that no associations other than those sponsored by the government will be permitted to exist, that education will be a function of government, strictly controlled by ideological considerations, and that no instruction of the young in any religious doctrine will be permitted.   All international communication will be cut off, and freedom of movement between Christian groups severely limited.

In such a situation, can the Christian society survive ? The answer would seem to depend on the extent to which its resources are in itself and not in circumstances, on the measure of its dependence for renewal on its living and present Lord, and on the strength of conviction found in the individual Christian and the Christian family.   Christians in communist-controlled countries have refused to be daunted by this new challenge, and are resolved to go forward into the new situation, confident in the power of affliction to cleanse the Church of its weaknesses, and in the capacity of the Christian society to make itself light and salt and leaven in any situation that the ingenuity or wrong-headedness of man may produce.

It has seemed necessary to lay stress on the challenge to the Christian society presented by the revolutionary situation in its more developed forms.   But it is important to bear in mind the principle of the non-contemporaneity of civilisations.   The whole world is never simultaneously in the same state of development, or affected by the same influences.   At an earlier stage of our study, it was convenient to divide the Christian society into three main areas, extremely diverse as a result of the different influences brought to bear upon them.   In the present turning point of history, a fourfold division would seem to be more appropriate :

1. Over a large part of the world's surface, and particularly in Africa and parts of Asia, the Christian society has full liberty of action, and manifests all the dynamic power of youth. Numbers are increasing with great rapidity. As in the early days in the Roman Empire, the Church seems to have the power to attract to itself some of the best elements in society, to develop from within itself creative leadership of the kind that can influence the minds of men outside the Christian orbit, and to affect society as it responds to the current of world opinion.

2. North America is still living in the pre-revolutionary age. Elsewhere, capitalism seems to have run its course as the means to an increasing satisfaction of the needs of men. There the phenomenon of an expanding economy is still to be observed, though its end may be already in sight. The churches also are living in the same epoch. They give evidence of increasing strength, and of a growing hold on the life of the community. During the great days of expansion, the settlement of the American west ran far ahead of the development of the Church, and the Church was left panting in the rear, always some distance behind in the attempt to catch up with a Frontier that was steadily moving away from it. When the expansion reached the Pacific, and about 1880 the process of settlement was at least in outline completed, the Church was given a breathing space in which to catch up. This process of consolidation still continues. Each year, the figures of Church membership show an increase, and a larger proportion of the population of the United States than ever before is in close fellowship with the churches. Those denominations which are most democratic in their organisation manifest the most rapid growth. It may be that much of this American Christianity is superficial ; nevertheless it is warm-hearted, generous, and marked increasingly by a sense of world-wide mission. In America, as elsewhere, immense changes are on their way. The American churches have so far been less

affected than any others by the necessity of adjustments to
meet the changes as they come.

3. In western Europe, the Constantinian situation
remains outwardly unchanged. The social position of the
churches is strong. There is still a diffused, though vague,
sense that there are Christian nations, and that there is
some kind of co-ordination between the Christian society
and society as a whole. Even in a deeply secularised
country like Sweden, ninety-five per cent. of the young
people come forward for Confirmation, though the great
majority of them never come to the Holy Communion after
they have been confirmed. But all available statistics, in
Roman Catholic as in Protestant countries, show that, in
spite of religious revivals and heroic efforts on the part of
the Church to recover its place within a changing society,
alienation between the ordinary thoughts of men and Christian standards, between the habits that effectively determine
the nature of a society and Christian principles, has gone so
far as to make the Christian organisation of these countries
little more than a shell with a vacuum beneath it. The
process of disintegration continues, and no effort on the
part of the Church has yet availed to stay its course.

4. In eastern Europe, and the parts of Asia that have
come under communist control, the Christian society is
fighting for its spiritual independence. No such situation
has arisen, on a large scale, since the collapse of the eastern
Roman Empire before the Muslims. There is no reason to
suppose that the communist domination will be less enduring
than that of the Muslim empires. The possibilities before
the Church in that area would seem to be three only. It
may become, as in the Muslim empires, a tolerated body,
existing but excluded from any influence on the men and
movements by which the course of history is determined.
It may make the wrong kind of peace, and find itself the
servant of a force the triumph of which throughout the
world would mean the end of the history of the Christian

society. It may be able to continue a martyr existence, in which the faith is held and the reality of the Christian society manifested, as in the early Church, in small groups bound firmly together by charity and hope.

Looking back on the history of the Church, it is easy to see how each phase has arisen out of that which went before. But every prophet who has gone beyond bare generalities has been confounded. God leaves a place in history for the unexpected and paradoxical. If the beginning of the Twentieth Century was a time of unfounded optimism, there is no reason why the middle of the century should be a time of equally unfounded pessimism. The Christian temper is realist. It takes account of difficulties and of opportunities. It regards every difficulty as an opportunity. It recognises that every opportunity may be a temptation. Each day every Christian is faced with numberless occasions on which decisions have to be made. It is out of the multiplicity of Christian decisions, unknown to any but God, that the fabric of the Christian society is woven. It is, humanly speaking, on the faithfulness of the unknown and unrecorded man that its continuance through the long centuries of history has depended. It is not likely that the future will introduce any new circumstances calculated to reverse this law, which has been found to be of universal application in the past.

CHAPTER XIII

THE CHRISTIAN SOCIETY AND THE CHURCH

SOONER or later, it becomes necessary to consider the Christian society, as it now exists in the world, in relation to the New Testament idea of the Church.

The new factor in the situation of the Christian society is that in the Twentieth Century it has become, for the first time in history, a geographically universal society. There are still a few countries, of which Tibet is the most extensive, in which, though there may be a few scattered believers in Jesus Christ, nothing like an organised society exists. Some of the remoter parts of Africa, of South America and of the islands of the sea have never yet been visited by preachers of the Gospel. In all the great non-Christian countries, there are large gaps in the structure of Christian "occupation." Yet, when all this has been fully admitted, it remains true that the Christian faith is by far the most widely disseminated of all the faiths, religious or secular, that have ever come into existence in the world.

But the picture presented by the society of today is very different from that of the small original Christian groups of New Testament times. It is known by a variety of different names. It is divided by differences of organisation and confessional loyalty. It has no organs of common action, and is therefore gravely weakened in the effectiveness of its witness and of its action on the society surrounding it. Apart from theological considerations, which are of the greatest weight, a mere policy of self-interest and self-preservation in the face of increasing dangers would seem to indicate the urgent necessity of closer integration, and of the recovery of that unity which, in New Testament thought, is one of the essential marks of the Christian society as the Body of Christ.[1]

The divisions among Christians are so conspicuous and so glaring that they cannot escape the notice of the most casual observer of the Christian scene. Converts in India make the complaint, not without justification, that, whereas they had experienced a unity in Hinduism, they have found themselves by the fact of becoming Christians divided among sects demanding an exclusive and segregating loyalty. Actually underneath all the divisions there is a sense in which all Christians have the experience of belonging to one another. In times of peril and of common suffering, barriers are broken down. In the face of the non-Christian religions, the things that divide Christians are seen to be of much less weight than the things that unite them. But such diffused fellowship as makes it legitimate to speak of one Christian society in the world is very much less than the unity which would make it possible to speak of one universal Christian Church, of which every Christian in the world is a member, and in which he feels at home.

The word *Church* appears to be commonly used, in modern speech, in no less than six different senses.

There is, first, the mystical sense of the word, in which the Church is understood as the body of Christ, the Bride, not having spot or wrinkle or any such thing, the Church as Christ intended it to be, and as in the purpose of God it already is. This is the concept which dominates the thought of the Orthodox Churches about the Church. When an Orthodox theologian speaks of the Church, it is this indefectible, exalted Church that he has in mind. He may not be greatly concerned about the relationship between this ideal Church and the existing societies which bear the name of Christ. He may agree that it is possible for individuals within the Church, or even for large Christian groups, to

[1] In a theological sense, the *Church* cannot be divided, any more than Christ can be divided. At this point especially our use of the term "the Christian society" manifests its convenience.

sin and to be in error.   But the Church, by its very nature
as the Body of Christ, cannot fail.   To speak, as many speak
today, of the sins and failures of the Church, sounds in his
ears as blasphemous as it would be to speak of the sins of
Christ.   If the Head is sinless, so also must the Body be.

Secondly, the word Church is used to express the fellowship of all those who now or at any time are or have been
of the company of the redeemed in Christ.   The membership of this great fellowship is known to God alone.   The
greater part of it has passed into the eternal world.   Of
those called Christians now living in the world, some may be
within the outward organisation of the Church, and yet
not be in fact within the Church itself, when the word is
taken in this sense.

Thirdly, *Church* may be taken to mean all those who at
any one time in the world's history are within God's covenant
of grace, through fellowship within the body which is the
regular and appointed channel of that grace.   Differences
of opinion may exist as to the nature and extent of that
body.   This concept of the Church is widely held.[1]

Fourthly, the word is used to describe the group of
Christians worshipping in a single place, and bound together
by a common loyalty and an experience in common of the
presence of Christ in worship.   This is good New Testament
usage.   The Church in Philippi or Corinth is just that local
fellowship in which the life of the risen Christ is continually
manifest.   There are those who would maintain that this
is the only legitimate use of the word, and that the nature
of the Church in all its fulness is found in such a local
fellowship of faith.   On this view, such local groups, though
bound together by ties of mutual recognition and affection,

---

[1] This view is admirably expressed in the *Appeal to all Christian People*
sent forth by the Lambeth conference of 1920: "We acknowledge all who
believe in our Lord Jesus Christ, and have been baptised into the name
of the Holy Trinity, as sharing with us membership in the universal Church
of Christ which is His body." *Lambeth Conferences (1867–1930)* (London,
S.P.C.K. 1948), p. 38.   This statement does not, of course, express the
whole of Anglican doctrine about the Church.

do not coalesce into *a Church*, but should rather be described in the plural as *Churches* ; and for this also there is good New Testament authority.

But circumstances have led to a wide extension of the local basis of the Church. Phrases such as "the Church of England", "the Church of Sweden" and so forth, have become part of ordinary Christian usage. As we have seen, long before the Reformation the phrase *ecclesia Anglicana* was in use, though without such a strong sense of separateness as came to be associated with it, when nationalism and distinct organisation had broken up the unity of the medieval *corpus Christanum*.

Finally, the word has come to be used denominationally, in such phrases as "the Methodist Church", "the Lutheran Church." This appears to be a recent development. Methodism, for example, grew up in the form of societies for special purposes within the Church of England. Even after its separation from the parent body, it had no strong Church sense of its own. It was only towards the end of the Nineteenth Century that the claim to be a Church, with standing equal to that of other churches, began to be formally made.[1] A further step is taken, when such a denomination, having become world-wide, takes on something of the lineaments of a universal Church. For such a usage there seems to be no basis in New Testament language or thought about the Church.

Each of these forms of language has its own theological presuppositions ; their diversity represents the difficulty by which the Christian society is faced as it strives to find its unity, and to express it in action in face of an increasingly hostile world.

There are churches which hold that there is no problem,

[1] The great Methodist leader of the end of the Nineteenth Century, Hugh Price Hughes (1847–1902), appears to have been one of the first to impress this Church consciousness on what had previously been content to be a dissenting body, a " society." See *Life* by his daughter (London, 1907), pp. 435–480.

since the original unity has never been lost, and is already present and expressed in an existing Church organisation.

The Roman Catholic Church claims that it is *the Church*. Founded on the Rock of Peter, guarded by his perpetual watchfulness against the least tincture of error, endowed by the Saviour with the gift of infallibility, it teaches all truth, reprobates all error, and speaks with authority to meet the changing situations of all times. It is still official Roman Catholic doctrine that it is absolutely necessary for the salvation of every man that he should be in communion with and in submission to the rule of the See of Peter. The rigidity of this view has been mitigated in recent years by the doctrine of invincible ignorance ; this leaves a door of hope for those who have never had the claims of the Roman Church clearly explained to them, or have been prevented by pre-existing prejudice from comprehending them. Some Roman Catholics in good standing would go yet further, and say that Christians of other than the Roman obedience may be of the soul of the Church, though they are not within its body. But these concessions do not in any way modify the claim of the Roman Church to be *the Church*, the Kingdom of God on earth,[1] endued with the plenitude of authority and power. The only way to the recovery of the broken unity of the Christian society is for all who have strayed from the true fold to return to it, that, according to the will of God, there may be one fold and one shepherd.[2]

The Roman Church has never at any time been able to make its claim effective throughout the Christian world. It does not seem likely that in any near future it will prove

[1] The identification of the Church with the Kingdom of God is the source of most theological error about the nature of the Church in the purpose of God.

[2] I have quoted John x. 16, according to the Vulgate, and not according to the true reading "one flock, one shepherd". The late Prof. F. C. Burkitt was wont to say that, from the time of Augustine on, this mistranslation had done more harm than any other single factor in the history of the Christian Church. The Roman Catholic view on Christian unity has been charitably but forcefully re-expressed by Pope Pius XI, in the Encyclical *Mortalium Animos*, published on 6 Jan., 1928, some months after the Faith and Order Conference at Lausanne.

to be the rallying point for all scattered Christians. That Church has, indeed, great strength. Its discipline and the clarity with which its positions are defined makes it more effective in the conflict with non-Christian systems of thought and organisation than any of the non-Roman churches. It has gained in prestige in the turmoils of recent generations in Europe. On the other hand, the increasingly rigid definition of doctrine, the addition to the faith of the dogmas of the Immaculate Conception of the Blessed Virgin (1854), and of the Infallibility of the Pope (1870), the recent developments in Mariolatry, seem to many theologians familiar with the history of the Church to be irreconcilable both with the ancient standards of Christian orthodoxy and with any legitimate theory of the development of doctrine. The extreme centralisation of the Roman system repels those who believe that the well-being of the Church demands greater flexibility, and such independence for the parts as makes it possible for each to make its own individual contribution to the development of the whole.

The Holy Orthodox Church of the East makes a claim not dissimilar to that of Rome. It points with pride to its unbroken succession, both in its hierarchy, and in the maintenance of the original deposit of the faith, without such changes as have been made in the west, for example by the unauthorised insertion of the famous *Filioque* in the Nicene Creed. With the lapse of Rome into heresy, the Eastern Church remains as the one true successor of the Apostles. Salvation and unity are to be found only in its fellowship. This Church alone has access to the treasures of grace guaranteed by Christ to His Body. Though some crumbs may fall from the table to those who call themselves Christians, but are outside the Orthodox family, it is only for the children that the feast is provided by the Master of the House. The Orthodox Church does not decide on the question whether non-orthodox can be saved, leaving that to the mercy and judgment of God, and for that reason does not proselytise.[1] But it holds that no unity of the Church is possible without the return of all Christians, including those of the Roman obedience, to the Orthodox fold.

In recent years, the non-orthodox churches have become more conscious than ever before of the wealth of Christian insight and devotion that has been maintained and built up by the Orthodox Churches in their long centuries of isolation. But there is no sign anywhere of any large movement to join the Orthodox Churches, or of a belief that this is the way in which the unity of the Christian society can be secured. The Orthodox Churches are weakened by their own inner divisions. Constantinople, followed by the Greek-speaking Churches, holds that the Ecumenical Patriarchate still possesses undiminished the authority given to it by the Council of Chalcedon, and that, since the defection of Rome, it has no rival in supremacy over the whole Christian world. Moscow holds a rather different view. When Byzantium fell in 1453, effective supervision over the churches of the world could no longer be carried out by its patriarch ; so, when old Rome had fallen into heresy, and new Rome into captivity, God called into being Moscow, the third Rome, to be the head and light of all the Churches.[2] The tension between the Greek and Slavonic Churches remains unresolved. The universal headship of either Byzantium or Moscow is not likely to be taken very seriously by Christians of other allegiances.

Some Christians firmly believe that any attempt to secure outward unity of the Christian society is a mistaken policy

[1] From an article by the Metropolitan Michael of Corinth, published in *Ekklesia* (1 March, 1949), and quoted in the *Ecumenical Review*, Vol. I, No. 4 (1949), p. 435.

[2] Moscow was recognised as a separate Patriarchate in 1589. Attempts have been made to claim an apostolic origin for this Patriarchate as for others; as in the answer of Ivan the Terrible to the Papal Legate Possevin: "We received the Christian faith at the birth of the Christian Church, when Andrew, brother of the Apostle Peter, came to these parts on his way to Rome. Thus we in Moscow embraced the faith at the same time that you did in Italy, and have kept it inviolate from then to the present day." Miliukov, *op. cit.,* p. 16.

doomed to frustration. All that is needed, they would allege, is the mutual recognition by all of the faith in Christ of others, and the development of the spiritual fellowship which is admitted by all already to exist. Such a policy of general goodwill sooner or later encounters the difficulty that a certain precision of definition cannot be avoided. The early Christians did not set out with the idea of defining exactly the faith which they professed, and for a considerable time were content to leave many problems unsettled. But as questions were asked they had to be answered ; any definite answer to a question inevitably involves the exclusion of its opposite. For friendship, sympathy and goodwill are enough. For co-operation in good works, not much more is required. But common life in one fellowship makes necessary sooner or later a definition of the terms on which the fellowship is maintained.

Others hold that the most that is possible at present is world-wide fellowship on the basis of some common purpose or some experience shared in common. The Nineteenth Century was rich in movements, which, starting from the evangelical experience of salvation through personal faith in Christ as Saviour, developed into world-wide movements of a non-denominational pattern. All these were fellowships within the churches of like-minded people who agreed to work together for specific aims. This was the original impulse which underlay the formation of the World Student Christian Federation and the international missionary movement, though each of these has in time broadened its basis and its aim. Similar in origin and purpose were the Young Men's Christian Association, and the Young Women's Christian Association. None of these bodies aimed directly at bringing the separate churches into fellowship. They rather disclaimed responsibility for the churches as such. But each served as a place in which Christians of different allegiances could come to know one another in a fellowship

of service, in which what later came to be known as the
ecumenical climate could be created, and in which the
problem of Christian divisions was constantly kept in the
minds of those who served together in limited areas of the
churches' concerns.

The characteristic feature of the Twentieth Century so far
has been the formation or closer integration of world-wide
denominational or confessional fellowships. The success of
missionary work gave the Protestant denominations a
significance such as they had not had in the earlier days of
Reformation history. World-wide extension, with its possibilities of centrifugal tensions, suggested the need of a
counteracting focus of world-wide fellowship. Some denominational fellowships are no more than loose federa-
tions, with occasional conferences for the exchange of ideas.
Others, particularly the Presbyterian Alliance and the
Lutheran World Federation, show signs of development into
well-integrated Church bodies, with a world-wide consciousness and organs of common action. A great change has
taken place since the days when local loyalty was the
determining factor in the organisation of the Protestant
Church bodies.

The Anglican Communion occupies a unique place in the
Christian world. It has gone further than any other
Christian body in the non-Roman west to develop a new
type of universality, as world-wide as the Roman (though
much smaller in the number of its adherents), but more
flexible and more readily adaptable to changing conditions.

We may note, as an interesting example of the influence
of secular and political society on a Christian society that
the development of the Anglican Communion has in some
ways closely followed that of the British Commonwealth.
What was the United Kingdom, with an appendage of colonies
hardly acknowledged and sometimes disliked, has grown
into a world-wide family made up mainly of self-governing
dominions, each of which is a fully independent nation.

Recently the already flexible organisation has been expanded
to make possible the inclusion of republics in a body of which
a king is the recognised head. The links which hold
together this assembly of peoples and races at most diverse
stages of political and social development are so intangible
as not to be readily expressible in any constitutional formula,
but have proved themselves stronger and more enduring
than those which have served many more apparently stable
organisms. Similarly, the Anglican Communion has grown
out of " the United Church of England and Ireland " into
a fellowship which stretches far beyond the limits even of
the British family of nations, and is held together by links
as strong and as intangible as those which maintain the
the British Commonwealth as a unity in the political field.

The capacity of the Anglican system to maintain itself
in complete independence of the state was shewn in the
Eighteenth Century in the persistence of the Episcopal Church
in Scotland through the years of savage proscription (1745-
88), which ended only with the recognition of the House of
Hanover by the Scottish bishops, on the death of Charles
Edward the Young Pretender. The first official breach in
the English monopoly was made by the Act of 1786, which
authorised the Archbishop of Canterbury to consecrate for
service in America bishops who, as American citizens,
could not take the oath of allegiance to the British crown.
The Oxford Movement, from 1833 on, had carried out its
memorable work of restoring, in the face of the prevailing
Erastianism, the idea of the Church as an independent
spiritual society, responsible only to the will of God. Yet
as late as 1857 many churchmen doubted whether a bishop
not appointed by the Crown would be able to maintain
the dignity of his position and to control his clergy. But
the persistence of George Augustus Selwyn (1809–1878)
won the day, and in that year the Church of New Zealand
obtained its constitution as an independent self-governing
Church within the Anglican fellowship. From that date,

progress was rapid. The Anglican Communion now includes self-governing provinces or regional churches, " dominions," in every one of the five continents. The isolated dioceses which are still under the Archbishop of Canterbury as quasi-metropolitan, and the missionary districts of the Protestant Episcopal Church in the United States, bear some resemblance to the colonies and protectorates, which are still found in some parts of the British Commonwealth.[1]

The Anglican Communion has no strong centre of unity. The Archbishop of Canterbury has, outside his own province, no control in any way resembling that of the Pope over the whole Roman Catholic body. The Lambeth Conference is not a synod ; its decisions have no authority, except in so far as they are formally accepted by the governing bodies of the constituent churches. No part has coercive authority over any other part. The whole body is held together by *communio in sacris*, by a common but flexible liturgical tradition, and by a mutual loyalty which seems to grow stronger as the formal ties are one by one eliminated.

More important still, the Anglican Communion has shewn in recent years a marked tendency to grow into fellowship beyond its own borders.

In 1931, full intercommunion was established, by the Bonn agreement, with the Old Catholic Churches of the continent of Europe (subsequently extended to include the Polish National Catholic Church of the United States). In this agreement, it was laid down that full communion is possible, if each Church recognises the standing of the other within the fellowship of the Catholic Church of Christ, but that neither is thereby committed to every doctrinal statement or every liturgical practice adopted by the other.[2]

---

[1] The history of this development has been graphically recorded by John McLeod Campbell in *Christian History in the Making* (London, 1946).
[2] See the full and reliable account in C. B. Moss, *The Old Catholic Movement* (London, 1949). The official documents are readily accessible in G. K. A. Bell, *Documents on Christian Unity, Third Series 1930-1948* (Oxford, 1948), pp. 60-63.

Some of the Anglican Churches now have relations of limited communion, formally attained and recorded, with the Churches of Sweden and Finland. Beyond these formal negotiations and agreements, there has been a tendency for parts of the body to branch out into relationships with other parts of the Christian society. For nearly a hundred years, the small Episcopal Churches in Spain and Portugal have been dependent for episcopal ministrations on the bishops of the Church of Ireland.[1] The Church of India has entered into relationships of limited communion with the Mar Thoma Syrian Church of Malabar, the reformed section of the ancient Syrian Church of India. This is the only example in the world of intercommunion between an eastern and a western Church. When the independent Church of the Philippines, the so-called Aglipayan Church, a body which had broken away from the Church of Rome at the end of the Nineteenth Century and had at that time lost the regular episcopal succession, requested the Church in America to help it by the regular consecration of some of its bishops, that Church, after full enquiry, decided to give the help asked for, it being made clear that no other part of the Anglican body would be bound by the action of one of its members.[2]

These developments raise the question how far the expansion of one denomination can go. Is a denomination to be regarded as a permanent feature in the life of the world-wide Christian society? Or should it face the possibility of its own dissolution in a wider unity, if it seems clear that its historic work is done, and that the values for which it has stood in its isolation can be fully incorporated into the life of a larger whole? The Anglican bishops, assembled at

[1] These included, in 1894, the consecration of Sr. Cabrera as bishop for the Church in Spain. This experiment has not since been repeated. The Spanish and Portuguese Churches use a form of the Book of Common Prayer with adaptations to their own use, and enrichments from the old Mozarabic sources. The work has been admirably done.

[2] Three "Aglipayan" bishops were regularly consecrated by three American bishops in Manila in April 1948.

Lambeth in 1930 and in 1948, were prepared to consider this possibility and to recognise that the Anglican Communion itself might in course of time be merged in a larger episcopal fellowship, and cease to have an independent and denominational existence. This is perhaps the first time in history that a great denomination has seriously faced and expressed the possibility of its own demise.

The Lambeth Conference of 1948 was, in fact, considering the wider implications of something that had already happened, since the Anglican Communion had had to face the fact of its disappearance as a separate entity in one part of the world through the merging of four dioceses in the new Church of South India.

During the last century of Church history, the tendency towards the formation of new denominations, still unchecked in the United States and in South Africa, has been more than offset by the contrary tendency towards re-integration and corporate union between previously separated bodies. In Scotland, almost all Presbyterians have been brought together in one Church of Scotland (1928). In England and the United States, mergers of separate Methodist communions have brought into existence great united Methodist bodies. In Canada, the United Church of Canada (1925) includes Methodists, Presbyterians and Congregationalists. The Church of Christ in Japan, a union of non-Roman churches imposed by the force of government in the war years, has not been able to maintain its full cohesion, but includes the same great bodies as the United Church of Canada. The Church of Christ in China covers a yet wider range, including both such bodies as the Baptist, which stand most strongly for the autonomy of the individual Christian congregation, and others, such as the Presbyterian, which have a stronger sense of Church order on a territorial basis. There is hardly a country in the world at the present time, in which negotiations between Church bodies are not proceeding with a view to full corporate union.

The experiment in South India is of special significance, for a number of reasons. The negotiations which brought the new Church into existence affected many countries, since the missions in South India had their origin in the British Isles, in the United States, in Australia and on the continent of Europe. A wider range of Church traditions than in other similar unions was brought into fellowship, as for the first time since the Reformation episcopal and non-episcopal churches found a way to unite. The problem was to bring together Anglican, Methodist, Presbyterian, Congregational and Continental traditions, without diminution and without mere compromise, in a genuine and organic unity. After twenty-eight years of patient negotiation, a decision was reached. On 27 September, 1947, the new Church came into existence.

The Church of South India declares its intention to maintain the faith which the Church of Christ has ever held.[1] But union was achieved on the clear understanding that detailed agreement on every aspect of faith and practice should not be a pre-condition of union, but could be attained only by the experience of living together in the fellowship of one Church. A period has been provided for the growing together into one of previously disparate bodies. For example, for a time two types of ministry, episcopal and non-episcopal, will continue side by side. All forms of worship previously familiar to the congregations will be maintained, until such time as the Church can work out its own liturgical standards, drawing on its own experience and on that of the universal Church of Christ. Forms of admission to full membership in the Church will for a time vary in different areas according to the traditions inherited from the past. The Church has willingly accepted these anomalies, as necessary to a form of union which aims at the enrichment

---

[1] Whether the new Church actually does maintain that faith, and whether the safeguards in its constitution are adequate to ensure that it does so in the future or not is the subject of continuing and at times acrimonious controversy.

of each tradition by all, and not at the suppression of any one by another.

The experience of four years of common life suggests that this is a pattern which may be widely followed elsewhere in the recovery of the broken unity of the Christian family. The evidence of those who have lived through the experience is that the growth in mutual understanding is far greater than would be supposed, if attention were directed only to the changes in organisation. It is possible to understand sympathetically the traditions of a Christian body other than one's own, but there is always an element of detachment, a lack of responsibility for that tradition and for those who maintain it. But if that tradition has entered in as a living element in the Church of which one is oneself a member, it is possible in a new way to apprehend its religious significance for those who have maintained it, to feel responsibility for the retention of all that is significant in it as a creative power in the life of the Church, and so to lose the sense of strangeness which always attaches to a tradition that has been studied, but has not actually been lived.

The Church of South India declares its intention to remain in fellowship with all those parts of the Christian Church from which its own life was originally derived, and to extend that fellowship more widely in India and elsewhere. This is a laudable purpose, and was involved from the beginning in the plan for bringing into existence a united Church. If the Church of South India were no more than a new regional Church, autonomous in its own area and bringing into fellowship a large number of Indian Christians previously separated by denominational allegiance, but without clear standing in the universal Church of Christ, it would merely perpetuate the worst features of the Reformation settlement, in which geographical location became the basis for permanent divisions within the Christian society. But the existence of such a Church, uniting diverse traditions, presents a serious challenge to the older churches from which it derives, and demands a reconsideration not merely of their relationships to the new body, but of their relationships to one another, and of the hindrances which still keep them back from according to one another full fellowship within the one Body of Christ.

The movement towards closer Christian fellowship has taken other forms than the unification of separate Church traditions. Within a year from the inauguration of the Church of South India, the World Council of Churches was formally constituted, on 23 August, 1948, as an instrument of fellowship and co-operation between churches which are able to come together on the basis of faith in Jesus Christ as God and Saviour.

The severe limitations within which the World Council of Churches has to work must be clearly recognised. The Church of Rome, on its own principles, can take no part in its affairs, though individual Roman Catholics have welcomed with enthusiasm what they have judged to be a genuine working of the divine Spirit of unity in divided Christendom. The Orthodox Churches are only weakly represented, those of the Slavonic world having for the most part refused to enter the fellowship. Nevertheless, the World Council of Churches, with its hundred and fifty-eight member churches in all parts of the world, does represent a new stage in the evolution of the Christian society. A wide range of Christian traditions, Orthodox, Old Catholic, Anglican, Protestant of many varieties, is represented in its membership. Older and younger churches meet on terms of perfect equality. No major area in the world is quite unrepresented ; and, most noteworthy of all, an Assembly of the World Council is not a gathering of individuals interested in the problem of Christian union and prepared to labour for its achievement ; it is an Assembly of representatives officially chosen by churches, which, as churches, have pledged themselves to the cause of fellowship, and in the words of the Message of the first Assembly, are determined to stay together.[1]

The ecumenical movement, to use the term which, unsatisfactory as in some ways it is, has become generally current, is only in its beginnings, but has had a long enough history for some of its effects to become apparent. The danger of any movement towards Christian unity is that it may result in a reduced Christianity, through agreement to overlook those uncomfortable factors in which division is most apparent, and to concentrate on that minimum of faith and practice on which all Christians are already at one. This danger has been successfully avoided. The ecumenical movement lives by the sharp mutual confrontation of the differing traditions in all their strength and all their fulness. But no one exposed, in the atmosphere of Christian charity, to this confrontation remains unchanged by it. Even those most attached to the tradition of their own Church discover in a new way the brethren from whom they have been previously separated, find themselves compelled to respect that which previously they had been inclined merely to disapprove, and are compelled to recognise the inadequacy of any one tradition, as it finds itself expressed in the empirical churches as they now are, fully to set forth the manifold wisdom of God revealed in Christ.

The recovery of the unity of all the parts of the Christian society remains a distant ideal, to be worked for in the spirit of the prayer of the Saviour "that they may all be one ; as thou, Father, art in me, and I in thee, that they also may be one in us ; that the world may believe that thou has sent me,"[2] but not to be quickly realised by human contrivance, or by a hasty synthesis that is less than organic in its recovery of the fulness of life. The World Council

---

[1] "Here at Amsterdam we have committed ourselves afresh to Him, and have covenanted with one another in constituting this World Council of Churches. We intend to stay together." *The First Assembly of the World Council of Churches* (London, S.C.M. Press, 1949), p. 9.

[2] John, xvii, 21.

of Churches cannot create that unity. Already certain tasks to which it can set itself, or which it can challenge the churches to undertake, have become apparent.

There is, first, the task of closer theological definition of those points at which the Christian confessions really are divided. Definition of agreement has proved comparatively easy ; the precise location of difference is much more difficult. The experience of debate in the ecumenical setting has shewn that the major differences within the Christian world do not at present run along the lines of confessional division. A "Catholic" in the Church of England may find himself at many points more closely in sympathy with Roman Catholics than with evangelical members of his own communion. An "Evangelical" may feel nearer to a Protestant Nonconformist than to an Anglo-Catholic of his own Church. The conservative attitude towards the Scriptures known, not very suitably, as fundamentalism, is found in almost all the great confessions. So is the attitude generally described as liberal. Pacifism is not the monopoly of the Friends, nor anti-pacifism of the state churches of Europe. Modern psychology has shewn that men are influenced more than they know by psychological factors and less than they imagine by convictions reached through intellectual processes and rationally held. It may be that attachment to confessional principles is due, more than men suppose, to traditional loyalty rather than to immediate spiritual experience, and that theological positions are, more than theologians like to think, rationalisations of unconscious motives of fear, self-preservation or aggression.[1]

This does not mean that the differences between the Christian traditions are imaginary, or that they have no serious intellectual and theological content. To attend an ecumenical gathering is to become aware in a new way of

[1] See C. H. Dodd, " A Letter Concerning Unavowed Motives in Ecumenical Discussions," published in *Ecumenical Review*, Vol. II, No. 1 (1950), pp. 52-56.

the depth of those divisions, and of their power to keep in separation those who most ardently desire to be in all things one. But it does mean that the whole problem of division and unity has to be surveyed afresh. To what extent is it possible for differing theological positions to be held within a single confession without disrupting its unity ? What are those theological differences which are of such weight as to justify the confessions in continuing in separation, in a world which cries out so urgently for the unity of the human race to be prophetically manifested in the unity of the Church ?

A second problem is that of the recovery of a measure of liturgical unity within the Christian society. This is not to be confused with the question of inter-communion, which is a matter of doctrine and church order, and not primarily of liturgical emphasis. The way in which a man has been accustomed to worship God has a deeper influence on his total reaction to the Christian faith than almost anything else. It is at this point that Christian divisions are most inveterate, and most securely rooted in the less than conscious levels of personality.

In one great area of Christian tradition, public worship is carried on in a language unknown to the people. The intellectual response, therefore, tends to be individual through the private prayers and devotion of the worshipper, which may bear little or no relation to the liturgical movement of the service. The common response, which may be deep, sincere and intense, is on a different level, in that obscure region in which racial memories are stored, and by which the basic patterns of character are determined.

In another area, the service is liturgical, but in a language generally understood. Here the intellectual demand is much greater, but the worshipper is taught to be conscious of himself as a part of the larger unity of the Church in time and space, rather than to seek the immediate satisfaction of his own individual and personal needs.

Yet a third type of worship is non-liturgical. Here the central concern is with a particular group of Christians worshipping on a particular day, and with their immediate edification. Much depends on the minister, in whose hands the whole conduct of worship is placed, and whose effectiveness or ineffectiveness may make or mar the whole act of Christian worship. But within this non-liturgical tradition there is a marked difference in tone between those confessions in which the appeal is primarily intellectual, through instruction in the word of God, and those in which emotional effects are deliberately aimed at, or at least recognised as a normal part and consequence of Christian worship.

Finally, in the less organised sects, there is nothing that could be recognised as liturgical order, but rather a free participation in worship of all those present, according to the custom of the Church of Corinth, as we find it described in St. Paul's first Epistle. The same dangers recur as in the primitive age. And, paradoxically, there is in such worship something of the same mass emotional reaction, on a less than fully conscious level, as can be observed in the most strictly liturgical tradition of Christian worship.

As soon as the ordinary Christian moves out of the range of worship to which he has been accustomed and to which he is attached, he feels himself ill-at-ease. Something is lacking which he feels to be necessary ; something is present of which he finds it hard to approve. Those reared in a liturgical tradition are distressed by the lack of form and order in much non-liturgical worship. Those accustomed to freedom of expression find themselves straitened by the rigidity of liturgical tradition. An artificial mixture of divergent traditions satisfies no one, and leaves an almost universal sense of frustration.

It is here that we face in its practical and most immediate form the problem of Christian union. If Christians cannot worship together happily, agreement at other points remains barren. But in worship, we are dealing with the obstinate

antinomies of human nature and of the human situation—
the tension between intellect and emotion, between the
individual and the group, between the transitory and the
eternal, between the needs of the contemporary generation
and the changeless structure of the Christian society. The
Christian confessions, in their separation, have emphasised
one or other of the antinomies. Over-emphasis in one
direction has led to a reaction in another. The fulness of
Christian worship cannot be restored, until all the emphases
are brought together again, in a unity that reflects the rich
variety of genuine Christian experience and corresponds
to the proportions of the faith as laid down in the original
Gospel of Jesus Christ. To recognise the complexity of the
problem is to take the first step towards a realisation of all
that is involved in the restoration of Christian unity.

Thirdly, a world-wide Christian movement must have
some recognised medium of communication.

Part of the strength of Islam lies in its universal use of
Arabic as a sacred language. It has been the misfortune of
the Christian Church that from a very early date it has had
no common language. Many of the difficulties in the days
of the great Councils arose from mutual misunderstandings,
exacerbated by mutual contempt, between the Fathers of the
Greek-speaking and Latin-speaking. Churches. During the
Middle Ages, western Europe was held together by the use of
Latin as the common language of all educated men.[1] With
the breakdown of the *corpus christianum*, even this common
medium of communication has been lost, and the Church
has suffered the fate to which humanity was condemned
by the curse of Babel.

Nothing in modern Christian movements is more surprising
and unexpected than the part played in them by the English
language. When Chaucer used the Mid-Saxon dialect of
English as the medium of the *Canterbury Tales*, there was

---

[1] In Hungary, Latin survived till 1848 as the language of the Diet. At
the Vatican Council in 1870, it was noticed that only the Hungarian bishops
spoke Latin naturally; other bishops orated in it.

nothing to indicate that he was helping to initiate a movement which would transform the least barbarous of the dialects of Britain into the vehicle of the most notable literature of the modern world, and would in time raise it to the level of a universal language. Yet such is the fact. English today is spoken as their native tongue by far more people in the world than any other language, except Chinese.[1] The political predominance of Britain and America has contributed to the spread of English as a means of communication far beyond the limits of those who speak it from their birth. If representatives of the nations of Asia meet in council, that is the only common language in which they can communicate. In an increasing number of countries, English has been adopted as the second language in the schools.

A parallel process has been observable in the affairs of the Christian Church. The multiplication of international conferences and world-wide societies has brought home to men anew the need of a common language. English has a long start over all its competitors. At the great missionary conference at Madras in 1938, attended by the representatives of sixty-four countries, English was the only language used. Increasingly those who take part in world-wide Christian movements find themselves under the necessity, whether they will or no, of understanding English, and, if possible, of expressing themselves readily in it. It is possible that this unexpected development is only a consequence of Anglo-Saxon predominance in the political sphere, and that the situation may change within a generation. It is possible, however, that the movement is only in its beginnings, and that mankind has before it, on a wider scale than ever before, the possibility of one common language as the means of communication between all educated men.

---

[1] Even this statement need some modification. The spoken dialects of China are mutually unintelligible. The standard language, Mandarin, is the possession of a comparatively small educated class.

The ordinary Christian may be interested in world-wide movements, and may lend them his conscientious support. Yet his primary concern must be with the Christian society at his doors, the world-wide society in its concretion as the local fellowship of worshipping people of which he is himself a member. The dismay, and at times, the despair of Christian people is that the Christian society in its actual forms and activities bears so little resemblance to what ideally it should be. Even the non-Christian knows what the Church of Christ ought to be—the servant of the world, the bearer of light, hope and love to humanity in its sufferings and perplexities. What is seen in the ordinary Christian congregation bears little relation to this. It appears to be marked by much the same selfishness and rivalries as the fellowships of the world. It seems to make claims that it cannot fulfil. Often it appears to be more concerned with its own rights and the maintenance of the injustices of the *status quo* than with that revolutionary adventurousness, without which the sovereignty of God cannot be made manifest among men.

The first task of the Christian society in its local manifestation is that it should recover its own nature as the Body of Christ. The failure of the churches has been that they have not been true communities of the Spirit. The recovery of community, true fellowship in the Holy Spirit, is now and at all times the pre-requisite to unity and to effectiveness in the world.

Sometimes the idea of the Church as a community is wrongly stated. It is possible for a group of Christians bound together by an intense fellowship in Christ to become the exclusive community, in which the members share not merely their worship, but also their work, their recreations and their thoughts. This involves falling again into the pietist error. The Church becomes so separate from the world as to lose its redemptive function, and by seeking too exclusively the sanctification of its own members, produces a form of piety which is neither robust nor infectious. The Church is by its nature a close and intimate fellowship, but it is so only in order that it may live in the world for the redemption of the world.

The marks of the Christian society, in its double character as separated from the world and identified with it, are clearly set forth in the New Testament picture of the earliest Christian fellowships.

The Church is, first and always, the Eucharistic fellowship. In the central act of Christian faith, the interaction of time and eternity is always present. Christians are already citizens of eternity, and therefore cannot be other than pilgrims in time. Here they have no ultimate objectives. If they are intimately concerned with the things of time, that is because actions in time have eternal consequences, and man, standing always under the judgment of God, is working out for himself here and now an eternal destiny.

Secondly, the Christian fellowship is one in which no member should be in need or want, should never be lonely or friendless or in despair, since Christians are called to have all things in common ; and, though the rules and methods of this Christian communism, are flexible, the obligation is absolute and unchanging.

Thirdly, the Christian fellowship is that in which any stranger should feel himself immediately welcome and at home. Suspicion, contempt and hostility should be excluded by the Christian law of charity. This charity demands that Christians should always believe and hope the best of all men, that they should be tender towards the failings of other Christians and of other men, and that they should have inexhaustible faith in the power of the grace of God to renew even those who have fallen most deeply from the way of life that God has revealed.

Fourthly, the Christian fellowship should be clear-sighted in the detection and uncovering of evils existent in the society immediately around it, tireless in protest against injustice, active in the relief of suffering, and patient in study of the means and methods by which injustice may be set right.

Fifthly, the Christian society must make it clear that its ultimate loyalty is always and only to Christ and to His word. If it accepts for a time association with the state or any other human organisation, it must be prepared at any moment to withdraw from that association, if its spiritual liberty and its power to bear witness are in danger of being infringed.

Sixthly, each Christian group must be conscious of its fellowship in Christ with all other Christian groups throughout the world, even though circumstances should make impossible any expression of that fellowship other than the fellowship of prayer.

Seventhly, each Christian group must be constantly aware that the Church is set for the redemption of the whole world, and that the purpose of God in Christ cannot be fulfilled, until the Gospel of the kingdom has been preached to all nations for a witness unto them.

The Christian society believes that it is supernatural in origin, since it was called into being by Christ Himself, and that it lives on earth a supernatural life, since it experiences the truth of the promise of Christ that He will be with it till the end of the days, and draws inwardly on the unfailing resources of His grace. But such claims, made in words, make little impression on the world, or on the man outside the fellowship. The just demand of the world is that the Christian and the Christian fellowship should be recognisably like Christ. This does not mean a monotonous uniformity, either of individual Christians, or of the various Christian societies, since the liberating power of Christ sets men and societies free to be that which most characteristically they are, and so to manifest the variety of God's grace in the development of individual difference. But where Christ is Lord, there is

unmistakably present, under every difference of organisation, expression and point of view, something that is
derived from Him, and could not be derived from any other
source.

CONCLUSION

WHEN Jesus Christ sent out His little company into the world, He warned the members of it that life in the world would never be easy for them. They were sent forth as sheep in the midst of wolves. The time would come when anyone who killed them would think that he was doing God service. The Master seems even at one moment to have faced the possibility that the servants would fail in their task: "When the Son of man cometh, shall he find faith on the earth?"[1]

The Christian society can live only in a state of constant tension with its environment. In order to be itself, it must withdraw into itself, and realise its vocation to be a society governed by laws entirely different from those of its secular environment. Yet it must perpetually enter into that environment, in order that through it the world may be saved. Without that utter self-identification of sympathy and self-giving, by which the Incarnation was marked, it cannot be effective as the redeeming society. But if that identification goes beyond the limit marked out by its essential difference, the Christian society makes too successful an adjustment to the alien world, and loses its capacity to serve as salt and light. As long as it is in the world, it cannot but be the judge of the world. The more true it is to itself, and the sterner its condemnation of all that is contrary to the will of God, the more certain it becomes that its lot will be hostility, misunderstanding and persecution. But it is all too easy for the prophetic attitude of judgment to pass into a shrewish discontent, in which any opposition to the Church and any infringement of its privileges is identified

[1] Luke xviii. 8.

321

with rebellion against God, and the defence of its *status quo* is identified with righteousness.

When the gate is so narrow and so strait the way, it is not surprising that the visible Christian society or societies have so often strayed and wandered in the wilderness. And yet the Christian fellowship has continued to exist.

It was not always certain that it would survive the storms of time. There have been areas and periods in which it has perished, either by the extremity of violence, or by inner inanition, or by such successful adaptation to the world as has caused its own inner distinctiveness to be lost. Professor K. S. Latourette, at the conclusion of his immense survey of the Expansion of Christianity, concludes that the advance of the Gospel in the world has not been a steady progression, but advance followed by regression, the regression again changing to further advance. One of his volumes bears the title *The Thousand Years of Uncertainty*, and deals with that immense span of time in which it was not clear whether Christianity or Islam would develop into the world religion of the future. Islam has retained its hold on the lands that it has won ; yet it is the religion of Jesus which has held on, and in the end has grown into the first world-wide religion in the history of mankind.

The conclusion of our study must be to ask what have been the inner resources that have made it possible for the Christian society to survive and grow in the face of so much outer adversity and so much inner weakness.

We may answer first with certainty that what above all else has made it possible for the society to survive is that, at its worst, it has never wholly lost its contact with Jesus Christ. When the author of the fourth Gospel wrote that " in him was life, and the life was the light of men," he wrote what is literally true. What streams out from Bethlehem and Calvary is the true life of men ; whoever touches Jesus of Nazareth, even distantly, touches life, and enters at least upon the possibility of being transformed after the likeness of the Christ. Not infrequently, the Christian society has borne so little visible resemblance to its Head that the observer has been inclined rather to blaspheme than to believe. But the connection has never been wholly broken, and so the society has continued in being until today.

Of the elements of stability in the life of the society, that which we have noted again and again as the most effective is the continuity of public worship. Without that personal experience in which individuals come to know Jesus Christ as God and Saviour, the Church loses its vitality and its power to grow. But the New Testament knows nothing of a purely individual salvation. The people of God are formed by Him into a society; it is only in the life of that society that they can discover what they are, and rise to the height of their calling. Even in dispersion or hidden in the catacombs, the society is still conscious of its corporate existence ; the faithful are knit together in one communion and fellowship, which separation and earthly hindrances cannot destroy. But the natural life of the society is the life of a family ; and, as in the life of a human family, the essential manifestation of the inner life is in the Father's house, and above all else, in the family Meal, in which unity is both recognised and re-affirmed, and life, divinely renewed, is sanctified by the mutual pledge of self-giving and service.

If public worship were made impossible for a century, it might well be that the Christian society would cease, as such, to exist ; if it can be maintained, the life of the society is secure. In point of fact, there has been no day in the history of the world since Pentecost on which Christians have not met together somewhere to commemorate the death and rising again of Jesus Christ. Whatever other successions there may be in the Church, and whatever their importance, this more than any other is the indispensable apostolic succession, in which the continuity of the body in time is maintained, and in which its unbroken fellowship with the historic Jesus of Narareth is assured.[1]

There have been times of great demoralisation within the Christian body. Good men have been driven to despair of the possibility of renewal. But over and over again it has been proved that their despair was premature ; though there has been an appearance of exceeding dryness, the society has yet had within it the power of renewal ; it has been able " through the scent of water to bud, and put forth boughs like a plant."

When renewal has come, it has always come through a return to the Gospels and to Jesus Christ Himself. This was true in the Thirteenth Century, when the little poor man of Assisi heard words of the Gospel as a direct challenge to himself, and set out to follow them more literally than any man for centuries had tried to do. The same was true at the time of the Reformation, when Luther turned back from the labyrinth of scholastic exegesis to the simplicities of the Synoptic Gospels. Those who imagine Luther to have been so concerned with the doctrine of Galatians and Romans as to forget all else do him injustice ; no man has ever written with greater insight and tenderness of the simple narratives of Jesus as He is seen in the Gospels.[2] Once again, in the Nineteenth Century, when scholars began to read the Gospels with new historical insight, what they were seeking was the living Jesus. Some of them laid

---

[1] It must be borne in mind that, in the historic tradition of Christian worship, the elements of *Word* and *Sacrament* have always been combined. Separation of these two elements, and over-emphasis on either of them, always result in serious spiritual loss.

[2] The English reader may readily be excused for this misconception, since so little of the real Luther has been made accessible to him. Professor Bainton of Yale has rendered a great service by his *Martin Luther Christmas Book* (Philadelphia, Muhlenberg Press 1948), with selections from Luther's writings on the Nativity. Let one quotation suffice: "Think, women, there was no one there to bathe the Baby. No warm water, nor even cold, no fire, no light. The mother was herself midwife and the maid. The cold manger was the bed and the bathtub. Who showed the poor girl what to do? She had never had a baby before. I am amazed that the little one did not freeze. Do not make of Mary a stone. It must have gone straight to her heart that she was so abandoned." (p. 39). Reading such words, one thinks of Albrecht Dürer's woodcuts, and understands why Dürer thought the world of Luther.

coarse and clumsy hands on the narratives; many of them missed much that was obvious to simpler readers. But the result of all their labours is that we have come nearer than any intervening generation to those concrete realities of the flesh and blood of Christ by which the Christian society lives. When biblical scholarship turned away from liberalism to a deeper understanding of the religion of the New Testament, it did not abandon all that the liberals had learned ; it added adoration to enquiry, and so came nearer to a true Christian understanding of the mystery of faith.

God has His own ways of working, and His miracles cannot be commanded by men. Renewal of the Church has rarely come in the place towards which men were looking. God takes hold on one of His hidden ones—on an elderly nun in a Spanish convent, on a tinker of Bedford, on a chemist's assistant in Yorkshire, on a young girl whose drawings were greatly admired by Ruskin—and somewhere in the world a flame is lighted. It may be a great flame or a small one ; but it is a true fire of God, shining in the darkness, and the darkness cannot overcome it.

The society cannot itself produce the renewal which it needs. It can be aware of its need for renewal, and can to some extent create those conditions under which the voice of the prophet, should he appear, can be heard. In each age, one particular need of men is more acutely felt than any other, to which the Christian society if it is to be the effective witness of Christ in the world must respond, and for which, out of the riches of wisdom hid in Christ, it must find at least a partial satisfaction. The gift of discerning the signs of the times is only sparingly given ; but it is one of the good gifts of God that the Christian society may ask and claim, in so far as it is faithful to its twin tasks of watchfulness and prayer.

The central problem of the mid-Twentieth Century seems to be that of the irreconcilability of justice and freedom. It was the view of Napoleon that, if people were offered the choice of liberty or equality, they would always choose equality—equality under the rule of an oppressor, rather than the perils of liberty to prey on one another. Contemporary history suggests that Napoleon was not wholly wrong. One half of the world, in its passion for social justice, seems ready to surrender the hard-won liberties, personal and political, of a millenium. The other half, clinging desperately to liberty, seems to lack the creative imagination needed to alleviate and remove the injustices of class, economic insecurity, race distinction and unemployment. It is the failure of the Christian society to speak a prophetic word on this subject, and to manifest within itself a life that transcends the antithesis, which makes the Christian faith seem to many an irrelevant archaism, and turns their eyes to other and newer gospels.

And yet, the Christian society, if its theology were sufficiently profound, has ready to its hand the principle from which a solution can be derived. Freedom and justice are both functions of obedience to the will of God. The servant of Jesus knows that there is no true freedom in the world, except that which His Master purchased through His perfect submission to the will of His Father. He knows also that justice will never be done among men until Christians take seriously the command to love their neighbours as themselves, and until there are a sufficient number of them to exercise a creative influence on society as a whole. But such abstract insight into truth becomes effective, only when the prophet arises who can give it content in relation to an actual situation, and can face very ordinary people with a challenge to which they must answer Yea or Nay.

It does not yet appear whether in this century the prophetic vision will be given or no. It is already clear that the Christian society is entering upon one of its periods of great peril. But this in itself need not cause the

Christian to lose heart. When God calls His people out into the wilderness, it is in order that He may speak comfortably to them, and give them a new revelation of His love. What faces the Christian society today is not simply local persecution or oppression. It is confronted by the breaking down of many familiar landmarks ; it had become too closely associated in the countries of its greatest influence with one form of social structure, and, now that that social structure is breaking down before our eyes, church-men are dismayed and perplexed. But, as so often, what at first seems to be the greatest disaster may in the end prove to be the greatest blessing. For a long time the pillar of cloud has seemed to be stationary. Now it has begun to move forward. The people of God are summoned to take up their burden, and to move forward in confidence in Him alone. If they learn to do so, they will find that in doing so their society has recovered its true nature.

For it is part of the essential nature of the Church in this dispensation that it is always a pilgrim Church. The story of the people of God begins with the migration of Abraham, a wilderness journey. The theme of camels and tents runs through all the Old Testament: "For we are strangers before thee, and sojourners, as all our fathers were : our days on the earth are as a shadow, and there is none abiding."[1] When the Son of Man came, He came as a wayfaring man, who had no place wherein to lay His head. The Apostles went forth, "lone on the land and homeless on the water" to do His bidding. And so it must always be, until the Son of Man comes again. But the Church is always in danger of falling into the sin of the builders of Shinar. To find a pleasant place and in it to build a tower of Babel seems to be an ineradicable instinct of fallen man. But the purposes of God can never be fulfilled, unless God Himself comes down to scatter the builders, and to send them forth again on their endless journey.

[1] I Chron. xxix. 15.

When the Church of God is compelled to become again a pilgrim Church, then it can rejoice in the sure confidence that its redemption draweth nigh. It is in the humble admission that here we have no continuing city that the Christian society becomes again what it ought to be. To go out from the known, the secure and the familiar is always difficult. But there are sufficient pilgrims, and in particular one Pilgrim, ahead in the way to give the assurance that the experiment will not be in vain. " For they that say such things make it manifest that they are seeking after a country of their own. And if indeed they had been mindful of that country from which they went out, they would have had opportunity to return. But now they desire a better country, that is, a heavenly : wherefore God is not ashamed of them, to be called their God : for he hath prepared for them a city."[1]

[1] Hebrews xi. 14–16.

INDEX OF NAMES

INDEX OF SUBJECTS